THE ROHINGYAS

AZEEM IBRAHIM

The Rohingyas

Inside Myanmar's Genocide

Revised and updated edition

HURST & COMPANY, LONDON

First published in the United Kingdom in 2016 by
C. Hurst & Co. (Publishers) Ltd.,
41 Great Russell Street, London, WC1B 3PL
© Azeem Ibrahim, 2018
This revised and updated edition published 2018
All rights reserved.
Printed in the United Kingdom

Distributed in the United States, Canada and Latin America
by Oxford University Press, 198 Madison Avenue, New York, NY 10016,
United States of America.

The right of Azeem Ibrahim to be identified as the author
of this publication is asserted by him in accordance with the
Copyright, Designs and Patents Act, 1988.

A Cataloguing-in-Publication data record for this book
is available from the British Library.

ISBN: 9781849049733 *paperback*

This book is printed using paper from registered sustainable
and managed sources.

www.hurstpublishers.com

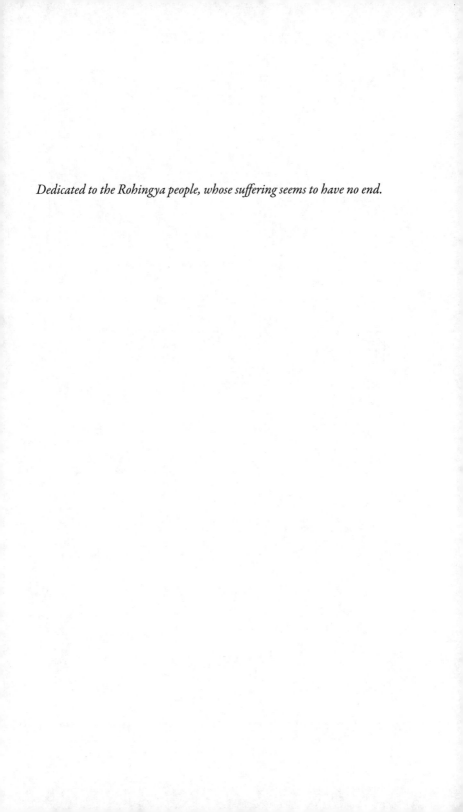

Dedicated to the Rohingya people, whose suffering seems to have no end.

CONTENTS

Acknowledgements   ix
List of Acronyms   xi
List of Key Individuals   xiii
List of Figures and Tables   xv
Map of Myanmar   xvi
Foreword   xvii

Introduction   1

1. A Short History of Burma to 1948   17
2. From Independence to Democracy (1948–2010)   35
3. The Return to Democracy (2008–2015)   55
4. Implications for the Rohingyas (2008–2015)   79
5. Genocide and International Law   99
6. Current Situation   113
7. What Can Be Done?   129

Conclusion   139
Epilogue, November 2017   143
Appendices   151
Glossary   157

Notes   161
References   207
Index   227

ACKNOWLEDGEMENTS

No book is written single-handedly. I have spoken with, and taken the time of, many dozens of people in the course of researching this book. It is always difficult to do justice to everyone, but I shall endeavour.

Above all I would like to give my sincere thanks to my friend and colleague Dr Roger Cook from the Scotland Institute and activist Jamila Hanan without whom this work would simply not exist. I am particularly grateful to my good friend and the Editor of the *Dhaka Tribune*, Zafar Sobhan who facilitated my first trip to the Rohingya camps and also arranged for Nobel Laureate, Professor Mohamamd Yunus, to pen the foreword to this book. That same first trip to the camps would not have been possible were it not for my guides and translators, Jaami A Farooq and Sayeed Alamgir from Cox Bazaar.

I am also grateful to several leading academics and activists who supported and contributed to this project. In particular, I owe a debt of gratitude to Ambassador John Shattuck whose experience from the Bosnia war was very relevant to this research. Also to Steven Kiersons from the Sentinal Project on Genocide Prevention; Shabnum Mayet, a leading activist and attorney from South Africa, Prof William Schabas, a world authority in International Law; Andrew Day, a leading voice and activist for the Rohingya, Alexia Solomou from the International Court of Justice; Emanuel Stokes, freelance journalist; Mohammad Ibrahim, Nay San Lwin, Erin Gallagher from Physicians for Human Rights and Dean Martha Minow from Harvard Law School.

Of my friends and colleagues, I would like to single out Keyleigh Long and Fiona McGreggor from the *Myanmar Times*. Both of whom I was very surprised to meet in Yangon and who helped me navigate the political wilderness of Myanmar and make my trip as fruitful as possible.

ACKNOWLEDGEMENTS

Thanks also to fellow author and academic Andrea Pitzer who bailed me out of a sticky situation whilst I was in Sittwe. A special thanks also goes to Sahira Sadiq for her valiant efforts in retrieving critical historical documents from the Indian National Archives in New Delhi.

Finally, I should like to thank my agent, Martin Toseland, my publisher Michael Dwyer and my wife Hena Ibrahim who supported me emotionally and practically during my long trips abroad.

Most of all I would like to give my deepest gratitude to all the Rohingya people I met and interviewed throughout my trips who I am unable to name for their own safety. Particularly my fearless guides who managed to smuggle me into and out of the IDP camps unscathed. They know who they are and I dedicate this book to them.

LIST OF ACRONYMS

ALD	Arakan League for Democracy
ANP	Arakan National Party
ASEAN	Association of South east Asian Nations
BCP	Burmese Communist Party
BIA	Burmese Independence Army
BSPP	Burma Socialist Programme Party
CRPP	Committee Representing the People's Parliament
DHRP	Democracy and Human Rights Party
ICC	International Criminal Court
NLD	National League for Democracy
NUP	National Unity Party
OIC	Organisation of Islamic Cooperation
RNDP	Rakhine Nationalities Development Party
UNHCR	United Nations High Commission for Refugees
USDP	Union Solidarity and Development Party

LIST OF KEY INDIVIDUALS

Kwan Kyi	Minister in the democratic government from 1948–62. Mother of Aung San Suu Kyi
Aung San Suu Kyi	Leader of the NLD
Shwe Mann	USDP party chairman until 2015 when he was removed by Thein Sein for being too close to the NLD. Ally of Than Shwe
Aye Maung	Leader of the RNDP/ANP
U Nu	Prime minister from independence in 1948 until the military coup in 1962 (with hiatuses)
Tin Oo	Vice-chairman of the NLD since 1988; had been the military's commander in chief up to 1976 when he was deposed after a failed coup
Aung San	Important military leader in the independence movement, assassinated in 1947. Father of Aung San Suu Kyi
Thein Sein	Myanmar's president since 2011, backed by the military and the USDP
Than Shwe	Leader of the government from 2004–11. Widely believed to still be influential and to control one of the major factions in the USDP
Ashin U Wirathu	Major figure in the 969 Movement, sometimes called 'Buddhism's Bin Laden'
Ne Win	General who organised the 1962 military coup; was forced to stand down after the 1988 popular revolt
Kyaw Zay	Important military leader in the independence movement; after independence led the military wing of the Burmese Communist Party

LIST OF FIGURES AND TABLES

1. Map of Myanmar xii
2. Languages of Burma, 1811 25
3. 1990 Electoral Results 41
4. 2010 Electoral Results 58
5. Map of Rakhine State Showing Locations of Internal Refugee Camps (2015) 88
6. 2014 Census Results 116

1. Map of Myanmar

FOREWORD

Muhammad Yunus

One of the fundamental challenges for a democracy is to work out how to ensure the voice of the majority does not trample the essential rights of minorities. Even as we applaud and rejoice in the new freedoms enjoyed by the people of Myanmar, the country's government must face this challenge as it evolves from autocratic rule into a democratic state. The tragedy of the Rohingya people, which continues to unfold in Rakhine State in the country's western corner, on the border with Bangladesh, will be its testing ground.

The rejection of citizenship rights for Rohingyas, denial of freedom of movement, eviction campaigns, violence against Rohingya women, forced labour, expulsion from their lands and property, violence and torture have made Myanmar's ethnic Rohingyas the most persecuted minority in the world. I humbly add my voice to the simple demand of the Rohingya people: that their rights as our fellow human beings be respected, that they be granted the right to live peacefully and without fear in the land of their parents, and without persecution on grounds of their ethnicity or their form of worship. A government must in the end be judged by how it protects the most vulnerable people in its society, and its generosity towards the weakest and most power-less. Let not the good work of this government be overshadowed by the con-tinuing persecution of the Rohingya people.

I urge the government of Myanmar to end all kinds of persecution and discrimination against the Rohingyas or any other ethnic and religious minorities. In addition, the international community needs to take a proactive role to end the ongoing isolation and persecution of the stateless Rohingya people. To end human rights violations not just in Myanmar but also around the world, the commitment of all stakeholders, including the United Nations, individual governments, humanitarian agencies, local communities and donors, is essential.

In tracing the plight of the Rohingya refugees, this book shows that the Rohingya refugee problem emerged out of a number of historical trajectories. It sets out all the issues in depth, and explores some of the approaches that are available to us to alleviate the situation—available to all of us, not just policy makers in the West. It contains a detailed account of the problems on the ground, their history and evolution, and their possible trajectories into the future. It also contains a great deal of hugely informative commentary and interviews with leading international policy makers, academics and humanitarians who are intimately acquainted with the many different sides of this tragedy and who will offer unparalleled insights into how to move forward. I have found it a stimulating read, utterly depressing at times, but ultimately hopeful—I believe that we can yet save the Rohingyas, and prove that we have learnt from the many tragic mistakes of the past.

I close with an appeal to the Myanmar government. You must amend the infamous 1982 law, and welcome the Rohingyas as full citizens of Myanmar with all attendant rights. In doing so you will end the possibility of the radicalisation of the Rohingyas and channel their energies for the development of Myanmar. You will remove the impetus for extremism and terrorism being generated by the current mistreatment of this vulnerable minority. A strong, stable and democratic Myanmar is not only in the interests of countries in the region, but will serve the cause of global peace and stability as well.

INTRODUCTION

This book argues that the reality facing the Rohingyas, a Muslim confessional ethnic group living in Rakhine province in western Myanmar, is the threat of genocide. Ever since Burma became independent in 1948 they have been targetted whenever ambitious (or desperate) politicians need to deflect attention from other matters. Both government officials and party leaders have called for their expulsion from their homeland, and the main opposition ignores their plight. The build up to the elections in late 2015 witnessed the final destruction of their civic rights in Myanmar (completing a process that began with the 1947 Constitution) and increasingly they are detained in what are now permanent internal refugee camps, where they are denied food, work and medical care.

If the regime fails to reign in the persecution of the Rohingyas (which only sustained international pressure will achieve) we will see a repeat of the by now familiar refugee crises, as the Rohingyas flee oppression. Moreover it is almost inevitable that there will be further inter-communal violence, aimed at forcing the remaining Rohingyas either to run away or succumb to mass murder. The charge of genocide is a serious one to make; the current situation in Myanmar fully justifies the use of this word.

Till recently the Rohingyas had attracted relatively little attention from the international press, even in the critical period leading up to only the third round of parliamentary elections to be held since 1990. If there is a common narrative it is that Burma (the name 'Myanmar' was adopted as part of a new set of laws in 1989) was a closed country of little direct interest to the world; that Aung San Suu Kyi, leader of the opposition National League for Democracy (NLD), having endured years of house arrest, is fully committed to a democratic future for all of Myanmar's ethnic and religious groups; and that instances of inter-ethnic or inter-confessional violence are to be expected in a country making the

1

difficult transition from authoritarian military rule to democracy. The problem is that all three of these beliefs are false.

Burma may have turned its back on the British-led Commonwealth when it gained independence in 1948, but it maintained substantial external links as a democracy (until 1962), under military rule (1962–2011) and subsequently. It is just that those links have been essentially pragmatic (especially under military rule), designed to allow the ruling elite to make money by trading away the country's wealth while at the same time buying arms. As we will see, the military regime (which remains essentially in power despite the notional return of democracy and the electoral defeat of its political party in 2015) does not like international criticism of its actions, but is far more responsive than is often believed. This means those who decide not to criticise it, or to set it red lines, are failing in their duty under international law.

As in its response to the political dynamics in regions such as the former Soviet Union and Yugoslavia, the Western media likes to identify clear heroes and villains. In Myanmar Aung San Suu Kyi clearly fits the hero category for this type of analysis. She has spent over twenty years of her life imprisoned in her own home, she has been awarded the Nobel Peace Prize, and she leads the main opposition party. However, as so often in the former Soviet Union, our chosen heroes are actually far more nuanced than our narratives demand. The other side of the story is that Aung San Suu Kyi herself is part of the Myanmar elite. Her father fought for the Japanese during World War II (albeit reluctantly) and was one of the leaders of the independence movement; her mother was a government minister from 1948–62. The NLD's deputy chairman was the commander in chief of the Burmese Army until 1976 when he was ousted after leading a failed coup. Equally, while the NLD may aim for democracy, in an ethnically complex country its electoral support comes almost entirely from the ethnically Burman community. Thus, in terms of its senior officials and the ethnicity of its electorate, the NLD shares much with the regime and the wider elite, and has had a difficult relationship with the ethnic minorities in Burma ever since independence. In particular, Aung San Suu Kyi has usually opted to avoid direct comment when the question of the systematic persecution of the Rohingyas is raised.

Another easy assumption is that Buddhism is a peaceful religion that shows no sign of the intolerance to other faiths that scars some forms of Christianity, Hinduism and Islam. Unfortunately this is not the case. Some who subscribe to Theravada Buddhism (which is also dominant in Sri Lanka and Thailand, where it is also associated with inter-communal violence) argue that for Buddhism to be safe all other religious beliefs must be eliminated. They also tend to look to the state for support and in a few extreme cases regard those who are not Buddhists as less than human.

In Myanmar, extremist Buddhist organisations have been at the heart of inter-communal violence ever since the return to relative democracy in 2011. Both the major political parties (the regime's Union Solidarity and Development Party, USDP, and the opposition NLD) are reliant on these organisations for much of their electoral support, giving them substantial influence over the political process. Equally there is emerging evidence that the old military regime funded and supported one major faction among the extremists to foster unrest. In turn, the existence of inter-communal violence keeps open the possibility of a return to military rule—in order, of course, to save the nation from violence.

This matters, as it means that Myanmar is not on a clear road to democracy. The violence against the Rohingyas is not an unpleasant, though predictable, side-effect of a society moving from authoritarian rule to liberalism. The repression of the Rohingyas is orchestrated, in part by those who believe there is no place in Myanmar for anyone who is not a Buddhist (and especially if they are Muslim), in part by ethnic extremists in other communities who want a racially pure state, and in part by the military regime, which is content to see a degree of unrest.

As this book argues, global indifference supports the regime and is leading to genocide. There is nothing to gain from not challenging the military and the notional opposition since, if they are left unchallenged, each year will see refugee crises, which are already destabilising the region. And, sooner or later, the world will wake up to a genocide on the scale that shocked the world in Rwanda in 1994.

Background

So how has this situation come about?

In a book primarily about contemporary events in Myanmar it might seem strange that, as we shall see, the answer partly lies in the history of the region before 1824 (when the First Anglo-Burmese War began). Nevertheless, this is the case. A key part of the narrative spun by the military, ethnic extremists, Buddhist fundamentalists and the NLD is that the Rohingyas have no right to be in the country. Time and again it is written that they are 'Bengalis' and should live in their own country—Bangladesh. This argument is widely believed in Myanmar and is one reason why the persecution of the Rohingyas is now so much worse than that of other ethnic minorities. Those groups may have sought to overthrow the state or have a history of armed resistance stretching over forty years but, oddly, there is no doubt that they are entitled to live within the geographical boundaries of the modern state (even if the regime does seek to steal their land and exploit and monopolise its mineral wealth).

What started out primarily as a scapegoating exercise by the military regime has unfortunately been absorbed by the Myanmar public. Discriminatory thinking against the Rohingyas gradually took root more generally, and today it has become deeply engrained. After 1962, the military junta in effect[1] created a new logic whereby only Burman Buddhists could really be loyal citizens (and if not ethnically Burmese then it was even more essential that they were Buddhists). This view has caught on. The Rohingyas, visibly 'alien' in the colour of their skin, in their language, and most of all in their religion, have borne the brunt of this discriminatory mode of thinking, even though they have not, historically, been the only minority ethnic group in Myanmar to suffer at the hands of the military. The approach that the successive military regimes took to build a new sense of nationhood in Burma resulted in a great degree of fear of outsiders, whether they were within or outside Burma's borders, and created a gnawing sense that other ethnic or religious groups form a constant and real threat to the viability of the country.[2]

The argument that the Rohingyas are really Bengali migrants who entered Burma during the period of British rule is widely repeated by Burmese officials in order to claim that the Rohingyas are not really Burmese.[3] Such officials, who quite unselfconsciously echo this colonial-era myth, include Ye Myint Aung, the Burmese envoy in Hong Kong, who described the Rohingyas as being as 'ugly as ogres' and as not sharing the 'fair and soft' skin of other Burmese ethnic groups.[4] Not quite the language one would expect to hear from a diplomat, but a common enough part of the discourse among the extremists and their apologists.[5]

Correcting the historical record

Chapter 1 discusses Burma's pre-1948 history in detail, but it is useful to set out the broad themes here. The first point to stress, and this is critical to any understanding of the Rohingyas' situation, is that until 1784 the histories of Arakan (now called Rakhine) and Burma were largely separate.[6] This matters because the debate about who lived in Arakan when it was conquered by the British in 1826 (having been part of the Burmese kingdom for a total of forty years out of the previous 500) is fundamental to understanding the modern-day persecution of the Rohingyas. However, and this cannot be overstressed, where people may or may not have lived in 1826 is irrelevant to their entitlement to citizenship today, and the criterion enshrined in the constitution and the statutes of Myanmar flies in the face of international law and the United Nations Charter. Nevertheless, the claims made around the 1826 issue are also false, and there is value in highlighting this fact.

Before dealing with the history of Arakan until Burma's independence, it is useful to very quickly cover the main dynamics in central Burma. The evidence is that the early communities who lived in that region were culturally linked to other parts of South East Asia.[7] Buddhism arrived in the region in stages but had become important by 800 AD.[8] Around this time there were also several waves of migration from Tibet and this saw the spread of an ethnically Tibetan-Burmese culture[9] and resulted in the establishment of the Pagan Kingdom.[10] This was the first state to both unify the entire Irrawaddy Valley and to be strong enough to push both west and east. During the period of its power, the Rakhine people crossed into Arakan and settled in the province.[11] They had retained a degree of independence from the Pagan Kingdom, while maintaining religious and linguistic links to central Burma. As Martin Smith says, 'The Rakhines, as an ethnic group ... appear to have come into the territory around the same time as the main body of ethnic Burman migration into the dry zone area of Upper Burma around the 9th or possibly 10th centuries A.D.'[12]

The Pagan Kingdom collapsed after a Mongol invasion in 1286 and Arakan broke away at the same time as the rest of Burma fragmented. By the 1750s the Burmese kings had again become a major regional power and made significant gains in a series of wars with neighbouring Siam.[13] Flush with success, they then invaded and conquered Arakan in 1784. It has been estimated that around 30,000 Muslims fled Arakan during the brief forty years of Burmese rule.[14] Unfortunately for the Burmese, their control of Arakan brought them into direct conflict with British-ruled India. In the First Anglo-Burmese War, Britain annexed Arakan in 1826. After two more wars, by 1886 all of Burma was ruled by the British (administratively as if it was part of India). In 1937 it was made a full colony in its own right (on the basis of the pre-1824 borders) and it became independent, in that particular geographical form, in 1948.

All of this matters for the simple reason that the regime, Buddhist extremists and Burmese nationalists now have a fixation on who was or was not living within these artificial borders in 1824–6.[15] While this is nonsense under the UN conventions on citizenship,[16] they are also inaccurate in their account of history.

It is thus useful to set out some of the historical record about the ethnic make-up of Arakan both before 1826 and during the period of British colonial rule. The available evidence suggests that a group speaking an Indo–Aryan language[17] migrated from northern India to Arakan in around 3000 BC. As will be discussed in Chapter 1, this group can be identified with the modern-day Rohingyas, and by 1000 AD they had largely adopted Islam and their language had absorbed other influences (from their trading across the Bay of Bengal) to the extent that it had diverged significantly from its original form.[18] When Arakan again split from the rest of Burma after 1300 AD, it became a multi-confessional (Hinduism, Islam and Buddhism were all present), multi-ethnic state. Most of its rulers were Muslims and the kingdom had close links (and enduring rivalries) with the Bengali kingdom to its north as well as with the various kingdoms in central Burma. Overall, as we will discuss in some detail, there is substantial evidence that an ethnic group, now known as the Rohingyas, lived in Arakan before the Burmese invasion of 1784.[19]

To address the charge of the extremists that the Rohingyas only arrived in Arakan during the period of British rule, it is useful to examine the census record of the British colonial era. Shortly after the British conquest, a survey carried out by Charles Paton indicated the population of the province was around 100,000.[20] As with many British censuses of the colonial period, he focused as much on religion as ethnicity and identified that there were 30,000 Muslims split between three ethnic groups: a large community mainly in the north (the Rohingyas); the Kamans (a group descended from Afghan mercenaries who had served the previous dynasty); and 'a small but long established Muslim community around Moulmen'.

If, as Buddhist extremists argue, there were no Rohingyas present in 1824, all the population increase in the number of Muslims since that date must have been a product of immigration from India. We will deal with this in some detail in the next chapter but for the moment it is enough to note that the British census of 1911[21] identified the Buddhists of Arakan (that is, the Rakhine) as having a population of 210,000 (compared to 60,000 in 1824) and the Muslims as numbering 155,000. As we will see, of the latter group, the Rohingyas likely made up the majority. Since, as will be discussed in Chapter 1, some 30,000 Rohingyas returned very soon after the British conquest, this indicates that both the Rakhine and Rohingya communities grew at similar rates in the first eighty years of British rule.

However, to be clear, there was indeed migration from British-ruled India to Burma before 1937.[22] This occurred in four main areas. The British established major rice fields in the lower Irrawaddy Delta and initially imported Indian labour (as the particular form of rice production they used was not practiced in Burma). Equally, they established significant rubber plantations and again imported labour to work in these. The British also generally favoured non-Buddhists in the colonial administration (as the various Christian and Muslim ethnic groups were seen to be more loyal) and, again, workers migrated from India to fill such roles. Finally, Indian workers came to be dominant in the docks and the wider transportation sectors. None of this significantly involved the Rohingyas, who mostly carried on working as farmers and fishermen on their own land rather than taking up work in the colonial administration.

Escalating discrimination and exclusion

British rule in Burma ended in 1948 and a multi-ethnic state blessed with potential riches but facing major problems (not least a severe financial crisis)[23] came into being. Almost immediately, the Burmese Communist Party launched a military campaign designed to overthrow the new government[24] at the same time as some British diplomats were encouraging the largely Christian Karen ethnic group to seize power.[25] All this set in motion a series of wars between the Burmese state and ethnic minorities on its borders; these wars have only recently died away (and still persist in some areas).

For the Rohingyas, independence brought a particular set of problems. They had remained loyal to the British when the Japanese had invaded in 1942. This, in turn, had provoked serious inter-communal strife with the Rakhine[26] and led to the fragmentation of the previously mixed Rohingya and Rakhine communities across Arakan. By the time the Japanese surrendered, most Rohingyas who had lived in the south had fled to the north of the province, and ethnic Rakhine who had previously lived in the north had fled south. Even worse, the British had promised partial independence to the Rohingyas but reneged on this once the war was over.[27] This led to a short-lived revolt[28] by the Rohingyas, and then some Rohingya politicians petitioned for the inclusion of the northern districts of Arakan into what was then East Pakistan.[29]

Compared to the sustained armed revolts of other ethnic groups, these attempts to gain a degree of self-determination were minimal but still led

Burma's new, post-independence rulers to see the Rohingyas as hostile.[30] Indeed, unlike most of Burma's many ethnic groups, they were not given full citizenship in 1948.[31] It is hard to understand why the Rohingyas were targeted in this way. They are ethnically different to most other groups in the country, and they are the largest Muslim community. Most likely they were simply a target of convenience, with the ethnic tensions provoked by World War II still very raw. However, Prime Minister U Nu indicated on several occasions that this was a temporary problem and that 'The Rohingya has the equal status of nationality with Kachin, Kayah, Karen, Mon, Rakhine and Shan'.[32] There is ample evidence in the Burmese legal framework[33] and in the practical decisions that were made that the Rohingyas were not seen as being especially different[34] to any other ethnic minority in the period of democratic rule up to 1962.[35] They are described as Rohingyas in the 1961 census, indicating an ongoing recognition of their existence as an ethnic group under that description.[36]

This relative tolerance started to change once the military came to power in 1962. However, the gradual and incremental nature of this process must be stressed. Some Rohingyas supported the military rule and served in parliament as members of the Burmese Socialist Programme Party. However, at the same time the generals were desperately trying to justify their own rule. In addition to their notional socialist allegiance (which in practice meant very little),[37] they decided if they could not have an ethnically pure state (which would have meant giving up all the wealth in the border areas to the north and east), they would use being 'Buddhist' as a test for being a proper citizen of the state.

The 1974 Constitution of the Socialist Republic of the Union of Burma[38] was a critical step as it removed the status the Rohingyas had been granted at independence and insisted that they accept identity cards that described them as 'Foreigners'. This led to a period of sustained violence against the Rohingyas and a large outflow of refugees, mostly to Bangladesh. The 1982 Burmese Citizenship Law[39] took this a step further: it started the modern-day obsession with who had lived in Burma in 1824 by stating that the Rohingyas were now foreigners, since they were deemed not to have lived in Arakan before 1823. In interviews I conducted in 2015 with Myanmar-based journalists and Rohingya politicians (whom I will leave anonymous for their safety), it became clear that this period saw a sustained campaign of propaganda and lies aimed at the Rohingyas to convince the rest of the population that this Muslim minority group, who spoke a language very different to Burmese, had no place in the country.

One question that does persist, and is harder to answer than it might first seem, is exactly why the Rohingyas became such a core target for the regime,

Buddhist extremists and the main opposition party. One argument is that they are a convenient target, being different in terms of ethnicity and religion. Another is that they are a safe target, as unlike other ethnic groups such as the Karen or Shan they do not have a long history of armed revolt, apart from the brief unrest in 1947. What is clear is that persecution of the Rohingyas, and the denial of even the most basic of their human rights, has become the one belief that the military, the democratic opposition and the extremists all share. In a perverse kind of way, it is in this ritual of persecution and oppression that the state and other political forces in Myanmar find harmony.

It is also worth noting that Rakhine was and is one of the poorest regions in Myanmar. It lacks the mineral wealth of other areas and is mostly reliant on fishing and agriculture (the port at Sittwe is the only major industrial conurbation). Locals interviewed by the author stressed that, as a result, there is a degree of prejudice among other Burmese groups who see Rakhine and the Rohingyas as being backward.[40] This in turn may explain why the Rakhine Buddhists are so ardent in arguing for their own 'superiority' over the Rohingyas, which is a driving factor in their persecution. In the rest of Myanmar, prejudice against the Rohingyas is common, but altogether relatively low key, and is really part and parcel of the wider anti-Muslim sentiment stirred up by the nationalist 969 Movement and other extremists.

All Burmese suffered when the 'Burmese Road to Socialism' proved to be an economic disaster[41] and 1988 saw a massive popular revolt that forced the generals to concede a return to democracy. New laws introduced in 1989 retained the discriminatory ethnicity laws from 1974, but a senior Rohingya official noted that the Rohingyas were still allowed to vote[42] in the 1990 elections and to stand for political parties[43]—either confessional parties or the military-backed National Unity Party or the new National League for Democracy. However, in a worrying sign of what was to come, the NLD (and its allies from the ethnic Rakhine community) tried to have Rohingya parliamentarians banned on the grounds that they must have used fake identity cards in order to stand for election.[44] Equally, renewed military attacks on the Rohingyas in 1991–2 saw a further 250,000 flee to Bangladesh and Malaysia.[45]

The military annulled the results of the 1990 elections and was able to hang on to power until 2008. At that stage a renewed popular revolt (the Saffron Revolution) and the impact of Cyclone Nargis[46] forced major changes. The 2008 Constitution[47] allowed for a return to a limited form of democracy but quite deliberately repeated the restrictive definition of citizenship from the 1974 legislation. Clearly the Rohingyas were to have no part in this democratic future.[48]

The run up to the 2015 elections completed this gradual process of destruction of the Rohingyas' civil rights. The 2014 census[49] forced them to choose between being described as 'Bengali' or not being able to register to vote. The first option carried the threat of deportation, the second of being forced into one of the refugee camps that had sprung up after the 2012–13 violence in Rakhine. Even worse, the regime then confiscated the 'White Cards' that had been the last form of official documentation held by many Rohingyas.[50]

Finally, very few Muslim candidates were allowed to stand for parliament in the 2015 elections[51] (and very few Muslims were eligible to vote).[52] A combination of judgments by the State Electoral Commission[53] and complicity by the major, supposedly multi-confessional, parties means that roughly 5 per cent of the population are now disenfranchised. This is quite deliberate and represents a complete repudiation of the ideals of some who fought for Burmese independence.[54] The current persecution and exclusion of the Rohingyas reflects over forty years of state propaganda designed to ensure that most Burmese now regard them as foreigners and as a threat to Buddhist culture. This narrative, disgracefully, has not been challenged by the democratic opposition party, even though it is led by a winner of the Nobel Peace Prize[54] who is widely praised in the Western media for her commitment to democracy.[56]

As one of the few ethnically Rohingya MPs elected in 2010 put it in an interview with the author:

> Myanmar people are suffering. If people are in hell, I would say Rohingyas are at the bottom of the hell, the worst case, unfortunately. So Myanmar government made the policy by using race or religion, nationality, and then almost all Myanmar ethnic have started hatred against Rohingya and hatred against Islam, and accusing collectively, 'These people are illegal immigrants.'[57]

This situation is no accident; it has been deliberately manufactured.

Contemporary Politics

Later chapters in this book will cover in detail the shifting political landscape of Burma since independence. In this section the primary goal is to set out some of the complexities of the current situation, in particular with respect to the November 2015 elections. Broadly there are five separate—though overlapping—groups of political actors. These are:

1. The military. Despite the changes since 2008, the military remains very powerful and many former generals sit in parliament as part of the USDP. They retain control of the country's economic wealth.

2. The two multi-ethnic, multi-confessional parties. The USDP was set up by the military to contest the 2010 elections (which it won); the NLD acts as the primary opposition party. At least in theory (and until recently in practice), both have memberships that are multi-ethnic and multi-confessional. However, since 2011 both have increasingly only spoken for the Burman ethnic community (who are mostly Buddhist).

3. Ethnic regional parties. Many ethnic groups such as the Shan, Karen and Rakhine have set up parties that reflect their own specific interests. The key exception is, of course, the Rohingyas.

4. Buddhist monks. These have become increasingly important in the political arena since 1998. Among the extremists there are two main organisations, the 969 Movement and the MaBaTha (the Patriotic Association of Myanmar). Both are at the forefront of all moves to demonise Myanmar's Muslim minority and have been implicated in almost all the major episodes of inter-communal violence since 2010. However, there are other groups of Buddhist monks who have challenged these movements' interpretation of their faith and their intolerance.

5. Civil society groups. Groups such as Pan Zagar have called for an end to anti-Muslim hate speech, but they are weak.[58] Other groups have convinced the NLD to campaign against recent laws banning marriage between Buddhist women and Muslim men.[59]

It is useful to consider each of these in turn, and to draw attention to where they have close links.

The military

Before independence there had been a substantial debate between those like Aung San (the father of Aung San Suu Kyi) who argued that the military should be subordinate to the civil authorities,[60] and those like Ne Win who saw the military as the only reliable institution in an unstable multi-ethnic, multi-confessional state. Ne Win won (especially as Aung San was assassinated before independence) and by 1962 had taken power in a military coup. Embroiled in wars with most of Burma's ethnic communities (and facing a serious challenge from the Burmese Communist Party), the military came to distrust the population of the country and looked for a unifying ideology. Initially this was the idea of a uniquely 'Burmese Road to Socialism,'[61] and this was allied to a sense that Buddhism could also form a unifying role.

Politically, the generals maintained the veneer of a civilian government. Thus, after 1974 they ruled through the Burmese Socialist Programme Party.[62]

Equally, the military contained multiple factions and this led to various attempted coups and changes in leadership. Ne Win finally fell in 1988 after pro-democracy demonstrations had shaken the regime. For the 1990 elections the military formed the National Unity Party, which performed disastrously.[63] When it was forced to reinstate some degree of democracy after 2008, it was clear it had learnt some lessons from this episode. Its new political vehicle was the USDP, and this time it took out an insurance policy against setbacks in the democratic process: 25 per cent of the seats in the new parliament were reserved for the USDP and these were allocated to serving officers.

The fundamental problem is that the military still controls Myanmar[64] and do not have the slightest intention of withdrawing from politics. It needs to retain political power to protect its substantial economic interests, and, importantly, its belief that only it can represent the nation is at the core of its approach.[65] This is not to say it is a unitary body: there are clear and ongoing indications of factional disputes,[66] in part about how to interact with the NLD, and also about the relative importance of international links.

However, rigging the electoral system (25 per cent of seats are still guaranteed for the military's political party) is not the only insurance policy it took out. There is growing evidence that the MaBaTha Buddhist extremist organisation was set up by the military as an alternative power base.[67] To understand why it may have done this, it is useful first to survey the rest of the current political scene.

The 'national' political parties

Currently there are two notionally multi-ethnic, multi-confessional parties: the military-created USDP and the opposition NLD. The latter emerged during the 1988 uprising,[68] initially led by a serving general, a former general (Tin Oo) and Aung San Suu Kyi. This coalition was not accidental. The NLD saw itself as reaching back to the anti-colonial tradition of being both a mass party and an elite organisation that also combined civilian and military elements. The problem was that in its initial incarnation it was indeed an elite party,[69] drawing its leadership initially from those in the governing elite who had fallen foul of Ne Win. While the party appealed to the protesting students, it had no direct connection with the bulk of the Burmese population. This connection was provided by the monks who were at the forefront of the protests. By allying with the monks, the NLD gained the support of a group who were widely respected by most Burmese and able to give the NLD the electoral base it needed.

The NLD boycotted the 2010 elections (partly because Aung San Suu Kyi was banned from standing) but did take part in the limited set of elections in 2012, winning forty-three out of forty-five contests.[70] It has since won a landslide victory in the 2015 elections, but problems remain for it. One is that Aung San Suu Kyi is still debarred from becoming president[71] (though she was allowed to run for parliament this time). This concern connects with the current factional dispute within the USDP, in which some elements may be prepared to do a deal with the NLD to retain some power after its electoral defeat[72] and may even be prepared to consider a form of national unity government between the USDP and the NLD. The immediate post-election period suggests that this outcome remains possible.

A second problem for the NLD is that while it seeks to be multi-ethnic, its electoral base remains the Burman ethnic communities (and it has expelled most of its Muslim members);[73] this leaves it very reliant on the Buddhist monks to influence the Burman electorate. Unfortunately, since 1988 the monks have become intensely anti-Islamic and they demand that the NLD support their positions; if it does not then it forfeits their support.

Regional political parties

The 1988 events also saw the emergence of a range of single-ethnicity parties that contested districts in their own state. The most important, in terms of this book, was the party formed to represent the Buddhist Rakhine community, initially called the Arakan League for Democracy (ALD). Its manifesto was explicitly anti-Rohingya from the start and called for the exclusion of the Rohingyas from the electoral process and the establishment of Rakhine villages in areas with a Rohingya majority.[74] Rohingya activists and politicians note that this party was closely allied to the NLD and joined with the NLD in challenging the validity of those elections which had been won by ethnically Rohingya candidates.[75]

Renamed as the Rakhine Nationalities Development Party (RNDP), it contested the 2010 elections and won the majority of seats in the province. The change of name has done nothing to dampen its hatred of the Rohingyas.[76] Its leadership has been heavily implicated in organising the 2012 and 2013 ethnic violence[77] that effectively forced many Rohingya into what are now permanent internal refugee camps. Its leaders[78] have also repeatedly called for the forced expulsion of the Rohingyas[79] and they have increasingly allied themselves with the extremist Buddhist groups.

Buddhist groups

The Buddhist monks are roughly clustered into three groups: the 969 Movement, the MaBaTha and a small group of mostly older clerics who reject the anti-Islamic rhetoric. None of these are political parties in any conventional sense, nor are they particularly tightly organised, but they are influential. The former two seem to be dominant and to see Muslims as threats to Myanmar's Buddhists, leading them to advocate discrimination and sometimes violence against them; their actions often seem calculated to 'driv[e] Islam completely out of the country'.[80] However, the two movements have very different origins despite close similarities in their rhetoric and actions.

The 969 Movement grew out of the 1988 uprising and, at least initially, was opposed to the military regime (many of its older leaders were imprisoned in the 1990s).[81] While it is clear the 969 Movement wields a great deal of influence over the NLD (in particular limiting their willingness to challenge anti-Muslim prejudices and especially to stand up for the Rohingyas),[82] some in the NLD have become worried about where the 969 Movement is trying to take Myanmar.[83]

In some ways, since its foundation in 2010 the MaBaTha has become more influential than the older 969 Movement. They now have a great deal of control over religious education in Myanmar,[84] which they use to teach their extremist anti-Muslim interpretation of Buddhism. They have also been running a number of campaigns to force Buddhists to boycott Muslim-owned businesses.[85] More critically, they have been at the forefront of every instance of violence against Myanmar's Muslim communities. In particular, the violence in Rakhine in 2012 and 2013 was orchestrated by an alliance of the RNDP and the MaBaTha.[86]

Recent evidence suggests a simple reason for the MaBaTha's influence: it seems to have been set up by the military as a front organisation.[87] Not only do the generals probably believe their own rhetoric that the Rohingyas have no place in Myanmar, but civil unrest is potentially very useful for them.[88] Having badly lost the 2015 elections, they may find it far easier to justify a coup on the grounds of major domestic unrest rather than one overthrowing a democratic government. In the meantime the MaBaTha have another useful role. The USDP struggles to appeal to many Burmese apart from those directly employed by the state.[89] In the same way that the 969 Movement allowed the NLD to broaden its electoral appeal, in 2015 the MaBaTha campaigned for the USDP.

In effect, the military is directly backing two different groups in contemporary Myanmar. It has, in the USDP, a notionally non-sectarian political organisation (and, to be fair, until the 2015 election campaign, one of its MPs was an ethnic Rohingya) with a guaranteed block of parliamentary seats. And it now has its own organisation of Buddhist extremists who both offer the means to channel electoral support to the USDP and to create violence that can later be used to justify a military intervention. It is against this background that many Western observers persist in believing that Myanmar is making a steady, if occasionally rocky, transition to democracy.[90]

Civil society

Although less important than the organised political parties and groups of Buddhist monks, Myanmar also has a small civil society movement. Networks such as Pan Zagar[91] deliberately challenge the incendiary language of the Buddhist extremists. They have some allies among those monks[92] who have challenged the ideology of the 969 Movement and provided protection to Muslims when they are attacked by extremists.[93] Women's groups led the opposition to the recent marriage laws[94] and are widely credited with ensuring that the NLD opposed this element of the recent set of anti-Muslim laws passed by parliament.[95] In turn, this rare act of opposition to anti-Muslim prejudice is now used by the MaBaTha and the RNDP as evidence that the NLD is pro-Muslim.

What should be done?

This raises the question of what can be done to improve the Rohingyas' situation. This book adds to the substantial evidence that Myanmar is not on a turbulent but inevitable road from authoritarian rule to liberal democracy. In reality, since 2010 the persecution of the country's small Muslim population has grown far worse and the lead up to the 2015 elections saw the quite deliberate exclusion of all Muslims from the electoral process. Equally, since 2010 we have seen substantial violence aimed at the Rohingyas,[96] their incarceration in what can only be described as outdoor prison camps,[97] and increasingly desperate waves of refugees.[98]

This leads to the first thing we can do. We can stop believing the pleasant myth that Myanmar is finding a way to democracy and that it has an opposition party committed to the good of all its citizens.[99]

This particularly affects the international community and its response. Too often the idea that Myanmar is isolated and resistant to pressure is used to justify inaction. This is not true. The regime needs international links in order to make money,[100] buy weapons, and attain a veneer of respectability.[101] It has also become very adept at playing its various international partners off against each other: for example, it effectively threatens the countries of the ASEAN (Association of Southeast Asian Nations) that if they persist in criticism then, regretfully, it will swing towards Chinese influence.[102]

At the moment, it is clear that the ASEAN has lost patience with Myanmar over the persecution of the Rohingyas.[103] ASEAN countries had to bear the brunt of the refugee crisis in 2015 and are aware that unless the situation in Rakhine improves, further destabilising refugee flows are now inevitable. Accordingly, a prominent group of ASEAN parliamentarians have argued that there is a need to abandon the traditional stance of non-interference in the affairs of member states and are demanding that Myanmar allows international observers into Rakhine and restores at least basic civil rights for the Rohingyas.[104] The rest of the international community would do well to back the current ASEAN initiatives.

Finally, there is a small but brave and committed, civil society movement in Myanmar. Directly backing this would probably do more harm than good since its participants would inevitably then be branded as stooges of external powers.[105] However, noting their importance and being less adulatory towards the NLD would send a powerful signal that the human rights of all those who live in Myanmar matter—not just those of particular ethnic or religious groups.

Myanmar now stands on the edge of genocide.[106] The Rohingyas have nothing left, most live in internal refugee camps[107] and they are denied basic health care and the ability to work. Due to these deliberate pressures they look to flee;[108] and many in the regime, of the regional Rakhine establishment and among the Buddhist extremists are keen to encourage them to do so—so keen that the use of violence to trigger a final exodus cannot be ruled out. This is genocide:[109] it is the deliberate destruction of an identified ethnic group. International indifference only encourages the regime to believe it can get away with it.

1

A SHORT HISTORY OF BURMA TO 1948

The attitude towards the Rohingyas that the Myanmar establishment displays, and its hostile actions towards the Rohingyas, are informed by a narrative that the Rohingyas do not have a legitimate place in the state. Usually this is simply expressed in openly racist terms (often linked to anti-Muslim prejudices), but there are some attempts being made to justify these prejudices using scholarship. As we will see in this chapter, not only is such scholarship badly flawed but, of course, it is completely irrelevant in any case.

The establishment narrative ignores the inconvenient reality that the territory occupied by historical Burmese states does not correspond neatly to the territory of Myanmar today: the modern province of Rakhine was only ever part of the earlier Burmese states for relatively brief periods of time. It is therefore no surprise that it has an ethnic mix very different to that of the rest of the country, especially as few modern states represent a perfect match between ethnic groups and political boundaries.

The history of the region of Burma has seen a sequence of ethnic shifts, conquest, expansion and collapse that is quite typical of the history of most regions in the world. In the last millennium-and-a-half, there has tended to be a core state or core in the Irrawaddy Valley, which repeatedly expanded towards and contracted from the periphery of the modern-day territory of Myanmar; it should therefore should come as no surprise that by the mid-1990s around one-third of the population of Myanmar was made up of ethnic groups distinct from the Burman majority.[1] This naturally reflected the history of interaction with China to the north, India to the west, Thailand and Laos to the east and Indonesia and Malaysia to the south. In particular, the mountainous regions to the north and east of the central Irrawaddy regions have long been home to a diverse range of non-Burmese ethnicities. Some of these groups live exclusively in modern-day Myanmar but many live on both sides of the various borders. Up to the nineteenth century, the evidence points to a degree of ethnic and religious tolerance,[2] even as the Burmese regions became increasingly dominated by Buddhism,[3] while the more marginal groups retained animist beliefs or adopted Christianity or Islam.

As discussed in the Introduction, all this means it is particularly important to separate the history of Arakan from that of Burma up to the 1800s. The core of the Burmese civilisation in central Burma, along the Irrawaddy Valley, is geographically and culturally linked to the Tibetan region, southwest China and the rest of East Asia. The south (the modern-day Mon and Tanintharyi provinces) is part of the wider Malaysian Peninsula[4] and has sea links to the south, including Sri Lanka and parts of Indonesia. In fact, this was the original vector for the early spread of Buddhism to Burma.

However, the Arakan region in the west has always been separated from the rest of Burma by a high and difficult-to-traverse coastal mountain range. As such, for most of its early history, both in terms of ethnic make-up and political-economic interaction, the natural links of the region were across the Bay of Bengal to India rather than with the rest of Burma. It was also a relatively poor province, reliant on subsistence agriculture and fishing, so it was generally of little interest to would-be conquerors. Indeed, early in modern Burmese history we see plenty of instances of warfare with Siam (now Thailand) over control of rich trade routes, but relatively little interest in Arakan.[5]

This state of isolation only changed from around 1000 AD, when the Rakhine ethnic group moved from central Burma to Arakan.[6] The modern-day province is named after this group. From then until late in the 1700s, Arakan had periods of dependence on the rulers of central Burma, periods of independence and even short periods when it dominated neighbouring Bangladesh. In 1784, Arakan was formally annexed by the Kingdom of Burma. However, this conquest brought the kingdom into conflict with the British, who also had an interest in the region. At the end of the First Anglo-Burmese War (1824–6), Arakan was appropriated by the British, and once again separated from Burmese rule. However, once the British had conquered the rest of Burma in the 1880s, the province was included in colonial Burma and, as a consequence, became part of Burma on independence in 1948. At that same time its administrative title was changed from Arakan to Rakhine.

Early history (to 1000 AD)

Burma

Archaeological evidence suggests that the earliest human settlements in modern-day Myanmar date back to 11,000 BC. By around 6000 BC there is evidence of a more settled culture, with cave paintings depicting domesticated animals.[7] One of the earliest sites showing evidence of agriculture has been found near Mandalay, and dates to around 500 BC. The styles of pottery, iron working and burial practice all show close links with those practised in Thailand and Cambodia at the same time. This suggests that the earliest settlements in central Myanmar were culturally linked to those elsewhere in South East Asia and that the earliest settlers in the region were related to other ethnic groups prevalent in South Asia. Groups such as the Mon (who live in the southern corner of Burma) still have much ethnically in common with the Khmers of Cambodia.

The first walled cities in the region appeared around 200 BC.[8] These showed design features common both to India and to Thailand, indicating the diffusion of Indian norms and culture across South East Asia in this period. Indian approaches to city-planning dominated, as did both Hinduism and Buddhism. These new religions arrived in the region at this period and mixed with the older indigenous animist beliefs. At this stage, central Myanmar was ethnically split between the Mon, who lived in the south, and the Pyu, who lived in the north.[9]

The Mon are widely credited with bringing Theravada Buddhism to Myanmar through their trading links with Sri Lanka. However, this did not immediately lead to the dominance of Buddhism, and the archaeological record of their main coastal city, Thaton, contains examples of both Buddhist and Hindu art. The city was conquered by the emerging Pagan Kingdom at the beginning of the eleventh century AD, marking the end of an independent Mon Kingdom, and the Mon were then largely absorbed into the new Burmese Buddhist culture, even though they have retained their own language.

The northern Pyu city states seem to have been ethnically related to the wider Burmese–Tibetan group, possibly indicating that they were migrants from Tibet, a characteristic shared with the later Burmese migrants. Indeed, the Pyu and the Burmese languages appear to have similar linguistic roots,[10] especially when compared to the differences between Mon and Burmese. As in southern Burma, the earliest religions in the region dominated by the Pyu were a mix of animist, Hindu and Buddhist, with the latter growing in relative importance over time. Buddhism was first recorded from around 500 AD. The Pyu occupied a region that also sat astride an important trade route between India and China and this may have given them access to wealth and exposure to external influences, but it also left them vulnerable to their more powerful neighbours.[11] The Pyu city states eventually fell after being weakened in a series of wars with the Chinese in the ninth century AD, leading to an incursion from Tibet of Burmese tribes taking advantage of ethnic ties and the weakening of the Pyu. The evidence for this period is partial and complicated, but one plausible explanation for this incursion is that the northernmost Pyu cities were already inhabited by people of Burman ethnicity as early as 900 AD.[12] In effect, this was less a process of conquest from Tibet and more one of two closely related groups intermingling as their relative power shifted.

In the ninth century these minor cities coalesced into the Pagan Kingdom,[13] during which time the Burmese peoples spread along the Irrawaddy Valley following the collapse of the Pyu city states. Burmese language and culture absorbed local influences from India and from the Mon in particular, but also derived linguistic and cultural elements from the wider region, from neighbouring states, and traders and settlers.[14]

Arakan

The earliest settlers in Arakan were probably closely related to aboriginal cultures that existed across South East Asia, Indonesia and Australia.[15] However, the earliest settled kingdoms that left an archaeological record were Indo–Aryan groups who arrived from the Ganges Valley as early as 3000 BC.[16] At the time of their arrival, minorities such as the Mru, Sak, Kumi and other Chin ethnic groups were already living in the region[17] and continued to do so in the remote hilly regions.

The nineteenth-century British historian H.H. Wilson suggested that the dominant culture in Arakan was Indian up to the tenth century AD, and that only then did growing interaction with Burmese culture begin.[18] Pamela Gutman[19] follows Wilson in arguing that the only way to understand the history of Arakan up to this point is to see it as a region of India rather than part of the Burmese world. In particular, the high coastal mountains and difficult terrain made overland interaction with the rest of contemporary Myanmar much harder than forging links across the Bay of Bengal.

Gutman suggests that whoever was in Arakan before the ninth century AD had ethnic links to Indian groups, rather than to groups in what is today

Myanmar. The Rohingyas, whose language is Indo–Aryan,[20] from the Bengali–Assamese branch, may well descend from these pre-ninth-century inhabitants of the region, whereas the Rakhine did not arrive until the ninth century. The Indo–Aryan roots of the Rohingyas are manifested in inscriptions from the Hindu temples at Anandra Chandra (eighth century AD), which display close similarities to similar inscriptions and buildings in India.[21]

The earliest rulers of Arakan were mostly Hindus,[22] reflecting the links to India. However, Islam arrived in the seventh century via trading links to India and Arabia, but the region remained multi-confessional, with Hindus, Buddhists and Muslims living together.[23] Under these influences, the Rohingyas' language evolved from its early roots with the adoption of Arabic and Persian words, and the script adapted to more closely resemble that of Bengali. Equally, as an ethnic group, the Rohingyas absorbed Arab and Persian elements in the period up to 1000 AD. Later, the close links with Bengal meant absorbing both Bengali and Mughal ethnic influences as part of the regular interaction with northern India.

As Burmese power consolidated in the central Irrawaddy region, the degree of interaction between Arakan and the Burmese kingdoms increased. The Rakhine ethnic group crossed the Arakan Mountains and settled in the region in around 1000 AD, and this was followed by a period of relative domination of the region by the Burmese Pagan Kingdom. In effect, from 1000 AD Arakan came to interact as much with the rest of Burma as it did with Bengal and northern India.

From 1000 to 1824

Burma

Burman ethnic groups steadily gained more influence in central Burma, and by 1100 they had conquered the Mon. This led to emergence of the powerful Burmese Pagan Kingdom[24] and this was probably the first largely ethnic-Burman state in Myanmar. As a consequence, many later rulers have sought to trace their lineage to this era, so as to claim legitimacy in ruling over the whole of Burma. Even the military regimes of the past sixty years have been very keen to stress the importance of this period, and have invested substantially in rebuilding pagodas that dated from the Pagan era.[25]

The Pagan Kingdom unified the areas previously divided between the Mon and Pyu under the first king of the dynasty, Anawrahta (1044–77 AD). The new regime adopted Theravada Buddhism as the state religion, built a substantial number of religious buildings and also incorporated older animist deities into a Buddhist religious framework. The bulk of the population adopted Buddhism, but there was as yet no movement to exclude other religious beliefs prevalent in the region. There also seems to have been a great degree of cultural pluralism, and the Mon community in particular seems to have contributed substantially to cultural developments of the era.[26] By the late thirteenth century, the Pagan Kingdom was a major protector of Buddhism, constructing monasteries[27] and using its state power to ensure a coherent religious community emerged. However, this substantial expenditure on religious buildings, arts and monks may have undermined the economic basis of the kingdom.[28] A small Mongol incursion (part of a wider series of attacks into South East Asia from Vietnam to Thailand) in 1286 brought about the rapid collapse of the kingdom and its fragmentation into a number of smaller city states.

But though central Burma became a patchwork of smaller polities, most of the successor states sought to draw their legitimacy from the Pagan period. Equally, in terms of architecture and art, the process of moving from norms shared with India and regions to the east towards a more indigenous Burmese aesthetic continued. The Ava Kingdom (1287–1752) came to dominate upper Burma around Kyaukse. Over time this became the dominant power and managed to unify the Irrawaddy Valley by about 1636. This expansion ended the power of the Shan Dynasty that had taken control of northern Burma after the Mongol invasion and had sought to remove Buddhist influence[29] from that region. The renewed Ava Dynasty again allowed Buddhism to spread. Most rulers were Buddhist and more and more of the population was converted.

The Ava Dynasty was succeeded by the Konbaung Dynasty (1752–1885). This period saw the emergence of Burma as a major regional power. It also saw the foundation of Mandalay (in 1857) as the capital of the new state. This assertive and aggressive dynasty won victory in wars against neighbouring Siam, and the resultant boost of wealth and power allowed the kingdom to annex Arakan in 1784.

But this then triggered a series of wars with the British, which led to the loss of Arakan by 1826. Full annexation of the rest of the country by the British followed in 1886.

In terms of religion, by the nineteenth century there had been a degree of fusion between state and religion, as the king saw himself as a protector of all Buddhist monasteries including those in provinces occupied by the British[30] after their conquest of Arakan. Though this linkage between religion and state fell apart after the British had conquered the entire country, it remained an important issue for many Burmese Buddhist nationalists.

In their turn, the British were mostly indifferent towards organised Buddhism and a number of monasteries fell into disrepair or were abandoned.[31] The British took a secular view of the administration of their colonies, mostly out of necessity, and especially refused to be dragged into disputes about religious practice and monastic discipline[32] within the Buddhist community. This indifference indirectly undermined the monastic structure because, by refusing to appoint a head of the *sangha* who would oversee discipline in the different monasteries,[33] the British allowed the hierarchical structures so critical to Theravada Buddhism to fall apart. Some Buddhists saw this as part of a British plot to promote Christianity but a more plausible explanation is simply one of disinterest. The consequence was a degree of fragmentation and the loss of an organised Buddhist voice. Some in the early nationalist movements took little inspiration from Buddhism as such,[34] but others considered regaining independence as a precondition for protecting Burma's Buddhist heritage.[35]

The failure to protect Buddhism is now seen by many pro-Buddhist commentators as the major failing of British rule—they criticise the British for failing in their duty as rulers to protect and promote Buddhism as an integral part of Burmese culture.[36] This attitude is derived from Theravada Buddhism's notion that the strength of the religion is reliant on a state that is committed to its protection.[37]

Arakan

While historical Arakan started to interact with the kingdoms of central Burma from the eleventh century onwards, the area was formally independent of Burma up to the end of the eighteenth century. However, the Rohingyas' dominance in the region ended with the arrival of the largely Buddhist Rakhine from central Burma[38] around 1000 AD. The Rakhine also incidentally share a Tibeto-Burmese ancestry with the Burmans. This has been reflected in the archaeological record—for example in the history of the coinage issued in the region—and fits with the wider period of regional power enjoyed by the Burmese Pagan Kingdom.[39]

This arrival of the Rakhine was followed by two centuries of close links with the kingdoms of central Burma, during the height of Pagan power. When the Pagan Kingdom fragmented,[40] Arakan regained its independence and engaged in almost six centuries of war, dispute and trade with its neighbours in both Burma and Bengal. From the thirteenth to the end of the seventeenth centuries there were periods of Burmese dominance, periods when Arakan was independent and even brief periods when the regional kings conquered sections of modern-day Bangladesh.

During this time the Mrauk-U dynasty ruled Arakan, presiding over a multi-ethnic mix of the various Chin ethnic groups (Mru, Sak, Kumi), the Rohingyas and Rakhine, and a multi-religious mix of Hindu, Muslim and Buddhist beliefs. Islam was already significant in the region and during the Mrauk-U dynasty it became dominant among the descendants of the earlier Indo–Aryan settlers (that is, it seems, the Rohingyas), even as the Rakhine retained their Buddhist identity.

The court increasingly looked to Bengal and India, and most rulers of the dynasty were Muslims. Many court officials were recruited from northern India. Equally, many mercenaries from Muslim regions served either in the local army or in those of its Bengali rivals. The Muslim group now known as the Kamans arrived in the 1660s as mercenaries recruited from Afghanistan. After their military power was broken they adopted a local dialect and are now, unlike the Rohingyas, one of the accepted ethnic groups within Myanmar. However, it seems likely that the Rohingyas were an important part of the ethnic mix of Arakan in this era. Nineteenth-century British reports make reference to how the local Muslims called themselves 'Rovingaw' or 'Rooinga' (see Appendix 1, which reproduces the title page of one such work).[41] More importantly, as early as 1799 Francis Buchanan made reference to 'Rooinga' in the area.

Buchanan suggested in 1799 that the natives of Arakan were either 'Yakein' or 'Rooinga' and he indicates there are two main communities. One is the 'Mohammedans who have long settled in Arakan and who call themselves Rooinga, or natives of Arakan'.[42] The other are the 'Rakhing ... who adhere to the tenets of Buddha'.[43] He also notes that due to fewer external interactions the Rakhing 'language is consequently purer than that of the Burmeses, who sustained several revolutions'.[44] This strongly suggests that after the arrival of the Rakhine in Arakan around 1000 AD the ethnic mix of the province remained static with relatively little interaction with the outside world. In turn, the *Classical Journal* of 1811 has a comparative list of numbers in many East and Central Asian languages and identifies three languages spoken in the 'Burmah Empire', including a direct reference to 'Rooinga':

2. Languages of Burma, 1811 (*Classical Journal*, 'Numbers in 200 Tongues', No. 535, London: 1811, p. 107)

Three in the Burmah Empire.

Rooinga	????	Banga	Myanman or Burmah	A few Chrisitans in Siam or Taimay	Taiyay	Tailong
1 awg	aik	ak	teet	noong	noo	aning
2 doo	doo	de	hueet	so	sang	sonng
3 teen	teen	teen	thoum	sam	sam	sam
4 tchair	tsar	sa-ree	lay	see	shee	shee
5 pan-so-ee	paus	pas	ngaw	haw	haaw	haw
6 saw	tso	tsoe	kiouk	hoc	hook	hook
7 sat	sat	hat	kuhneet	kyaet	sayt	seet
8 aw-ton	as-to	awt	sheet	payt	payt	paet
9 no-naw	no	no	ko	ka-wo	kaw	kau
10 dus-so-a	dos	dos	tazay	seet	sheet	ship
20						
100						

An 1815 German compendium of languages of the wider region by J.S. Vateri also mentions the existence of the Rohingyas as an ethnic group (in this case spelt as 'Ruinga') with a distinct language.[45]

Thus there is plentiful evidence for the existence of the Rohingyas in Arakan by the early nineteenth century in a sequence of works published at the time. None of these sources had any partial political interest in the ethnic makeup of the region: none of them had any reason to invent the existence of a group such as the Rohingyas any more than they had an interest in suppressing such groups, and all clearly point to the fact that there was a major ethnic group in the region with a distinct language at the time, clearly identifiable as the Rohingyas. Notably, all three (Buchanan, Vateri and the *Classical Journal*) were produced during the brief period of Burmese control between 1784 and 1824, a time when other evidence points to an outflow of Muslims fleeing persecution.[46]

By the late eighteenth century, the Konbaung Dynasty of the central Burmese Kingdom had been strengthened by success in its wars with Siam.[47] Taking advantage of the weakness of the Bengali kingdom, it expanded into Arakan. One motivation for the Burmese attack was to ensure the Buddhist purity of Arakan and to reduce what were seen as dangerous ties to Islamic states to the west. In reality, the conquest created major tensions with British India.[48]

After its annexation of Arakan, Britain developed an increased interest in the wider region, and a series of conflicts followed. As ever, conquest of a small portion of a country meant the British then feared attack from the remaining independent areas. In turn those fears were linked to specific incidents to give a pretext for further conquest. The results were predictable. The British had annexed the entire territory of Burma by the mid-1880s.

The colonial era (1824–1948)

Outline

Up to this point in time, the histories of Burma and Arakan were largely separate, or at least had no more in common than most neighbouring states do. But from 1784 the two were going to be inextricably linked. After the British conquest of Arakan in 1826, tensions persisted with the Burmese kings. The Second Anglo-Burmese War took place in 1852 and resulted in British control over southern Burma, which left upper Burma completely isolated from the rest of the world. The Third Anglo-Burmese War ended in 1885 and by 1886 the British had created a formal division between 'Ministerial Burma' (basically Rangoon and the Irrawaddy region) and the 'Frontier Areas'.[49] In turn, this created a clear division between a central region dominated by the Burman majority and outlying regions in which a complex patchwork of ethnic groups lived alongside one another. These divisions created strictly enforced internal borders and were combined with limits on internal migration. Burma was designated as a separate administrative state to India in 1937 and the borders were drawn on the basis of state borders that had existed just before the war of 1824–6. So the new administrative unit thus integrated Arakan into what was to become, a mere ten years later, the newly independent country of Burma. This purely administrative decision is what led to the situation we are in today.

Burmese nationalists resented British rule and one source of unrest was the lack of support the British gave to the Buddhist religious hierarchy.[50] Under the previous kingdoms, secular authority had in part been derived from being willing to support Buddhism. So to Burmese nationalists the British were seen as illegitimate rulers, because they failed to meet the established demands of the political culture in the country, and fulfil the expectation that 'legitimate' rulers must protect and promote Buddhism as an integral part of Burmese culture.[51]

The British preference for employing Indians in the colonial civil service and administrative structures further aggravated the situation. The result was that anti-British feeling was stronger in the Buddhist, mainly ethnically Burman communities,[52] while many minority ethnic groups were pro-British—particularly the Muslim Rohingyas and the Christian Karen. The link between religion, ethnicity and anti-British sentiment had a profound influence on the dynamics of the independence movement which would ultimately lead to the emergence of the Myanmar we know today. This had immediate consequences, as the independence movement sometimes took on a confessional and ethnic character. For example, the anti-colonial riots of 1938 were as much aimed at the Muslim community[53] as at British power. These riots followed on from the unsuccessful rural Saya San uprising in 1930 that had explicitly aimed to restore the pre-colonial Burmese polity.[54] The seeds for deep divisions in the country along religious lines had already been sown.

Things really came to a head during World War II. Burma became caught up in the war in 1942 when the Japanese invaded the area. Initially their arrival was welcomed by some Burmese nationalists who, as with the Indian Congress Party, saw the defeat of the British Empire as a step on the road to independence. However, the Rohingyas remained loyal to the British (as did many other non-Burmese ethnic groups), leading to significant ethnic strife[55] between the Rohingyas and Rakhine ethnic communities. It has been estimated that some 307 villages[56] were destroyed, 100,000 Rohingyas lost their lives and a further 80,000 fled the region[57] as a result. The Japanese also made matters worse when they carried out multiple massacres of the Rohingyas to punish them for their pro-British stance.[58] And one further consequence of the ethnic violence in 1942 was that it eliminated the old patchwork of ethnicities in Arakan and led to ethnic segregation between a largely Muslim north and a Buddhist south.

In turn, the British recruited soldiers from among the displaced Rohingyas, and, looking for allies, promised the Muslims of northern Arakan relative independence and the creation of a Muslim National Area, in exchange for their contribution to the war effort. But, as in many other cases, they went on to commit a huge historical error and reneged on this promise once the Japanese were defeated.[59]

In 1947 some Rohingyas formed their own army and sought the incorporation of northern Arakan into the newly created East Pakistan,[60] now Bangladesh. This initiative failed, but after Burma achieved its own independence in 1948, some Arakanese Muslims went on to petition the Constituent Assembly in Rangoon for the integration of Maungdaw and Buthidaung districts into East Pakistan.[61] This was to have dire long-term consequences. It drove the Burmese authorities to regard the Muslim population of Arakan as hostile to the new regime[62] and to see them as outsiders whose loyalty lay with a different state. These events helped create a belief that only Buddhists could really be part of the new state, an attitude reinforced by the attempt of the Burmese Communist Party to overthrow the new state after 1948.

The other side of the liberation struggle in this period was even more complex. The Burmese Independence Army (BIA), led by the 'thirty comrades' (including General Aung San), was originally formed to help the Japanese against the British, and during 1942–5 mostly fought for the Japanese,[63] especially against the Chinese troops that were supporting British and American efforts to keep open a supply line to China. In addition, British accounts of the war make frequent references to local acts of sabotage[64] so, as with the Indian National Army, it was clear that many Burmese nationalists took the view that the Japanese were useful as a tool to weaken the British. Aung San had gone to Japan in 1941 and was made chief of staff when the Japanese declared Burma independent in 1943.[65]

By 1944, increased Japanese repression and violence led many of the independence leaders to see the British as the lesser of two evils, especially as it was clear that the Japanese were losing the wider war.[66] Aung San started to negotiate with the British and the independence movement subsequently switched sides and took part in the 27 March 1945 uprising against the Japanese. To Burmese nationalists this was originally 'Resistance Day' and later became 'Armed Forces Day', representing a key step on the road to an independent Burma. To others it was an opportunistic shift of allegiance when it was clear the Japanese were beaten.[67] But the symbolic role of the nascent army in this revolt fed into the mindset of the military after 1948 that the only guarantor of the nation was the military's power and that it faced powerful internal threats.[68]

After the Japanese surrender in August 1945, the BIA waged a low-level insurgency against British rule from 1946 to independence in 1948. Upon independence, it became the core of the new national army.

Shifting demographics in Arakan

Unfortunately, the issue of who actually lived in Arakan in 1824–6 is now a major part of the narrative of extremist Buddhists. The arguments revolve around which ethnic groups were deemed to be part of what is now Myanmar at the date of the British conquest, which has been chosen as the significant historical milestone for deciding which ethnic groups properly belong to which territory. The extremists claim that the Rohingyas only arrived in the region at a later date, due to British influence. This chapter addresses their claims in some detail and engages with the arguments of writers such as Derek Tonkin[69] and Jacques Leider.[70]

As with all nineteenth-century colonial powers, the British needed to keep on top of the demographics of their colonies and so carried out a number of censuses in the region. Though carried out in the interests of the colonial power, these are informative as to the shifting demographics of Arakan and the rest of Burma and provide a substantial amount of evidence, but also, unfortunately, leave some gaps.

As we have seen, Charles Paton carried out a major survey of Arakan in 1825–6. Ostensibly working for the British Colonial Office, he was actually gathering information for Britain's secret spy agencies. But whatever his mission, he left behind a compelling account of life in Arakan in 1826.[71] He detailed the ethnicity of the leaders of various villages and estimated that there were 60,000 Rakhine Buddhists, 30,000 Muslims and 10,000 from other ethnic groups (see Appendix 2).

Paton followed the later British practice of identifying groups as much on the basis of religion as ethnicity. He identified the 'Mugh' with the group more commonly known as the Rakhine but did not subdivide the Muslim population into ethnic groups. But he does make one important and interesting distinction. The local aristocracy ('The Mussalaman Sirdars') are noted as speaking a language easily recognisable to someone who can speak the main north Indian dialect. The local peasantry (from the same ethnic group) are deemed to speak a language unrelated to 'Hindoostanee'. This fits what we already know. The elite in the old Arakan kingdom had close political, cultural and ethnic ties with Bengal, and easily spoke a variant of Bengali. Their peasantry spoke the local Rohingya language, which provides further proof that a large Muslim community was living in Arakan by the start of the nineteenth century and that this had long been linguistically distinct from northern India.

When Burma became an administrative unit distinct from India in 1937, the British commissioned a report looking at population changes in the region since 1872.[72] This report, written by James Baxter, focused on the question of whether or not Indian migration had reduced employment opportunities for the local Burmese population. Baxter's report involved, for example, reclassifying the 1871 census figures such that the Hindu population in Arakan was identified as Indian in origin (having migrated in search of work under British rule). It also made an effort to distinguish between the various Muslim communities in the province as opposed to simply combining them by religious affiliation. From this, Baxter acknowledged that,

> there was an Arakanese Muslim community settled so long in Akyab District that it had for all intents and purposes to be regarded as an indigenous race. There were also a *few* Mohamedan Kamans in Arakan and a small but long established Muslim community around Moulmen which could not be regarded as Indian.[73]

I emphasise the word 'few' since it is important. The British census is clear that there were three Muslim groups: the Kamans, a group living in Akyab (the Rohingyas), and a small community at Moulmen. Baxter adds that it would be incorrect to 'assume that all the ... Mohamedans were Indian'.

Derek Tonkin has claimed that the Rohingyas are not among the communities of 'long established' Muslims, since Baxter did not use the term "Rohingya" to refer to the Arakan Muslims. He adds that 'at no stage during their administration of Arakan from its capture in 1825 to independence in 1948 did the British even once use the designation "Rohingya" to describe these communities'.[74] It is true that Baxter does not use the word 'Rohingya' but, as we have shown, there are plenty of examples of this name being used both before and during the colonial period. As discussed, the British censuses were done in the interests of the imperial power. Practically, for most of the colonial period, the British were interested in only those aspects of their subjects that could be used as indicators of their loyalty or lack of it. In the case of Burma, religion was more important than ethnicity in this respect.

Tonkin also claims that the idea of Rohingya identity is purely a construct of post-1948 ethnic politics. The word 'Rohingya', he says, 'came into use after independence in 1948, notably in the wake of a "jihadist" uprising which plagued Arakan ... until 1961 when Northern Arakan was designated the Mayu Frontier District and placed under military administration'. The Burmese government, he says, sometimes used the word thereafter, but this usage stopped after the 1962 coup.[75] The word 'jihadist' is often used by Burmese Buddhists to describe the brief revolt of 1947, and has connotations of Al-Qaeda-type terrorism. It is of course true that Mayu was administered by the military after 1948, but it was not the only frontier area of Burma to be administered this way after independence and in 1964 Mayu again became administratively part of Rakhine, thenceforth treated as a normal region of the country. Finally, as we have already shown, the advent of military rule in 1962 indeed saw a gradual increase in the persecution of the Rohingyas.

Other, less sophisticated, writers conflate the common argument that the increase in the Muslim population was purely the result of British policy with a claim that this was also designed to spread Wahhabist ideology:

> Most of the Bengali immigrants were influenced by the Farai-di movement in Bengal that propagated the ideology of the Wahhabis of Arabia, which advocated settling ikhwan or brethren in agricultural communities near to the places of water resources. The peasants, according to the teaching, besides cultivating the land should be ready for waging a holy war upon the call by their lords.[76]

The argument is that a substantial number of Muslims moved from Bengal to Arakan, when both were ruled by the British Empire, at the behest of Saudi Wahhabis.

The remainder of Tonkin's article, 'Rohingya' a Political, not Ethnic Label', is a detailed argument about which dialects were spoken where. He concludes it thus: 'The only reasonable conclusion is that "Rohingya" was never used historically as an ethnic designation'. Rather, he says, it was 'fashioned after the Second World War to define the majority of Muslims resident in the north of Rakhine State'. Therefore, 'it should not surprise us in the least that the Myanmar Government decline to accept "Rohingya" as an ethnic designation, insisting instead on 'Bengali' to which the great majority of Rohingya could very probably trace their heritage and ancestry'.[77]

The notion that the concept of the 'Rohingyas' is a recent construction is one that the regime favours. Jacques Leider is another who argues for this idea. He has written extensively about the Rohingyas and his articles present a variation of the same core arguments propounded by Tonkin. Specifically, he too argues that the name 'Rohingya' is a recent construct[78] which has been deliberately adopted by a group who, he contends, really are simply Bengali Muslims. His writings acknowledge that 'nobody doubts the historical existence of that [Muslim] community'[79] in Arakan, but crucially he argues that the Rohingyas are not descendants of the pre-colonial (that is, pre-1824) community that lived in Arakan. He thus ignores the fact that the Rohingyas are the largest Muslim minority in Myanmar and are concentrated in Rakhine: if they are not the descendants of the pre-1824 community, then who is? He emphasises that the ethnic designation 'Rohingya' did not appear in the 1826 census carried out by the British shortly after they conquered the region.[80] But, as we have seen, this is because the British opted to classify on the basis of religion and not ethnicity.

Linked to this, Leider and others argue that the various kingdoms that existed in Arakan from 1300 (when the area again became independent of the kingdoms in central Burma) were Buddhist rather than Muslim and that the population up to 1824 was ethnically Burman. As an example, Leider asserts that the independent kingdom that had existed in the western coastal regions up to 1794 was a Buddhist kingdom: 'the history of Arakan in the early modern period (15th to 18th centuries) is foremost the history of a Buddhist kingdom'.[81] This state is supposed to have drawn in some Muslims from the neighbouring Bengali kingdom as soldiers, traders or slaves. Leider presents inter-communal relations in this period as involving Muslim and Buddhist communities living 'side by side',[82] but says that this harmonious balance was disrupted in the colonial period when the British allowed mass immigration from Bengal.[83] To Leider, the current crisis stems from the belief of many Buddhists in Myanmar that the Rohingyas are outsiders, with no historical rights, but who are astute at manipulating international opinion.[84] Thus it should come as no surprise that the views of many Burmese Buddhists are echoed in the narrative of the 969 Movement.

There are plenty of pro-Buddhist websites, reports, articles and books that present far less subtle versions of such arguments. Some of this material is quite explicit in its goal of addressing what it sees as a mortal threat to Buddhist Myanmar and argues that the idea of the 'Rohingyas' is a recent invention. For example, take the book by Zan and Chan called *Influx Viruses*,[85] which claims:

> There is a new trend concerning the so-called Rohingya. This trend, fashioned by some Islamic radicals after Burma's independence, his been problematic, and a grave concern for (a) the Arakanese, (b) the people of Burma and (c) historians and scholars. A proper understanding of the importance and nature of illegal Muslim immigrant flow is crucial to comprehensively address the imperative issue of development contest. Rohingya movements have been accompanied by certain dangers and challenges, particularly for the Arakan State...[86] [grammatical errors and spelling mistakes in the original text have been retained]

The rest of *Influx Viruses* is a long diatribe about the alleged falsehoods put forward by those unfriendly to modern-day Myanmar. It argues for the essentially Buddhist and Burmese characteristics of the kingdoms in Rakhine before 1785, but goes further than Leider in claiming that the Muslim presence in the region before 1824 was minimal.

But the 1871 census notes that the 64,000 'Mussulmen' in Rakhine differ 'from the Arakanese but little, except in their religion and social customs which their religion directs'.[87] If we set aside the lordly indifference of the colonial power to the real differences between those they ruled, this is indicative that for all practical purposes the Rohingyas and the Rakhine were very similar populations which had lived together for a very long time indeed.

Summary

The historical pattern of the expansion and contraction of a core state based around particular ethnic and religious communities is not unusual. Equally, many modern post-colonial states were effectively delineated for the administrative convenience of the imperial power, and Burma was no exception. The consequence is a post-colonial world where many states have complex mixes of ethnic groups, and there are many regions with ethnic groups splintered across multiple states. However, what this does not mean is that ethnic groups different from the core group have no right to exist. Indeed, most modern states have managed to respond to these complexities in a decent and humane way. Unfortunately this is not the case in Myanmar. Here, the dominant narrative of many Burmese about the Rohingyas is one of illegitimate 'invasion' by a threatening 'outsider'.

This chapter has made it clear that for a long period, the history and ethnicity of Arakan developed separately to that of the rest of Burma. Political integration is relatively recent and all the evidence is that the Rohingyas were living in Arakan even before the Buddhist Rakhine arrived.

This is not to say that the nuances of early history should have any legitimacy in determining who is a citizen of a modern state. No matter what the Myanmar authorities have to say about the supposed history of Rakhine and the Rohingyas, there is no getting away from the fact that no state can render stateless, as a matter of policy, people born in its territory, under the UN Charter.[88] If a person is born on the territory of a country, and has no other legal citizenship, then they must be given citizenship by that country. The Rohingyas are Burmese by birth and according to international law. Where their distant ancestors may have come from and why is entirely irrelevant. And no amount of history, veridical or fabricated, can change that basic fact. No amount of history can then justify any attempt at ethnic cleansing.

Unfortunately, the pre-colonial history of Burma does matter, insofar as one version of it forms a major justification for the persecution of the Rohingyas. The reality in today's Myanmar means it is very important to look at these attempts at rewriting history in order to understand the mindset of the aggressors and see exactly how this phenomenon builds into a precursor to genocide. And it is here also that the international community can bring a lot to the table and provide the necessary objective analysis of the history of the region in order to refute the falsified narrative used by those who call for the expulsion of the Rohingyas from Myanmar. The average citizen of Myanmar has a right to know their own history, and has a right not to be deceived by the absurd propositions of Buddhist extremists in Myanmar.

2

FROM INDEPENDENCE TO DEMOCRACY
(1948–2010)

Domestic events

British colonial rule ended in Burma on 4 January 1948[1] and the new country was based on the boundaries that pre-colonial Burma had briefly expanded to by 1824, as defined by the British colonial authorities in the mid-1930s when Burma was administratively separated from India. On independence, Burma was considered a rich country, with well-developed agriculture, major mineral reserves, and a well-educated population.[2] In particular, the British had expanded rice production in the lower Irrawaddy region (in part by bringing in Indian labourers) and this had led to Burma becoming one of the major producers in the world, providing the means to both feed the local population and to export to other, food hungry, states in the region.

On the other hand, the new state inherited a complex mixture of ethnic groups and religious beliefs, as regions populated by non-ethnic-Burman groups were included in the new country. Districts such as Shan, Kachin and Sagaing to the north and Chin to the west were all largely inhabited by non-Burman ethnic groups who were to face severe repression during the period after independence,[3] as were the Karen who lived both in the Irrawaddy Delta region and in what became Karen State to the east. The map at the beginning of this book shows the provincial boundaries of post-independence Burma including Arakan, renamed Rakhine.[4]

At its creation Burma also faced a significant internal debate among the new ruling elite. Some saw the new state as the means to create a Buddhist and

Burman polity with other ethnicities and religious groups excluded. To them, this was overcoming the critical failure of British rule—that it had not actively sponsored the Buddhist hierarchy and the infrastructure of monasteries and temples, as the Theravada Buddhist theory of the just state required of its rulers.[5] Others, such as General Aung San,[6] argued that the new state should be inclusive and that all who lived within its borders were now to be seen as Burmese citizens. Within the army there was a different debate, between those who saw the role of the military in conventional ways (as the armed forces of a state but under civilian control) and people like Ne Win (the organiser of the 1962 coup) who wanted to see the military take control,[7] since they believed that only the army truly represented the Burmese people.

With the assassination of General Aung San in 1947,[8] these debates shifted in favour of those who wanted the new state to be an embodiment of Burman Buddhist beliefs and who believed that the military was 'the only institution that has discipline, loyalty, unity and deep commitment to protect the sovereignty and independence of the country'.[9] This in turn provoked some splits among the former independence movement, and some leaders, like Kyaw Zay, went into internal exile to lead the military wing of the Burmese Communist Party. Some members of the civilian government, including Aung San's wife, Khin Kyi,[10] continued to argue for a secular future for Burma. In effect, it was not until the military took power in 1962 that the logic of equating being Burmese with being Buddhist came to be deeply entrenched, and even then it was a gradual and incremental process.

The Burmese military, also known as the 'Tatmadaw', as a result came to see itself as the cornerstone of the new state. It also quickly came to the conclusion that it faced powerful internal threats,[11] especially now that it had chosen a sectarian, exclusivist definition of what being Burmese meant.

In reality there was some truth in the military's fears, but what was to come was also in part a consequence of the drastic measures it imposed out of little more than paranoia. By effectively telling those who wished for a secular Burma, or who came from non-Burman ethnic groups, that they were not proper members of the new state, it set the stage for a series of revolts. Shortly after independence, in March 1948, the Burmese Communist Party, possibly with Chinese backing,[12] launched a military campaign to bring down the new government.[13] By the early 1950s they had been beaten back but remained a significant military force, and were only driven out of central Burma in the early 1960s. In turn, the Karen ethnic group rebelled against the central regime and also against the Shan–communist alliance,[14] which had retreated into the mountainous regions in the north-east, close to the Chinese border.

There, there were several active military groups, and fighting between the Shan and the Karen was not the only inter-factional dispute. In the period after the end of the Chinese Civil War in 1950, the CIA was actively trying to fund Kuomintang[15] units in northeast Burma to invade China.[16] This situation persisted in the 1950s and fused with the chain of rebellions of the border tribes against Burmese rule and the fighting between the various ethnic groups. The CIA-backed campaign was of particular concern to the Burmese authorities as they feared the Chinese would use the existence of Kuomingtang units as an excuse for invasion. Equally, such a flagrant intervention in their domestic affairs did little to mitigate the military's already strong distrust of foreigners, who were seen as following their own agendas to the detriment of Burma.

In consequence, by the late 1950s the army was embroiled in a complex set of civil wars on Burma's borders and the pressures created by this militarisation of society led to the partial instigation of military rule in 1958, and then to the 1962 coup which saw the official establishment of a military regime.[17] But more than this, the permanent wars that followed independence meant the military lost all distinctions between their internal 'enemies' and civilians[18] who happened to live in one of the rebellious areas.

It also established a pattern of rivalry and tension between those doing the fighting and those ruling in Rangoon, which continued even after the military officially seized power. This led to warlordism, as regional commanders asserted their independence in the regions where they were notionally fighting to re-assert central control. And later, as the wars continued, an officer class formed that was able to grow rich from controlling the economy, especially opium production, while the rank-and-file soldiers were reduced to growing their own food and stealing from the civilians they were meant to protect.[19]

The dispute about the role of Buddhism was also not settled by independence. During the democratic period from 1948 to 1962 Buddhism was mostly seen as a moral basis for public life, but there was less sense that it was an essential part of 'being Burmese'. During the 1970s and 1980s the military co-opted organised Buddhism as the state religion.[20] In the absence of a homogeneous ethnic identity for much of the population of the country, they increasingly resorted to seeing Buddhism as the essential criterion for being a 'true Burmese', as they set about nation-building. In the early years of military rule, Buddhism was secondary to the ideology of the 'Burmese Road to Socialism', but it was nonetheless important to the military as a source of legitimacy. Later, monasteries, which had fallen into disrepair under the British, were restored, and grants awarded to support monks.[21] By supporting the Buddhist hierarchy, the generals claimed they were fulfilling the Theravada expectations of just rulers.

The establishment of military rule did nothing to bring an end to the series of military campaigns aimed at the hill tribes in the northern, eastern and southern borders, and this situation, over time, led to substantial human rights abuses and the creation of a large refugee problem. Typical of this was the plight of the Karen people. By 1990, over 31,000 had been displaced into refugee camps in Thailand and left totally dependent on foreign aid,[22] and many others were internally displaced within Burma. Their situation was made worse by military cooperation between the Burmese and Thai regimes, ostensibly in an attempt to curb heroin production and export,[23] but in reality aimed at imposing central control over a region that had become de facto independent of both states. Indeed, there is evidence that both the regime and armed opposition groups used the production and export of drugs to fund the conflict.[24] Equally, both the military and the various hill tribes have made regular use of child soldiers:[25] every faction in the wars that have scarred Myanmar since 1948 are guilty in this respect.[26] All this adds to the mindset of the military that the entire nation forms a potential threat to its existence. This has continued to the present day where the army presents ongoing intercommunal violence as a fundamental reason why they cannot relinquish full power to the ostensibly democratic institutions now in place.[27]

In 1974 Burma's constitution was formally changed to that of a one-party state, entrenching army rule, though notionally through the civilian Burma Socialist Programme Party.[28] Subsequently, the leadership of the army became increasingly divorced from the country it ruled. Relatively pampered, it captured most of the wealth and increasingly came to see the rest of society as a threat to its order.[29] By this stage, the military's rule was more about retaining its own economic power than representing and preserving Burma. Over time, it took control of key assets and ensured that any foreign investment enriched the military leadership.

But there were also frequent factional disputes over the division of the spoils and the best way to preserve military rule. These disputes within the military elite may go some way to explaining the decision to overthrow Ne Win in 1988 when it appeared that the pro-democracy movement was making gains, and also the removal of Than Shwe after 2010 when there was a need for the ruling party to appear to be part of the new democracy. Both should be seen as the outcomes of tactical disputes about how best to retain power, either by further repression or by appearing to embrace change. Neither actually mean the generals have a real commitment to democracy, or are prepared to see their real power base (and thus the source of their economic wealth) undermined.

The Burmese Road to Socialism and the strain of constant war proved to be an economic disaster. All Burmese apart from the ruling elite suffered throughout military rule,[30] and there are numerous well-documented instances of forced labour[31] and other human rights abuses. Popular anger erupted in 1987 when Ne Win decided to cancel most bank notes on the grounds that they represented unlucky numbers. The only notes left in circulation were the 45 and 90 kyat notes (Ne Win believed these were lucky numbers as they were divisible by nine).[32] This destroyed people's limited savings overnight at a time when the population was already suffering from the ongoing economic crisis.

As we have seen above, Buddhism played a complex role during the military dictatorship. It was co-opted by the state as part of the ruling ideology and the military tried to gain popular support by funding monasteries and monks in the 1970s and 1980s. On the other hand, Buddhist monks were critically important during the 1988 revolt.[33] Monks and students protested together: 'students sported their symbol of the fighting peacock, and monks carried their alms bowls upside down to show they would not accept handouts from the military, again as a protest'.[34] While the army put down the revolt by shooting at the protestors,[35] the alliance of convenience between pro-democracy demonstrators and Buddhist monks endured, and continues to have significant implications for contemporary politics in Myanmar.

However, some military leaders felt the initial wave of repression was too harsh, and that the violence that followed was itself becoming a threat to the legitimacy of the military establishment. As a result, General Ne Win was removed from power. His successor, General Saw Maung, took over and initially carried on with the repression, subsequently claiming: 'the country has come back from the abyss, and I saved the country for the good of the people, according to law'.[36] However, he also sought to defuse the tensions by promising a return to democracy. Saw Maung was the first of the senior military leaders to rule Myanmar who had joined the army after independence. Over this series of transitions, the formal aspect of the regime ostensibly morphed from military to nominally civilian administration, but the reality was very much a case of the same establishment in charge. At each stage, the real goal was to retain control over Burma's wealth and the privileged status of the military.

Even so, the 1988 events had a significant impact and forced changes in the political structure of the country. First, the notionally socialist nature of the regime was changed with the adoption in 1989 of the name Union of

Myanmar. And second, the ruling elite was forced into holding relatively free elections in 1990.

The 1988 events also saw the emergence of a new political movement—the National League for Democracy (NLD). This was created after the 1988 uprising, but its style of organisation and its political approach were based on well-established traditions in Burmese history.[37] From the 1920s, in opposition to both the British and Japanese, an important approach to politics was to combine illegal opposition (which by definition meant the actions of a minority) with a mass movement.[38] In the 1920s and 1930s this meant armed struggle, but the NLD's focus is on non-violent resistance. However, the concept of bringing together an elite model of politics and mass participation remains theoretically important to the NLD. The idea of mass resistance was important in the frequent street protests against the military which gave the leaders of the NLD a ready-made mass movement.

The NLD drew some of its legitimacy from its interpretation of the splits in the military in the period up to 1962, in particular about the role of the army in society. This coalition of interests with a part of the military was reflected in its initially appointing Brigadier General Aung Gyi as its chairman, former general Thura Tin Oo as its vice-chairman, and Aung San Suu Kyi.[39] Aung Gyi left after two months to form his own party, claiming that the NLD was a communist front, and he was replaced by Aung San Suu Kyi. Tin Oo remained involved in the NLD, and he represents the extent to which the leadership of the NLD was embedded in Burma's elite,[40] having been forced to resign as commander in chief of the army in 1976 after a failed coup and when his wife was accused of taking bribes.

In effect, the NLD emerged as a coalition of three different elements of Burmese society. It had links to the military, in particular those who had fallen out of favour in the various factional disputes that occurred after 1962. In Aung San Suu Kyi, it embodied the linkage back to General Aung San and those who had hoped for a secular, civilian Burma. Finally, it attracted the electoral support of the students, monks and other Burmese struggling against the military, but had limited popular appeal outside the ethnically Burman communities.[41] This led to a very particular type of organisation. On one hand, it was an elite party representing two slightly divergent elements in the Burmese elite, and on the other hand it became a mass party almost by accident.[42] As we will see, this has left the NLD very dependent on the Buddhist monks, as they form the link between an elite leadership and the popular masses[43] and this, in turn, has severely limited the NLD's appeal outside the Burman ethnic majority.

In the run up to the 1990 elections, many of the opposition supported the NLD, but equally, most ethnic groups organised their own regional parties. In Rakhine, the Arakan League for Democracy (ALD) emerged as one of these local parties, but they only accepted membership from Rakhine Buddhists, deliberately excluding the Rohingyas, and called for the establishment of ethnically Rakhine communities in the north of Arakan.[44] The successor to this party, the Rakhine Nationalities Development Party (RNDP) was to be instrumental in organising the 2012 massacres.[45] Thus, unique among the patchwork of ethnicities and political movements, the Rohingyas were severely impeded from having any direct representation in the elections (and, due to the citizenship laws, most were denied the vote). Despite this exclusion, an important side note for us is that in the 1990 elections some ethnic Rohingyas were allowed to organise their own political party and even won some seats.[46] And the decision to allow some Rohingyas to stand in 1990 was the result of the regime's interpretation of its own citizenship rules,[47] allowing Rohingyas with identity cards issued in 1982 to vote or stand for election.

In turn, the generals set up the National Unity Party (NUP) as a political front to legitimise their continuing rule. The poll proved to be a debacle for the ruling party. Aung San Suu Kyi's opposition NLD won over 80 per cent of the seats.

3. 1990 Electoral Results[48]

Party	Seats Won (total 485)	% of Seats Won
National League for Democracy (NLD)	392	80.8
Shan Nationalities League for Democracy (SNLD)	23	4.7
Arakan League for Democracy (ALD)	11	2.3
National Unity Party (NUP)	10	2.1
Other Parties (23) and independents	49	10.1

In total, twenty-seven parties won seats, the majority of these being smaller ethnicity-based parties winning seats in their own provinces. In particular, the ALD won eleven out of twenty-seven seats in Rakhine. Rather than acquiesce to electoral defeat, the military annulled the elections on 27 July 1990, announcing that the ruling junta would remain in power until a new constitution was created. Most of the parties that had contested the election were banned, but the NLD was allowed to function legally, in principle, while their power was curtailed by harassing and often simply arresting their representatives.

The NLD, in response, created the Committee Representing the People's Parliament (CRPP) to act in place of the banned assembly and elected the leader of the ALD to be its first speaker.[49] In effect, one of the first voluntary acts by the NLD was to closely ally itself with a Buddhist confessional party that was already calling for the expulsion of the Rohingyas, its leader stressing 'a Rakhine claim to the west bank of the Nat River, which Rakhines had "inherited from their ancestors" but been forced to evacuate during the wars'.[50]

A Rohingya activist who had stood for election told the author that there was a particularly anti-Rohingya aspect to the crackdown and one that indicated a worrying trend of collusion between the NLD and the military in this respect. One charge that was used to justify stripping parliamentarians of their seats was that of using fake identity cards. Conviction led to sentences of up to forty years in prison.[51] This form of repression was specifically aimed at those from the Rohingya community who had won seats and may reflect pressure from the NLD and its Rakhine allies to remove any political representation for the Rohingyas. One way to do this and thus boost the other parties' relative share of the seats in the national parliament was to claim that those Rohingyas who had stood for parliament must have used fake identities.

This is important as it illustrates how prejudice against the Rohingyas has evolved and been stoked up by political elites for their own political expedients. Up to 1974, while facing many of the problems that all minority groups faced under military rule, the Rohingyas were still allowed some degree of participation in the limited political process allowed under the Burmese Road to Socialism, and some members of the Burmese Socialist Programme Party were ethnically Rohingya.[52] Even in 1990, they retained a degree of political involvement but this was to be steadily eroded in the period up to the partial restoration of democracy in 2010 and, as we will see, has been radically eroded since then.

After the 1990 elections, repression continued in the regions in the north and east of the country, and there were an estimated 120,000 refugees in camps on the Thai–Burmese border,[53] mainly fleeing ongoing violence between the regime and the hill tribes.[54] In addition, UNHCR (the Office of the United Nations High Commissioner for Refugees) estimates there were some 450,000 internal refugees. This suggests that the level of violence in the border regions was less one of low-level insurgency and more that of a full-scale war as the regime sought to defeat those it saw as its enemies. Even since the move towards democracy in 2008, repression of the minorities in the mountainous border regions has continued, despite the armed conflicts having officially ended.[55]

Overall, by 1992 it appeared as if the military had faced down the political and social unrest in central Burma and regained full political control. However, the repression continued, as did economic hardship for almost all citizens of Burma.[56] An internal coup was attempted in 2001,[57] reflecting yet another factional dispute within the military. More serious for the regime were ongoing economic problems, and these created the next real challenge to the junta in a wave of open popular revolt in 2007, led by Buddhist monks, and, this time, widely televised in the West. The combination of a charismatic leader with Western links, Aung Sung Suu Kyi, and easier television access meant greater awareness in the West of events inside Burma than at any time since the late 1950s. In reality, the military repression after 1992 had resolved nothing and, as we shall see, all it took was a single unexpected event to force the regime to grant major concessions.

International relations

There was an international element to the domestic politics of Burma in this era.[58] As noted above, at least one of the border wars that were such a feature of the 1950s was closely related to US attempts to destabilise the new Chinese Communist regime. Equally, the military in particular had a profound fear of foreign intervention, whether in the form of invasion or of external interference in domestic politics. Despite this apparent preference for isolationism, there were important international influences on Burmese domestic politics even if, for the most part, the outside world took little interest in the problems of Burma throughout this period.

Britain, as the former colonial power, originally envisaged that Burma would join the Commonwealth on independence in 1948.[59] However, the new state, suspicious of its former colonial ruler, declined the invitation. Given the larger challenges of Anglo–Indian and Anglo–Pakistani relations after those countries became independent in 1947,[60] Britain abandoned its initial attempts to influence the new country.[61] Britain had originally provided aid at the request of the new government to stabilise its finances, and, as elsewhere, offered to allow the new country to continue to use sterling as its currency. More importantly, the British were trying to construct an alliance of former colonies, and Australia and New Zealand to construct an anti-Communist bloc across South East Asia.[62]

However, the new Burmese government saw the British as seeking to continue their colonial dominance by other means and the British were further tainted by their support for Karen aspirations to greater federalism. By mid-1949, Burmese–British relations had effectively ended over revelations that at least some British officials had plotted a coup to bring the Karen to power, as they were seen to be more reliably anti-Communist than U Nu's official government.[63]

In the 1950s, insofar as Burma had systemic external links they were with international bodies such as the early versions of what became the Non-Aligned Movement (it cooperated closely with India[64] in order to set this up as a formal organisation). Burma also was a member of the United Nations and its broadly neutral stance (between the Soviets and Americans) meant that U Thant was elected secretary-general of the UN in 1961.[65] Burma was to remain a member of the Non-Aligned Movement up to 1979 and has maintained its UN membership, despite being regularly criticised for human rights abuses.

Although after 1962 the military regime formally claimed it was socialist, it had little contact with the USSR, the People's Republic of China[66] or the later socialist regimes in Vietnam and Cambodia (beyond some arms sales), and it attempted to keep neutral in the Sino–Soviet split. In effect, a pattern of limited international interest in Burma's affairs was established, apart from the interest that some logging and mining companies took (they generally found it easy to accommodate the regime's 'eccentricities').

The military came to believe that Myanmar faced a unique set of development challenges and that there was little for it to gain from close involvement with the outside world.[67] However, the reality was that the regime was less isolationist than is sometimes believed. They embraced a very practical approach to international relations, less in terms of alliances and more in terms of pragmatic exchanges to gain something they sought or to sell commodities they were able to extract from provinces they controlled. Their foreign policy was framed by a mindset that saw any external pressure as illegitimate and intrusive, but equally the successive regimes knew that in order to realise the wealth of Myanmar (even if only for their own enrichment), they needed a degree of international interaction. However, they managed to ignore international pressure over human rights.[68]

At the regional level, the period after 1950 also saw difficult relations with the neighbouring powers of Malaysia, Thailand and East Pakistan/Bangladesh—usually fuelled by tensions arising from border disputes between the Burmese government and various tribal communities with links to those neighbouring countries. Burma's participation in regional groupings such as ASEAN was partial as regional tensions reduced the scope for practical cooperation.

Despite this pattern of partial involvement with other countries, Burma found a close ally in North Korea.[69] In many ways this exemplifies the self-serving pragmatism of their approach to international relations. This was a bumpy relationship that commenced in the 1970s with arms sales, but relations worsened after the North Koreans tried to assassinate a South Korean delegation in Rangoon in 1983. However, mutual interests brought the two states back together by the 1990s.[70] The Myanmar regime was happy to divert food from its starving population to pay for weapons and for some time explored the option of buying longer-range missiles and even submarines. This might have also included a search for a nuclear weapon,[71] but it seems most likely the regime decided against this, not least as it feared such a move would have challenged the Americans too directly[72] as well as worrying the Chinese and the Indians.

Ties with North Korea have become substantial and important to both countries. For example, Myanmar obtained help in an extensive programme of developing its own military infrastructure. In particular the regime wanted a network of tunnels to hide its equipment (including medium-range rockets) in case of an attack. Historically the Burmese army had been primarily an infantry force used in the border wars and for internal repression. The modernisation of the army and the adoption of modern weaponry and tactics have been linked to a desire to protect the 'leading role' in national politics allocated to the army in the 2008 Constitution.[73] Nevertheless, there is little evidence the Burmese army can use the highly expensive equipment they have bought from North Korea, Pakistan or Israel,[74] so the weaponry is probably more important as a status symbol than for actual usage.

In a way, Burma's relationship with North Korea captures all the contradictions of their approach to foreign engagements.[75] A degree of trading of food for advanced weaponry happened from the 1960s, not least as neither the USSR nor China would sell the Burmese regime missile launchers without also insisting on their own technicians being deployed, and not just for training, but to ensure control over usage. North Korea had no such requirements and was willing to approach the relationship as a purely commercial deal.[76] In effect, North Korea was an ideal partner. Unlike the US, it did not insist on at least lip service being paid to human rights, and unlike China it harbours no ambitions to link the infrastructure of Myanmar into its own geopolitical goals.[77] And so long as isolationism has not got in the way of either the acquisition of weaponry or the making of money, the regime was keen to retain this foreign policy stance.

However, post-2008 Myanmar has had to balance external pressures from China and the US about its North Korean ally. To date, the regime has proved unwilling to break from North Korea despite US pressure, for example Defense Secretary Chuck Hagel's demand in 2015 that 'it's important that Myanmar sever ties with North Korea'.[78]

The military remains obsessed by fears of invasion.[79] In the early years after independence the largest fear was of China, but the regime regards almost all external powers as potential threats. After the repression of the pro-democracy movement in 1988, a fear of a new enemy emerged as the decision to ignore the 1990 elections brought the regime into conflict with the EU and the US, which both imposed sanctions. This intensified in the early years of the Bush presidency when Burma was publicly linked with regimes such as North Korea, Iran, Belarus and Zimbabwe as 'outposts of tyranny'.[80]

To the generals, this diplomatic isolation was linked to moves to have the UN Security Council declare Burma a threat to regional security, international praise for Aung San Suu Kyi and open support for other opposition groups. The return to public unrest in the form of the 2007 Saffron Revolution was seen by the generals as being the result of foreign intervention (and linked to fears about the various US-inspired 'colour' revolutions in former Soviet republics).[81] Their paranoia about invasion reached new heights when the US, Britain and France sent warships to the area to help in the aftermath of Cyclone Nargis. Such fears were stoked by the French, in particular, stressing that the regime was a barrier to the delivery of aid and that military force might be needed to ensure that relief reached those suffering in Myanmar.[82]

The overall defensive and suspicious mindset of the military to the outside world has been a regular part of their response to criticism of the persecution of the Rohingyas. They use nationalism in fused with Buddhism to reject external influences and solidify military rule. In a multi-ethnic state, as we saw earlier, the army sees itself as the only body that captures the true spirit of the nation:

> Our state has been in existence as an independent nation for thousands of years ... It is our bounden duty to defend and safeguard, with our lives, the independence and sovereignty which our martyrs and patriotic heroes wrested back, and to ensure their perpetuity as long as the world exists.[83]

This led to the view that the security of the state relies on maintaining rigorous independence from any external pressures which might seek to interfere with the generals' interpretation of Burmese interests. This was set against a constant fear that external regimes, such as India, China or the former colonial rulers, were actively trying to conspire against Myanmar and seize its assets. Finally, there was, as we have explored earlier, the effort to build a mono-cultural nation based on the idea that the proper and true Burmese citizen was both a Buddhist and of Burman ethnicity.

However, as we have seen, the concept of self-reliance has constantly competed against the need to trade. Trade allowed access to weapons, but it also allowed the generals to monetise their control over Myanmar's assets. This tension came to a head with the discovery of large offshore oil and gas supplies in 2007, leading companies, particularly from China, India, Australia and South Korea, to seek, and eventually secure, exploration licences from the state-owned Myanmar Oil and Gas Enterprise (MOGE).[84] While these are notional joint ventures, the reality is that the foreign partner has to pay all the costs. In addition, India was involved in massive investment in the port facilities at Sittwe and China is funding a pipeline from Sittwe to Kunming in southwest China.[85] This pipeline was part of $8bn of Chinese investments in infrastructure projects in Myanmar in 2009. Politically, the Chinese also agreed to block cross-border movements of ethnic rebel groups, and stated that it wished to see 'stability' (that is, a continuation of the regime) after the November 2010 elections.

In effect, while it is conventional to describe Myanmar as isolated and immune to international pressure, the reality is slightly different. The generals do not care for lectures on how they should behave, and are intensely suspicious that external powers are seeking to intervene in Burma for their own interests. However, they want arms (even if just as prestige projects) and, more importantly, want to realise the wealth they have gathered on the international stage. Increasingly, they also want international investment to improve the country's infrastructure and ease the process of extracting mineral wealth.

Impact on the Rohingyas, 1948–2010

For the Rohingyas, the period immediately after independence meant restrictions, as the region was deemed a frontier area, reflecting the tensions of the war years and the short-lived revolt of 1947. However, compared to the significant armed revolts by the communists, Shan and Karen tribes, Arakan remained peaceful.

Key to the steady increase in the level of discrimination and violence aimed at the Rohingyas has been the shifting legal definition of Burmese citizenship. The story that the Rohingyas are somehow alien to the state of Myanmar now finds its expression even in the constitution and the law of the country. One of the preconditions to genocide is the systemic denial of standard legal rights to an identified group. In the Introduction it was noted that a key part of the persecution of and discrimination against the Rohingyas is denying that they are legitimate citizens of the state they were born in and live in.[86]

Successive UN reports have emphasised that 'race and ethnicity cannot be determining factors in the granting of citizenship. Instead, the law needs to provide for objective criteria that comply with the principle of non-discrimination, such as birth in the territory and descent (with citizenship being passed through a parent who is a citizen).'[87] The 1947 Constitution[88] of Burma placed considerable stress on the question of citizenship, and also retained the aspect of administrative convenience[89] in decision-making that had been a feature of British colonial law. Of importance in terms of citizenship was the clause:

> The President of the Union may exempt any person or any class of persons either wholly or partially or temporarily or otherwise, from all or any or the provisions of this Act contained in any of the sections subsequent to section 5 and may at any time revoke any such exemption.

The democratic period, 1948–62

Despite the relatively peaceful nature of Arakan, even in the late 1940s the Rohingyas were placed into a special category compared with other ethnicities in Burma. The democratic government of Prime Minister U Nu in the 1950s accepted that the Rohingyas were an indigenous ethnic group,[90] but they were not one of the named ethnicities given full nationality in the 1947 Constitution. In a public speech on 25 September 1954 U Nu stated: 'The Rohingya has the equal status of nationality with Kachin, Kayah, Karen, Mon, Rakhine and Shan.'[91] A radio station was established that broadcast using their dialect[92] and the legislation setting this up makes direct reference to Rohingya as one of the minority languages needing to be reflected in the diversity of broadcasting.

It is not clear why the Rohingyas were singled out. There was anti-Muslim sentiment arising from the British having sometimes preferred Muslims over Buddhists, and having facilitated Indian immigration into the region, which caused some locals to struggle to find employment. But other Muslim ethnicities, both in Rakhine and the rest of Burma, were granted full citizenship. The

1947 revolt and the decision in 1948 to petition for inclusion in East Pakistan did not help but were minor events compared to the revolts by the Shan and Karen (both of whom were on the list of accepted ethnicities). One argument is that even before independence, the issue of migration from India was a source of irritation to the Burmese majority. There was some truth in their concerns: Baxter's 1941 report noted there had been labour substitution[93] arising from migration from India in three areas: the docks, the recently established rice fields and rubber plantations, and the civil service. However, the Rohingyas, being mainly engaged in agriculture and fishing in their own village communities, had not been present in these roles.

The 1947 Constitution formally acknowledged that all ethnic groups in Burma were immigrants[94] and that the differential treatment of the Rohingyas would be subsequently addressed. In particular, it was intended that citizenship would be granted on the basis of having lived in the territory of Burma for at least eight out of the previous ten years. As a result, Article 11 (iv) of the constitution awarded the Rohingyas National Registration Certificates with full legal and voting rights.[95] The Rohingyas were told they had no need to apply for a citizenship certificate 'as you are one of the indigenous races of the Union of Burma'[96] (see Appendix 3).

The wider evidence is that in the 1950s the Rohingyas were acknowledged to be a separate ethnic group, part of the complex pattern of ethnicities in Burma, and relatively well integrated into Burmese political and social systems. In the period between 1948 and 1961 a small number of Rohingyas (between four and six) were serving as members of parliament, and even after the military coup several Rohingyas remained in parliament as supporters of the Burma Socialist Programme Party.[97] In 1959, a Rohingya student association was one of the approved groups at Rangoon University[98] (see Appendix 4).

To all intents and purpose, the Rohingyas were treated like any other ethnic group and it is reasonable to assume the government intended to normalise their status at some stage. Equally, there was no denial that the Rohingyas existed as an ethnic group. A military report from 1961 describes the Muslim population in the Mayu frontier district (bordering East Pakistan) as Rohingyas.[99] The 1961 census indicated the Mayu district was 75 per cent Rohingya,[100] and this district was formally transferred from the frontier administrative districts to the Ministry of Home Affairs and incorporated into Rakhine province. This treatment is in contrast to other ethnically dominated border districts and indicates that relations in the area were relatively normal, with no ongoing armed revolt.

Instead, the main targets of discrimination at this stage were those who were deemed to be Indian migrants, who were denied citizenship and treated as foreigners. This in itself was contentious under the UN Charter, but was aimed at the mostly Hindu Indian migrants who were brought by the British to Burma to work in the rubber plantations (work that few Burmese were prepared to undertake). However, this distinction between the labour migrants and the Rohingyas was slowly eroded after the military took power in 1962.

Military rule, 1962–88

Up until 1965 the military regime did little to attack the Rohingyas directly and some Rohingyas continued to sit in parliament supporting the goals of the Burmese Road to Socialism. A 1964 school encyclopaedia describes the ethnic makeup of the Mayyu region as '75% of Rohingya and a few of Rakhine, Dai Nat, Myo, KhMee. Rohingya are Islam'.[101]

However, the Rohingyas were steadily losing their existing rights, and the 1974 Emergency Immigration Act imposed ethnicity-based identity cards (National Registration Certificates), with the Rohingyas only being eligible for Foreign Registration Cards (non-national cards).[102] It is important to note that this renewal of attacks on the Rohingyas came at a time when the economy was in crisis and the regime needed to distract attention. This pattern of the Rohingyas being a target of opportunity has been repeated ever since, not least because, unlike the Karen or Shan tribes, they are not armed (indeed, they have deliberately avoided armed revolt after the experience of 1947), making them a safe and easy target for the regime.

The 1974 Constitution of the Socialist Republic of the Union of Burma defined citizenship (in Article 145) as follows: 'All persons born of parents both of whom are nationals of the Socialist Republic of the Union of Burma are citizens of the Union'.[103] This was a critical step because, since the Rohingyas were not formally treated as citizens in 1947, they could not now be citizens of the state. Their National Registration Certificates (from the 1947 legislation) were replaced with Foreign Registration Cards. The next legal step was the 1982 Burmese Citizenship Law, which created four categories of citizenship: citizen; associate citizen; naturalized citizen; and foreigner. Different categories were assigned to ethnic groups on the basis of their residence in Burma before 1824. Anyone not belonging to these categories, specifically the Rohingyas, was deemed to be foreign.

Citizenship, in turn, was redefined as follows:

> Nationals such as the Kachin, Kayah, Karen, Chin, Burman, Mon, Rakhine or Shan and ethnic groups as have settled in any of the territories included within the State as their permanent home from a period anterior to ... 1823 A.D. are Burma citizens. The Council of State may decide whether any ethnic group is national or not.[104]

Thus, citizenship was linked to membership of defined ethnic groups that were deemed to have lived in Burma before 1823. This law was important, as it was the first time so much had been made of the question of who lived within the borders of pre-colonial Burma in 1824. As we have discussed in the previous chapter, this is a contentious issue, but the evidence is clear—the Rohingyas formed a substantial part of the population of Arakan both when the Burmese kings conquered the region in the 1780s and when the British annexed it in 1826.

In effect the 1982 law deemed any ethnicity other than those explicitly named to be foreign.[105] Critically, again, the key judgement was one of administrative decision-making, not subject to any legal process. Naturalisation was offered under the following circumstances:

> Persons who have entered and resided in the State anterior to 4th January, 1948, and their offsprings born Within the State may, if they have not yet applied under the union Citizenship Act, 1948, apply for naturalized citizenship to the Central Body, furnishing conclusive evidence.[106]

Paragraph 43[107] then sets out in detail who can make an application for naturalisation, but the one category that is excluded is someone born to two parents neither of whom are already citizens (the Rohingyas are therefore, by definition, excluded). In turn, Paragraph 58 goes to considerable length to set out the various reasons why this form of citizenship can be revoked. 'Foreigners' have no rights to citizenship under this act, reflecting their status under the old British colonial laws.

Under the 1982 legislation, the Rohingyas were denied full citizenship due to the ethnic classifications used in 1948 (when they were not designated as one of the core ethnic groups living in the new state).[108] In addition, the legal structures were left vague, with substantial amounts of administrative discretion, and their few legal rights were undermined by the regular passing of Martial Law legislation.[109] On the other hand, as discussed below, this ambiguity was used to allow the Rohingyas to participate in the 1990 elections.[110]

Denial of citizenship led to restrictions on movement and access to education, as well as the loss of land holdings. The 1974 constitutional and legal changes also saw an increase in the levels of violence by the state towards the

Rohingyas, and this led to a growth in the number of refugees fleeing to Bangladesh.[111] Soon after this, the 1977 Nagamin (Dragon King) campaign was designed to identify every individual in Burma as either a citizen or a foreigner.[112] In Rakhine, this was interpreted by the Buddhist community and the army as a licence for attacks on Rohingya communities, and by 1978 over 200,000 more Rohingyas had fled to Bangladesh.[113] In turn, Bangladesh returned most of these refugees back to Burma.[114]

Military rule and the return to democracy, 1988–2008

Political unrest after the 1988 revolt and the annulled 1990 elections saw an increased deployment of the Burmese military in northern Rakhine.[115] Nonetheless, as discussed earlier, some Rohingyas had been allowed to contest the 1990 elections[116] on the basis of the 1982 citizenship laws.[117] The renewed attacks in the period 1991–2 saw 250,000 flee to Bangladesh, and again were marked by the use of forced labour,[118] beatings, rape and land theft.[119] The latter involved the construction of villages in northern Rakhine for non-Rohingyas built on land taken from older Rohingya settlements[120] and often built with forced Rohingya labour. The villages were then populated by Burmese who were brought into the region and given substantial agriculture production targets by the military. There are reported instances of Rohingyas leasing back the land from the new owners in order that the production targets be met.

Not only were the Rohingyas displaced from their villages by the new villages or army bases,[121] but those forced to return from Bangladesh found their previous communities had been destroyed and re-appropriated by groups favoured by the state. Typically, this led to renewed tensions, and subsequently more repression and a continuation of the refugee flow[122] to both Bangladesh and Malaysia.

Bangladesh consistently and forcibly sent back refugees to Burma,[123] including those who had fled in the 1970s and again in the early 1990s, in violation of various UN declarations on universal human rights and the rights of refugees.[124] Those who fled to Malaysia have often been allowed to stay, but as stateless refugees, since the Burmese government will not accept them back[125] and the Malay officials are prepared neither to force their removal nor to provide them with proper refugee status.

A target of choice

There is a clear racial aspect to the overall pattern of legal discrimination against the Rohingyas.[126] However, it must be stressed that the persecution and discrimination against the Rohingyas was not a particular feature of Burma at independence. Instead, they were subject to the official distrust of all non-Burman groups and the situation has been quite deliberately worsened since then. There is ample evidence from the 1950s and 1960s that the Rohingyas were just one of many ethnic groups in the country who faced discrimination, but were also an accepted part of the ethnic patchwork.

One important reason for the change to more direct persecution in the 1970s was that the Burmese Road to Socialism was proving to be an economic disaster. The regime needed an easily identifiable group it could victimise and against which it could construct wider discrimination. The Rohingyas fitted this role. They were unarmed, ethnically easily identifiable, spoke a non-Burmese language and were Muslims in a country where 90 per cent of the population was Buddhist.

Ultimately, the military regime used the concept of a Buddhist identity as the basis of citizenship to deny rights to minorities in Burma.[127] This was done gradually and partially, since there were some groups such as the largely Christian Chin who were unlikely to convert to Buddhism. In the early 1960s this was applied in a limited way as the regime used Buddhism as one pillar of its legitimacy but, as the economy worsened, finding internal 'enemies' became ever more important. Further acts in the 1990s imposed restrictions on the Rohingyas, since they were deemed to be foreigners,[128] including limiting them to having no more than two children, introducing forced birth control, and restricting marriage. These restrictions resulted in officials invading people's homes to check who was living there.[129] In addition, the Rohingyas have no automatic rights to travel, even between townships in Rakhine, without authorisation. Permission to leave the region and travel elsewhere in Burma is very rarely granted.

If this legislation and discrimination was simply a historical legacy of the period of military rule and dictatorship, it might be possible to hope the situation will correct itself as the democratic process develops. However, as we shall see in the next chapter, the shift to democracy has worsened the legal position of the Rohingyas and has seen a dramatic escalation in the violence they face.

3

THE RETURN TO DEMOCRACY (2008–2015)

The impact of Cyclone Nargis

The repression after the 1988 revolt did not resolve anything. The opposition survived and slowly the NLD and organisations of Buddhist monks forged a closer alliance. Equally, for most Burmese life became harder. In September 2007 there were widespread protests, known as the Saffron Revolution; these too were harshly put down.

The 2007 wave of unrest was again triggered by economic mismanagement, and monks again made the symbolic gesture of overturning their alms bowls[1] to signal their rejection of the regime. In turn, the army attacked and closed a number of monasteries. The revolt was successfully supressed, but the Saffron Revolution cemented the alliance between the NLD and the monks and this left the regime even more isolated and vulnerable as it lost the legitimacy it had sought from the Buddhist religious establishment. Furthermore, monasteries were increasingly providing education and food relief for those left impoverished,[2] giving the monks a renewed status among the population and increasing their influence relative to that of the military establishment.

However, it was the impact of Cyclone Nargis in 2008 that proved to be pivotal in forcing at least the appearance of serious political change. Cyclones are a typical part of the Burmese climate and often hit the region during the spring monsoon (usually March to May). Nargis was unusually fierce in part due to the geography of Burma. Most such cyclones travel north across the Bay of Bengal towards Bangladesh and lose power when they hit the coastal hills and mountains of Arakan. This time the storm directly stuck the Irrawaddy Delta and, caught up on the coastal swamplands, it did not lose power for two days. It wreaked destruction leading to the loss of 65 per cent of Burma's rice fields and 95 per cent of the buildings in the delta region.[3] In addition, the Irrawaddy flooded for up to 50 km from the coast, causing widespread damage. The economic dislocation was profound and it has been estimated that up to 138,000 people lost their lives.

The regime acted predictably. It initially refused to ask for help and it was not until 9 May (a week after the cyclone struck) that it agreed to accept the aid on offer. Initially only ASEAN members were allowed in but, after pressure from the UN, by 23 May the regime agreed that other international aid organisations would be allowed to help. As discussed above, there was a degree of military threat[4] involved in forcing this decision, with especially the French arguing that the regime was becoming a danger to its own people.[5] Even as it was, reluctantly, accepting aid, the regime was still exporting rice to pay for weapons and to earn foreign currency. Equally, the regime initially tried to control the distribution of aid to those it saw as loyal supporters.[6]

The regime's response was poor for a number of reasons. At its core, the army had long been an instrument of domestic repression and was ill-suited to helping the people of Myanmar. However, the Irrawaddy Delta is also home to part of the Karen ethnic group, who have been in revolt against Burmese rule since the 1960s. Thus the army's natural disposition to see civilians as their enemies was worsened due to the hostility of many in the region. Equally, while cyclones are normal, the most destructive usually hit Bangladesh, and the Myanmar regime was unprepared for the worst storm to hit the country for generations.

The conspicuous absence of the military when they were needed to help was in contrast to their overbearing presence during the violence of the repression of the uprising in 2007. Civilians in Rangoon started to ask: 'where are all those uniformed people who are always ready to beat monks and civilians? They should come out in full force and help clean up the area and restore electricity'.[7] Overall, this mismanagement of the crisis further reduced the legitimacy of the regime in the eyes of the population, and perhaps contributed to pressure that forced the military to allow fresh elections in 2010.

Rewriting the constitution, and the 2010 elections

The 2008 Constitution (The Constitution of the Republic of the Union of Myanmar) allowed for a return to a limited form of democracy. Power was to be notionally moved from the military to a civilian government elected by some form of franchise. However, the 2008 Constitution is a deeply flawed document. It enshrined the privileges of the military[8] and did nothing to challenge the notion that only the army could act as the guarantor of Myanmar. Banners and slogans such as that displayed in Appendix 5 continue to be common throughout the country.

Even worse, it perpetuated the obsessively restrictive approach to citizenship that has bedevilled the constitution of Myanmar since independence. At its core was the idea that only those ethnicities who had lived in Myanmar in 1824 could be citizens now, and the citizenship restrictions of the 1974 Emergency Immigration Act were retained in Article 345:

> All persons who have either one of the following qualifications are citizens of the Republic of the Union of Myanmar:
>
> (a) person born of parents both of whom are nationals of the Republic of the Union of Myanmar;
> (b) person who is already a citizen according to law on the day this Constitution comes into operation.[9]

In reality, this legislation is even more restrictive than the 1974 Act, as it restricts citizenship to those already deemed to be citizens or children born to two parents who are already citizens. In consequence of this legislation, the Rohingyas have been denied membership of the country they were born in and are subject to persecution in their daily lives. This is in open breach of the UN 1961 Convention on the Reduction of Statelessness, in which Article 1 states: 'A Contracting State shall grant its nationality to a person born in its territory who would otherwise be stateless'.[10] The government in Myanmar is aware of the implications of these policies and has complained that:

> Through international media, Bengali [Rohingya] groups are widely publicizing the extent of government controls over them. Whilst the Government deems such measures as necessary in the context of the country's situation and the non-citizen status of this group, the international community condemns these measures as violations of fundamental rights. This ... has undermined the country's reputation and affected its international relations.[11]

In protest against the imprisonment of its leaders, the NLD decided not to contest the 2010 elections.[12] Instead, they announced that they would promote democracy via a 'mass movement'[13] and carry on with their extra-parliamentary activities. One practical problem with this approach was that their activist core remained basically drawn from students. Their alliance with the Buddhist monks gave them a large constituency but this focus prevented them from being able directly to engage with and mobilise the potential political muscle of the workers or peasants. This has allowed the military to manage the threat of the NLD, and has left the opposition vulnerable to the specific interests of its two main constituencies.

In 2010 the NLD also attacked those elements of the pro-democracy movement that did decide to contest the elections. Not surprisingly, the elections were consequently won by the military-backed USDP, which claimed to have received 80 per cent of the vote:

4. 2010 Electoral Results[14]

National Parliament election results, 2010*

	USDP	Ethnic	Pro-Democracy	National Unity Party	Independent	Cancel/ed
People's Parliament (Lower House)	258	47	9	12	0	4
Nationalities Parliament (Upper House)	129	26	7	5	1	0

* The military appoints 25% of all seats to its soldiers: 56 additional seats in the Nationalities Parliament, 110 additional seats in the People's Parliament.

However, not only did the NLD boycott the 2010 elections but the USDP took a number of steps to boost its own notional support. Employees of state-owned enterprises, as well as civil servants, often voted en bloc and in advance of the notional polling date.[15] In effect, the USDP, even in the absence of its main rival, resorted to the crudest form of client voting[16] where by those who rely on the state for their livelihood are expected to vote for the party that provides them patronage.

The military junta was formally dissolved in 2011 and further by-elections were held in 2012 in forty-five constituencies. These were seen to have been much more fair than the elections in 2010; the NLD participated and won forty-three of the contested seats[17] (and 65 per cent of the popular vote).[18] For many Western observers, the 2010 and 2012 elections were ample proof that Myanmar was changing for the better. A media-friendly politician appeared to be leading a movement towards democracy and the regime was opening up to foreign investment.

Politics in Myanmar, 2011–15

At a national level, the trends established in the period 2008–11 continued in 2011–15. The principal political dynamic has become the interaction between the military, their political wing (the USDP), the NLD and the growing influence of extremist Buddhist monks. To fully explain the current threat to the Rohingyas it is necessary to see how these three forces interact and, combined, make it hard for the Myanmar government to ease the repression (even if that were what it wanted to do).

The military and the USDP

The notional move to democracy has not changed the military's deep-seated tendency to see both domestic society and the international community as enemies.[19] As of now, the generals retain effective control over the economy (especially natural resources) and have spent the last seventy years at war with Myanmar's ethnic minorities. These two factors are deeply intertwined, as most of the mineral wealth lies in territory occupied by ethnic groups such as the Karen and the Shan. So far, the West has been too willing to deal with the military, believing either that it can be reformed, or that it is a force for stability[20] and that the military is right when it argues the NLD is not yet 'ready for government'.[21] Despite losing the 2015 elections, the reality is that the military is desperate to retain economic dominance, and their strategy 'is all about the land … the control of it and the prospering from its fruits'.[22] In addition, as discussed above, it has developed a mindset whereby only ethnically Burman Buddhists can hold power if the state is to endure.[23] In reality, if Myanmar has a future as a state, it has to acknowledge its ethnic diversity and it must be essentially federal in structure. In this respect, the army is a major obstacle to progress. It is content to see some degree of internal conflict (such as within Rakhine), as this fits its narrative that only it can preserve the state.[24]

Some US-based commentators seem to believe that it is possible to deal with Myanmar's army as a military institution separate from one that is involved in politics and controls the riches of the country.[25] But the problem is that the military does have a virtual monopoly on the resources of the country, and any riches to be gained from developing or exploiting these resources will end up flowing to the generals and their group of cronies, regardless of changes in the electoral process.[26] Thus, any wishful thinking about the gains that the whole of society might make from foreign investment comes at a time when there is growing doubt that the military has any intention of 'withdrawing from politics',[27] let alone from the commanding heights of the Myanmar economy.

More generally, there is evidence of an intra-military dispute about the reform process and this seems to be affecting both the stability of the USDP and its interaction with the NLD. In late 2013, the USDP—in effect the old military regime dressed up as a political party—indicated that it supported repealing the clause in the constitution that bars Aung San Suu Kyi from being president on the basis that she married a foreigner.[28] But by late 2014 it had changed its view and was now supporting the continuation of this ban. One possible reason for these shifts is growing discontent with President Thein Sein among the older officers, as supporters of the ousted Than Shwe seek a return to power.[29] If so, this is better seen as a dispute as to the best way to secure continued military control over the country's wealth than a dispute than about the transition to greater democracy, especially as the military leaders have argued that the NLD is not ready to take power.[30] In addition, since 2014, Aung San Suu Kyi's previously good relationship with Thein Sein has broken down[31] as the NLD has become more of an electoral threat. As this book goes to press, they are involved in negotiating a transfer of power in the parliament from the USDP to the NLD.

By 2014, there was evidence that the move to democracy was stalled, that Thein Sein was tightening his grip on power and was driving his rivals from positions of influence. These tensions were particularly evident in the relationship between the USDP and the NLD in the run up to the November 2015 elections. In mid-August, Shwe Mann, the USDP party chairman and speaker of the parliament, was briefly arrested and removed from his post.[32] Various theories have been put forward as to why this happened, including that he was too close to Aung San Suu Kyi and was likely to facilitate a post-election deal favourable to the NLD. Subsequently, Shwe Mann has openly met Aung San Suu Kyi,[33] fuelling suspicions of a deal between a faction of the USDP and the NLD. There is evidence in support of this interpretation, as Shwe Mann has been described as an 'ally' by Aung San Suu Kyi: 'Now the picture is clearer as to who is a friend and an enemy, and our relationship with our allies is stronger'. The NLD, she said, would 'work with the ally'.[34]

From the available information, Shwe Mann was also open to some revisions of the 2008 Constitution to remove military privileges that it enshrined.[35] In turn, indicating how opaque Myanmar politics has become, some commentators suggest that both the promises of reform and his apparent overtures to the NLD should be seen purely in terms of internal USDP factional disputes.[36] In effect, gaining a reputation as a potential reformer might have helped Shwe Mann to become more powerful than Thein Sein. Since he was also seen as being closer than the latter to the deposed Than Shwe, his fall should be seen as the public face of a power struggle within the military.

That this might be the case is also backed up by the fact that the USDP has slowly been repositioning itself less as a party of retired officers and more as a normal political party, which has made many elements from within the army officer corps unhappy. However, the USDP has not resolved its underlying problem of a lack of popular support and the elections since 2010 have indicated that it cannot rely on sufficient votes from military or state employees to offset the NLD's popularity. Thus, the position of the military is partly threatened by the outcome of the 2015 election, in which the USDP lost almost all of the seats it took in the 2010 elections, when the NLD did not contest most districts. As such, some factions of the USDP have been looking for a means to remain in power by doing a deal with the NLD.[37] Of course, as in the period after 1990, the threat of a major electoral defeat raises the fear of a military coup.

If this were to happen, it would help the military if it could present this to the outside world not as sour grapes over electoral defeat but as a necessary step to avert chaos. In effect, a post-election rise in tensions in, for example, Rakhine might be very convenient for the military as a justification to ignore the results and, instead, maintain their own power. The military might be brutal, venal and corrupt, but they also believe their own claims that only they really embody the spirit of the nation and only their power holds Myanmar together.

The role of the NLD

After boycotting the 2010 elections, the NLD changed tack when the ban on Aung San Suu Kyi taking part in elections was lifted.[38] As a result the NLD took part in the small number of by-elections that occurred in 2012 and won most of the seats where it stood.[39] While this provided clear evidence that, at least in Burman-dominated regions, the NLD retained massive popularity, the return to the political arena brought a further shift in tactics. After 2011 Aung San Suu Kyi started to temper her criticism of the regime in terms of both progress towards democracy and the treatment of ethnic minorities.[40] The decision of the NLD to re-enter electoral politics brought direct benefits to the regime. President Obama hailed it as evidence of what he called 'flickers of progress'.[41] Equally, for the first time it was announced that Myanmar would take its turn as chair of the ASEAN group of nations after 2014,[42] which might partly be seen as a reward for the improvements in democracy and human rights.

As we have seen in the section on the USDP, the result has been a period of relative goodwill between it and the NLD. With no elections imminent after the limited set in 2012, the two parties could afford to co-exist and both gained from the relationship. The NLD was able to exploit its legal status to build a wider party apparatus and the regime gained international approval for appearing to oversee a move towards democracy. Of course, as we will see later, this era of cosy co-existence was also marked by open violence in Rakhine and the systemic destruction of the few rights that the Rohingyas had retained during military rule.

However, the build up to the 2015 elections tested the relatively good relations between the NLD and the USDP. In the run up to the 2015 elections, there was growing evidence that while the NLD now forms a part of the Myanmar political system, it lacks the power to directly challenge the military's control over the state, retaining weaknesses that were evident in 2010.[43] Recent events connected with the August 2015 ousting of the USDP president Shwe Mann over his links with the NLD indicate a degree of cross-over of political interests between the two parties[44] but also shows that the generals remain determined to ensure they retain control of Myanmar's wealth. As discussed above, Shwe Mann represented the faction in the USDP that, expecting to lose badly in 2015, was seeking an accommodation with the NLD.

Growing tensions with the USDP have seen a return to some degree of direct repression. For example, in September 2014 the journalist Par Gyi, who was closely associated with the NLD, was shot while in police custody and subsequently buried in a field. The Myanmar authorities claim he was trying to escape. When his body was exhumed it showed clear 'signs of abuse'.[45]

This shift in NLD–USDP relations matters. One interpretation is that the generals are now prepared to gamble on losing international goodwill by declaring a coup. Equally they may attempt to change the constitution (again) to retain economic power regardless of electoral results. In either case, it is hard to see what the NLD can do in response. This indicates that several key weaknesses in the NLD's strategy remain in place. Despite this, the size of the NLD victory in 2015 may give them sufficient power to deter any attempt by the generals to seize power, but this still leaves the question as to whether the NLD is able to wrest economic power from the military.

First, while the NLD is electorally popular in the ethnically Burman regions, it is not a mass party. It relies, for its connection with the bulk of the population, on its (sometimes uncomfortable) alliance with the Buddhist monks. Second, it remains very dependent on Aung San Suu Kyi for much of its popular recognition. This relatively weak basis for political operations means that the well-organised Buddhist groups have considerable influence over the NLD's practical politics—especially in relation to non-Burman ethnic groups. Thus to understand the final strand in contemporary Myanmar politics, we must turn to look at the Buddhist confessional groups that have become so important since 2008.

The role of Buddhism since 2007

After independence, Buddhism was briefly seen as setting a moral structure for the new state rather than as a marker of who really belonged in the new country. However, under the military the conflation of loyal citizenship with being ethnically Burman and religiously Buddhist was made. This became more marked as the Burmese Road to Socialism failed as an economic doctrine and the regime looked for a new approach to shore up its popular appeal.

Nevertheless, in both 1988–90 and 2007–8 Buddhist monks played a critical role in the popular protests against the regime. In this respect, Buddhism can be argued to have played a positive role in forcing the transition from military rule towards democracy in the period 1988–2010. By joining the student revolts, the monks gave them wider credibility, provided the NLD with the mass movement they sought, and indicated that the regime was losing control of the country—certainly, they brought a great deal of moral authority to the revolt. Many monks were imprisoned or killed[46] as a result of their involvement, which constituted a further reason why the reputation of the military and the USDP suffered after the protests.

But for Myanmar's non-Burman, non-Buddhist minorities, the alliance between the monks and the NLD was not so positive. There are, of course, significant exceptions. Some monks have visited the Kachin regions and sought to work with the largely Christian community there. One monk walked across Rakhine in support of peace and reconciliation,[47] and in 2014 monks also supported local people protesting against mining and forced land evictions.

However, the link between the NLD and the Buddhist monks could hinder Myanmar's development. The ideological leaders of the persecution of the Rohingyas come from among the monks, and they may put pressure on the NLD to link Burmese citizenship to Buddhism.

The influence of the extremist monks is also one of the many reasons why the military remains complicit in anti-Rohingya violence. Attacking the

Rohingyas is something the religious extremists, the military, and even some members of the NLD can all agree on.[48] As 'protectors of the nation',[49] joining in such attacks is one way that the military can demonstrate that they are in tune with religious sentiments and thus gain Buddhist support for their rule. Thus attacking the Rohingyas has become, to some, a public way to emphasise one's commitment to Buddhism. Also, as indicated earlier, some degree of civil unrest may be welcome to the military—it provides a pretext for their retention of power and even, if needed, grounds for a military coup[50] if they are in danger of losing power over the current democratic structures.

The Theravada Buddhist tradition

As we have seen, Buddhism has played a complex role in Burmese history. The Pagan Kingdom and its successors in one sense effectively fused state and religion and acted as sponsors for the Theravada strand of Buddhism, but equally they seem to have been broadly tolerant of ethnic minorities and non-Buddhist religious groups. One critique of British rule was that its indifference to safeguarding the Buddhist hierarchy was the mark of an illegitimate regime. The leadership of the Buddhist monks today looks back to the relationship they had with the kings before British rule. In effect, Buddhism in Myanmar has a long history of relying on the state in a two-way relationship. The kings provided the state power needed to enforce Buddhism and the Buddhists provided legitimacy, as 'the ultimate wielders of violence, for the support, patronage and order that only they could provide. Kings looked to monks to provide the popular legitimacy that only such a high moral vision can confer'.[51]

The Theravada strand in Buddhism is common across Sri Lanka, Myanmar and Thailand.[52] Equally, in all three countries there are ample examples of the local Buddhist leadership acting with complete intolerance towards other religious minorities, and one reason for this is the interpretation of Buddhism common to this strand. It is not that Theravada Buddhism is always about extreme nationalism and intolerance towards other beliefs, but that there are elements within its belief system that make it very vulnerable to being captured by those who wish to construct an exclusive, confessionally pure, polity.

In this context, the key tradition in the Theravada *sasana* (teaching) is that which links religion to state power. As we saw in the previous chapter, the Pagan rulers, in search of legitimacy, deliberately provided this protection and allowed Buddhism to spread. Any state tolerance of non-Buddhist religions is thought to threaten the existence of both state and religion. Theravada Buddhists cite approvingly the actions of a Buddhist king in Sri Lanka who defeated a Tamil invasion. Since he fought a defensive war to protect the *sasana*, he was absolved of any responsibility for the loss of life. Indeed, he was assured that only one-and-a-half 'people' had actually died: these were an enemy soldier who had fully converted to Buddhism and one who had taken partial vows.[53] The rest of the dead were non-Buddhists, and thus not really human and not worthy of pity. Their deaths were no stain on his eternal character.

The defence of the *sasana* is not always passive. It was the excuse used for the invasion of Arakan in 1784, since that kingdom was deemed to be insufficiently Buddhist[54] even though the Rakhine ethnic group represented a substantial Buddhist population. The presence of a large Muslim population was thought to put Buddhist traditions under constant threat. The irony here is worth noting. The invasion in 1784 was carried out in part as there were so many Muslims in Arakan. This contradicts the fantasy promoted by the regime and Buddhist extremists that there were very few Muslims in Arakan before the British conquest in 1826 and that the Rohingyas only arrived in the province in the colonial era.

However, by treating those of a different faith as not human in the ordinary moral sense, this doctrine lends itself very easily to mass violence against any other groups. As with many extremist movements, the underlying mindset is that almost any act can be justified by the final goal. In the case of the 969 Movement, the goal is to steadily increase the centrality of Buddhism to the governance of Myanmar. In this respect, this interpretation of Theravada Buddhism has something in common with extremist Islamic jihadist doctrines.[55] They too argue that it is essential for the state to only accept those with very particular beliefs and that the existence of those who dissent from their narrow doctrine is a threat to the entire political structure. In consequence it easy for jihadist movements to justify extreme violence,[56] as their end goal is, in their terms, morally just.

As Matthew Walton argues, 'Buddhism and nationalism have become almost inseparably intertwined [in Myanmar].'[57] In this respect it is worth noting that Theravada Buddhism is followed by significant numbers of those in Myanmar who are not of Burman ethnicity and it is precisely this that makes it attractive to those seeking to find a common basis for citizenship in the country. If Myanmar cannot be reduced to just the ethnically Burman, then it might be possible to reduce it to just having a single religious belief-system: Buddhism offers the extremists a label that could unify all the citizens they wish to have in their nation. Furthermore, Islam is increasingly identified by the extremists as the religion that is particularly incompatible with their ideal political order, as they fear that the real goal of all Muslims is to displace Buddhism. This fear finds its expression in claims such as: 'only small parts of Asia are Buddhist now; in the past, Indonesia, Bangladesh, Afghanistan, and many other places, including Turkey and Iraq, were Buddhist countries, but now they are lost'.[58]

The Dalai Lama has challenged this interpretation of Buddhism and has reported that he urged Aung San Suu Kyi to act over the continued repression of the Rohingyas in particular and Muslims in general.[59] He deemed her refusal to respond as 'very sad. In the Burmese case I hope Aung San Suu Kyi, as a Nobel laureate, can do something'.[60] He later raised the issue of the plight of the Rohingyas once more, stating that 'If Buddha would come at that moment, he definitely would save or protect those Muslims'.[61]

Unfortunately, the Dalai Lama represents a different strand of Buddhism, and this severely limits his influence. He comes from the Vajrayana[62] tradition, a sub-school of Mahayana Buddhism, which became dominant in Nepal from the fifteenth century. The Vajrayana tradition tends to stress social inclusivity but places greater emphasis on individual actions. It shares with the Mahayana tradition a focus more on the acts of the individual[63] as the basis for individual enlightenment. As such, it does not have Theravada Buddhism's focus on the wider polity as having to be pure from other influences, nor does it stress the importance of life within a monastic setting as a precondition for further spiritual progression. For many practical intents and purposes, the Theravada tradition has little in common with the strands of contemporary Tibetan Buddhism. Thus, while in the eyes of the West the Dalai Lama appears to speak for all Buddhists, in contemporary Myanmar, as one journalist argued, the 'views of the Dalai Lama are equivalent to the pope speaking to Protestants'[64] in the context of early modern Europe's religious wars.

The Dalai Lama is not the only person of international renown to have tried to contest the extremist narrative, especially now that the Buddhist extremists are identifying anyone who does not fully agree with them as traitors. Concern about this trend has led UN Secretary-General Ban Ki-moon to warn that such groups risk 'being swept up by a rising tide of extremist sentiment against other groups ... This betrays the peaceful teachings of the founder, Lord Buddha'. He insisted that Myanmar's 'leaders must speak out against divisive incitement ... They must promote interfaith harmony. And they must stand against impunity for provocations and violence'.[65]

The 969 Movement

One important group of Buddhist monks is the 969 Movement. This movement grew out of the 1988 revolt and is still currently involved in campaigns against those it deems insufficiently Burmese.[66] Their fundamental ideological principle is a form of exaggerated paranoia that it is not enough that Buddhism be protected by a state that is Buddhist, for the existence of other religions within that state is a permanent threat to Buddhism's continued existence. In consequence, the 969 Movement has attacked confessional Muslims regardless of their ethnicity across Myanmar in pursuit of its goals of a religiously pure state.

One of their important leaders, Ashin U Wirathu, has been called 'Buddhism's Bin Laden'[67] due to the extremism of his views. His defenders sometimes claim this label is applied only due to media lies, as 'the media are all owned by Muslims, and they paint only negative pictures of him'.[68] However, his publicly available speeches and YouTube channels leave little doubt as to his true views[69] and his open incitement of violence. Although U Wirathu is often presented as the leader of the 969 Movement, it is probably more accurate to characterise him as leading a particularly influential faction within a movement that has multiple centres of power all drawing on traditions from within Theravada Buddhism.[70]

While it has had a great deal of influence over the developments in Myanmar's politics since 2008, the 969 Movement is pressing for even more illiberal laws and repression of the non-Buddhist population. They are intent on preventing either the NLD or the USDP moving to a more humane policy and they have recently started to denounce the NLD as being insufficiently anti-Muslim and no longer protecting the Buddhist/Burman purity of Myanmar.[71]

The 969 Movement, in its extremism, has moved significantly beyond what can be seen as orthodox Buddhist norms. In fact, it is prepared to acknowledge this and glory in the paradox. Thus U Wirathu blames Muslim shopkeepers for inspiring him to call on his followers to boycott their shops, as such actions 'are not discrimination' but done to 'protect our people's interests'.[72] He also argues that Muslims already boycott Buddhist shops. Equally, the recent ban on inter-faith marriage is justified not in terms of Buddhist teachings but as a measure needed to protect the Buddhist community.

In this the 969 Movement draws inspiration from its co-religionists in Sri Lanka, who argue that violence and discrimination is legitimate as long as it has an acceptable purpose. In both cases the persecution of a different religious and ethnic community is justified if it 'protects' Buddhist culture. Thus the leaders of the 969 Movement deny responsibility for violence, even as they encourage it, since in their minds their only goal is to promote and protect Buddhism, and, as noted above, the victims are not really properly human.

Of course, in this way they can advocate the most horrendous atrocities while maintaining that they are not, in fact, advocating violent behaviour. The monks are already denying their responsibility for current events by saying they have not advocated violence, but can argue that nevertheless the violence that has occurred is acceptable.[73] An argument they often make is that if there is no intent to promote violence, say by speech, then there is no moral responsibility if that speech leads to violence.[74] This matters, because many people in Myanmar listen to what the monks say and respect their views,[75] giving their words an importance it may be hard to understand in contemporary Western society. Not least, as discussed below, extremist Buddhist movements have become major providers of basic education for many of the poor.

Even beyond the extremists of the 969 Movement, Myanmar is becoming more religiously intolerant. Pressure from extremist Buddhist groups led President Thein Sein to pass the Population Control Health Care Bill[76] which sets limits on family sizes and which critics argue will be applied only to Muslims. In 2014 an opposition politician, Hin Lin Oo, was sent to jail for criticising the 969 Movement,[77] and in early 2015 a New Zealander and two Burmese men were sentenced to thirty months' hard labour for insulting Buddhism,[78] when they created an online advert for a bar which depicted the Buddha wearing headphones.

The MaBaTha

More worryingly, extremist Buddhist groups are not just organising public demonstrations, but are also taking a growing degree of control over the country's educational system,[79] supplementing state schooling with Sunday schools. The textbooks they use are produced by the MaBaTha, the Organisation for the Protection of Race and Religion, a group that seeks to discriminate against other religions.

As Matthew Walton has noted, this points to the complexities of the situation especially in terms of how the Buddhists are perceived by the wider population. To many in Myanmar, such schools are important because of their Buddhist teaching rather than because they teach an anti-Islamic message. MaBaTha is, in principle, primarily focused on protecting Buddhism from what it sees as threats, and not all its senior members agree with the violently anti-Islamic message promoted by its leadership.[80] Nonetheless, the core message coming from these religiously inspired schools is not one of tolerance but one that seeks to claim that Buddhism is under threat from Islam.[81]

The MaBaTha, in conjunction with the 969 Movement, also runs 'buy Buddhist' campaigns to ensure that Muslim businesses are boycotted.[82] To promote this goal it has shifted politically to create a parliamentary alliance with the USDP so as to ensure discrimination is enshrined in legislation. The 'buy Buddhist' campaign has also gained state support[83] as the USDP is unwilling to upset an important part of its potential electorate.

This has spilled over into a campaign to close (mostly Muslim-run) slaughterhouses, which stems from fear that Muslims will eat all of the cows in Myanmar (thus harming agriculture). In Labutta (in northern Rakhine), under pressure from the MaBaTha, the local authorities first tried to prevent local farmers selling cows to some Muslim slaughterhouses, and then refused these slaughterhouses licences to operate. This hits both the economic livelihood of the Muslim community in the area and their religious practices. To the extremists, this is not an attack on Muslims as such, but on a critical way in which Muslim religious practice differs from what is acceptable within Buddhism: 'We are not deliberately targeting (Muslim) businesses. They would kill animals as they believe this is how they gain merit. That's the main difference between us and them'.[84] Naturally, some extremists go further and suggest that the Muslims only run slaughterhouses because 'They are practising how to cut our throats'.[85]

The MaBaTha has also been implicated in campaigns of intimidation against any Buddhists who dare to speak out against its agenda.[86] As with the West's assumption that Aung San Suu Kyi is beyond reproach, there is a need to challenge the view that Buddhism is inherently non-threatening. Like all religions, it can be many things to many people, and can be both tolerant and just, yet also can lend itself to extremism. In Myanmar, Sri Lanka and Thailand—where religion has become confused with ethnicity—it can be used as an excuse by extremists to justify violence against those of different faiths or ethnic groups. At the moment, there is no evidence that either the regime or the opposition is prepared to stand up to the Buddhist extremists, and both have alliances with factions within the groups of extremist monks.[87] As one Burmese journalist noted, 'the two strongest institutions in our country—the military and monk organisations—are driven by men, and promote nationalism and religion. That influences our media coverage'.[88]

The prejudice against the Rohingyas runs deep in the Buddhist community at the moment. And in a perverse example of how even the most benign religious idea can be twisted to serve an agenda of intolerance, many Buddhists justify the suffering of the Rohingyas in terms of reincarnation: if their lives are so awful now it is due to their sins in past lives.[89]

However, there is another aspect to the MaBaTha that is increasingly coming to light. The reason why a movement that did not exist before 2010 is now so influential is that it is funded and supported by the regime.[90] Monks who were arrested during the Saffron Revolution have been offered money and state patronage to join the MaBaTha and promote its core message of hatred of all Muslims.

Alternative voices in contemporary Myanmar

The material above may give the impression that anti-Rohingya racism is now the norm in Myanmar. It certainly is depressingly common. However, as in all societies, many are prepared to speak out against racism and bigotry. Similarly in Myanmar, some brave citizens have spoken out against the conflation of Buddhism with anti-Muslim prejudice.[91] Networks such as Pan Zagar have courageously taken on the extremists, explicitly rejecting the 969 Movement's fusion of being Buddhist and hatred of Islam.[92] Pan Zagar has explicitly called for action against hate speech, and unlike the monks of the 969 Movement, accept there is a link between speech and actions: 'Let's watch what we say so that hate between mankind does not proliferate'[93] has become one of their key slogans. This forms part of a slowly emerging counter narrative to that of the 969 Movement, for example as captured by another popular slogan: 'Don't spark hatred with your words'.[94]

Such dissent can have personal consequences, especially when the 969 Movement calls its opponents 'fake countrymen' and 'traitors on national affairs'.[95] As a result, some report feeling intimidated into keeping quiet, a worrying sign in a country sitting on the edge of genocide:

> About a year ago, a friend in my neighbourhood put stickers on his van that said: 'I will not be the cause of racial or religious conflict.' A little later, he peeled them off. 'I was worried people would be angry or violent towards me when they saw the sticker,' he said. 'The van is for business.' Who would I be to disagree? The stickers were from a campaign organized by youth groups opposing the spread of religious violence following the riots in Meiktila. My friend supports his family by driving that van.[96]

Other instances of civil groups challenging the 969 Movement include women's groups who opposed the proposed ban on inter-faith marriage as an assault on women's rights[97] in contradiction of the 969 claims that such laws were essential to protect women from Muslim violence. In this case, Suu Kyi actually did meet the activists, but those standing up to the 969 Movement continued to receive death threats.[98]

Others too are speaking out. Journalist and filmmaker Mon Mon Myat has spoken about the need to respect all Myanmar's ethnic communities in the move towards democracy.[99] Equally I met a number of journalists who work in Myanmar who told me that the government now feels that some extremist monks have gone too far[100] but, like the NLD, it may no longer be in a position to challenge them directly. As we have seen, the regime has an ambiguous view of international pressure, but would like to see the EU and UN sanctions lifted so they can continue the vital business of making money for themselves.

This does indicate that the 'vision' for Buddhism espoused by the 969 Movement and MaBaTha—the paranoid vision that if Myanmar is to have a Buddhist future, this must be grounded on the exclusion of all non-Buddhist groups—is not going uncontested even in the current climate. That is no small feat. But that will be far from sufficient as things stand. One problem in imagining a Myanmar where Buddhism is secure enough to co-exist with other faiths is the lack of an alternative perspective from the main opposition party, the NLD. This is the most disappointing fact about the situation in Myanmar, but perhaps also the area where the international community may find that it has the most leverage to improve the situation of the Rohingyas, and also those of other victimised groups.

There is also dissent from within the Buddhist community against the extremists. A practical example of the potential limits to the 969 Movement's power took place at Lashio, just north of Mandalay, in 2013. While the role of the Buddhist establishment is mostly one of condoning or encouraging persecution, this was an instance where the Buddhist community played a positive role. An outburst of inter-communal violence was triggered when a Muslim man set fire to a Buddhist woman after dousing her with gasoline.[101] The ensuing violence saw one Muslim killed and numerous Muslim businesses and houses burnt to the ground. To escape, local Muslims received help from the local army who took them to a monastery where they were fed,[102] and the monks intervened to protect Muslims from further physical violence.[103] Equally, unlike during similar events in Rakhine, the army and police moved to restore order the day after the riots and arrested twenty-five locals for carrying out acts of violence.

There seems little doubt that the reason why an isolated act of madness resulted in a full blown orgy of intercommunity violence was the environment of interreligious mistrust stoked by the 969 Movement.[104] Nevertheless, the events at Lashio expose many of the contradictions in contemporary Myanmar. Many monks have chosen instead to stress the traditions of peace and tolerance within their religion.[105]

This is one example of the dissent to the 969 Movement and the MaBaTha from within the Buddhist monastic communities. Others have occurred. In 2014 some monks worked with the local Muslim community in Mandalay to defuse tensions and promote inter-faith relations.[106] Near Meikhtila some monks also opened their monastery to offer shelter to Muslims being attacked by supporters of the 969 Movement. Importantly, there is also evidence that this reflects a generational divide, with older monks who took part in the 1988 revolt being more likely to speak out against the 969 Movement than younger monks. Sitagu Sayadaw, a senior monk who was imprisoned in 1988, has, for example, criticised those advocating violence and spoken out in favour of interreligious peace initiatives.[107]

International politics since 2010

There has been an important international dimension to Myanmar's domestic politics since 2010. In particular, the regime has gained much from appearing to allow a democratic transition and to accept the NLD as a democratic alternative. This has seen EU sanctions lifted, other sanctions reduced and a massive influx of foreign investment.

Post-2010, Myanmar's international links have expanded, but in essence the focus has continued to be on trade rather than significant political engagement with the outside world. Capital inflows have increased from $320m in 2009–10 to $1.42bn in 2012–13, and then to an estimated $5bn in 2014–15.[108] The largest share of this investment is in telecommunications, followed by oil and gas, real estate and tourism. In addition to this massive expansion of much-needed investment, the current regime benefits from the lifting of sanctions and a generally positive international reputation. And it is reaping the economic dividends—though the benefits are going to the military rulers, not the bulk of the population.

However, even with states like India and China, tensions remain. India has concerns about the security of the poorly delineated border between the two countries,[109] and has taken in a number of Rohingya refugees. India was active in Burma even before 2007, primarily building infrastructure and in terms of oil and gas extraction.[110] However, it now has concerns that the repression in

Rakhine threatens the security of the region around the Bay of Bengal. To India, Myanmar is a major trading opportunity, and it hopes that a successful transition to democracy will ease a number of problems, but Myanmar also continues to be a theatre for India's ongoing dispute with China[111] as both powers tussle for trading dominance.

China, while essentially supportive of the regime, wishes to see the conflicts in the northern provinces ended, in part to ease the creation of communication links, but also to reduce the flow of refugees into China.[112] In pursuit of this goal, China has effectively become a part of the events driving the various ethnic conflicts in northern Myanmar.[113] A wider issue is that it is often Chinese-funded investment projects fuelling local disputes about land ownership across Myanmar,[114] in effect destabilising the very regime China relies on to safeguard its investments. Both the recent conflict involving the Kachin and an escalation of tension in the Shan region are connected to major Chinese infrastructure projects. China seems to be playing favourites among the armed groups in the region as it seeks to safeguard its border, its investments, and the transport links being developed from China to the Bay of Bengal. In an echo of the 'Burma Road' used to send supplies to China during World War II,[115] Myanmar is now seen by China 'as the bridge to the Bay of Bengal and the waters beyond'.[116] From this point of view, the only reason China might worry about the persecution of the Rohingyas is if the situation threatens their commercial interests.

More widely, China has been described as the 'elephant in the room'[117] with a 'firm reach into almost all corners of Myanmar society'.[118] Practically, the Chinese appear to strongly support the military rulers and have no reason to support democratic change. However, recently, they have started to court the NLD and they invited Aung San Suu Kyu to Beijing in July 2015.[119] This may have been a pragmatic preparation for the outcome of the November 2015 elections. China now has long-term interests in Myanmar, as creating the necessary transport infrastructure in the country would allow it to link land-locked provinces such as Yunnan to the sea.[120] Safeguarding these projects is probably of more importance to the Chinese than the actual make up of the government in Myanmar—as long as that government can deliver the required level of security.

Elsewhere, authoritarian regimes have found China a willing partner when they wish to avoid Western pressure around human rights and corruption.[121] This matters, as US–Chinese dynamics are becoming increasingly important for the future of Myanmar. If both China and the US perceive themselves to be in a zero-sum game for influence, this will dampen either state's willingness to really challenge the regime over human rights abuses[122] for fear that the other power will step into the vacuum. There is evidence that the US is more than prepared to do a deal with the existing military in return for vague promises of reform.[123] The US wants listening bases along the Andaman Sea, while China's expansion into this region fits with its other initiatives to establish control over Asian trade routes, such as its massive investment in Karachi, Pakistan.[124]

Myanmar's formal move towards democracy has led to increasing contacts between the Burmese leadership and the US. Hillary Clinton visited in November 2011, and British Prime Minister David Cameron followed soon afterwards. This led to British and US pressure to lift EU and UN sanctions in 2012. That year also saw visits to the country from Tony Blair, EU Commission President José Manuel Barroso and, in November, President Obama (this visit coincided with the announcement of an independent inquiry into events in Rakhine). In all the international rivalries and competition for trade, the plight of the Rohingyas is easily overlooked. President Obama did mention the 2012 massacres in Rakhine when he visited, but this was one sentence in a speech that otherwise concentrated on praising the military and the opposition for managing the transition to democracy.

The EU has been another international actor with interests in Myanmar. It imposed sanctions after the 1990 crackdown, but since 2011 it has clearly decided that encouraging the regime is the only valid strategy.[125] As we shall see, it was very quick to absolve the regime of any responsibility in the 2012 ethnic violence in Rakhine[126] and subsequently lifted all its sanctions (apart from those connected to arms sales).[127] Since then it has been a major donor, in particular of help that it believes will assist the transition to full democracy.[128] Pragmatically, compared with the US, India and China, the EU is a minor actor in Myanmar, but it does set the tone of the response of the international community. As we will see, there are strong grounds for arguing that this belief in a gradual but inevitable transition to democracy that will benefit all the citizens of Myanmar is flawed.[129]

The US is clearly unhappy about the continued North Korean presence, but the fact that the Myanmar regime seems content to ignore this is indicative of its strong resistance to influence.[130]

Another important set of external relations is with ASEAN. This regional grouping tends to emphasise the concept of non-interference in members' affairs. This has led to an unwillingness to criticise Myanmar even if, mostly due to a range of territorial disputes, Myanmar has rarely played an active role in the group. An important reward for the relatively free 2012 by-elections and the apparent acceptance of the NLD as a legitimate opposition was that Myanmar became chair of ASEAN in 2014 for the first time. However, the 2015 refugee crisis (discussed in the next chapter) led to a breakdown in relations. In effect, Myanmar's policies were threatening the security of other states, and Malaysia in particular firmly placed the blame for the crisis on Myanmar's treatment of the Rohingyas. The criticisms were direct, and included demands for the Rohingyas to be granted citizenship.[131] Myanmar, perhaps not surprisingly, refused, and its relations with ASEAN have reverted to being limited to attendance at formal meetings.

Myanmar's interactions with ASEAN are perhaps indicative of its wider approach to international relations. As a group, ASEAN is worried about China's rise to regional dominance: while they welcome the trade and economic development opportunities, they fear the spread of Chinese power.[132] On a number of occasions, Myanmar has traded on this fear when ASEAN places it under pressure. In effect, Myanmar has forced ASEAN to minimise criticism on the grounds that this will drive the regime to become less dependent on its ASEAN links and more reliant on China.[133]

This indicates that the regime may well like to have multiple partners and is not worried if they have conflicting goals. If China and the US were not competing with one another in Myanmar, one or the other might be more willing to take steps to criticise the regime and perhaps punish it for ongoing human rights abuses. North Korea in this sense is an ideal bargaining card. It provides something very useful to the regime (arms sales), and its influence can be used as an implicit threat to all of the US, India and China—in effect, can they risk antagonising the Myanmar regime if it will then turn to a closer link with North Korea?

The shifts in international relations reflect a convenient narrative available to Western leaders. Myanmar is on the road to some form of democracy, the economy is open for foreign investment and there is a media-friendly opposition leader available. Myanmar is now seen as an opportunity and many states, both regional and international, are keen to exploit the mineral wealth of the country.[134] And whatever problems we see today, they can be dismissed as nothing more than bumps along the road as Myanmar moves towards democracy, liberalism and Western values.

Thein Sein has clearly benefitted from his apparently reformist policies. *Foreign Policy* named him 'Thinker of the Year' in 2012, and UN Secretary-General Ban Ki-moon has praised his 'vision, leadership and courage to put Myanmar on the path to change'.[135] As such, the relative liberalism of the period 2011–14 (a period without any electoral events that could threaten USDP control) can be seen as a deliberate strategy designed to maximise international investment and gain legitimacy.

There is evidence this has worked so far. Many external bodies seem to want to believe that Myanmar is becoming more democratic and any problems are the minor setbacks that accompany the process of moving from an authoritarian regime to a democratic one. This is a dangerous assumption and the reality remains that Myanmar's future success depends on it respecting the rights of all of its citizens, especially those from the most persecuted groups.[136] As the refugee outflows in 2015 have shown, the persecution of the Rohingyas has the capacity to undermine the stability of much of the neighbouring region. Progress is not just about the convenient veneer of regular elections.

Still, the fact that recent years have seen substantial flows of international capital into Myanmar is hugely significant, because it gives the international community leverage to comment on the country's domestic politics, and allows us to intervene on behalf of the oppressed minorities—should we commit to doing so. All regimes take some note of international opinion—and at this point in their history specifically, Myanmar is more responsive to international opinion than at any time since it has gained independence. At the moment, in the rush to praise the limited moves towards democracy[137] and to ensure a share of the investment boom, foreign states are not fulfilling their moral, and arguably legal (under UN legislation), obligation of holding the regime to account for ongoing abuses against minorities.

As in other recent instances of genocide, such as Rwanda, international indifference to the realities of a country is dangerous. If the regime feels it has no reason to fear external pressure, it is more likely to indulge in further, perhaps escalated, repression. Rohingya activists are clear that the Myanmar regime will only agree to intervene against their persecution if threatened by international sanctions. To the regime, building up the economy is the means to a strong military. As one activist told me, 'When I talk to the ... people with the ruling party ... their interest is to ... make Myanmar economically strong [because] if the economy's not strong, defence is not strong. Because they love the word of a British defence minister. Defence minister of Myanmar quoted the word of defence minister of UK. He says, 'Without good economy ... strong defence is not possible.'[138]

The regime's logic, and its vulnerability, is clear. It wants a strong economy so that it can act as it wants without fear of external pressure.[139] The current regime does not want economic growth to benefit the bulk of Myanmar's people. Nevertheless, it might be prepared to recognise the Rohingyas if it believes this is needed to secure economic growth.[140] It is aware of external debates, and the need to at least avoid open conflict with external powers. As one Rohingya activist put it, 'if we stop international pressure, they will relax. So at the one side, international pressure should continue, I fully agree with that'.[141] As I will argue later in this book, at the moment the international community has more leverage over the regime than it seems prepared to use. This indifference may well have fatal results.

4

IMPLICATIONS FOR THE ROHINGYAS (2008–2015)

As noted in the previous chapter, the 2008 Constitution actually strengthened the 1982 Constitution's denial of citizenship to the Rohingyas. Moreover, after 1988 the NLD formed a close alliance with the regional ethnic Rakhine parties. Even in the 1990 elections, these parties were arguing for the expulsion of the Rohingyas from the north of the province.[1] Increasingly, the local Rakhine population has backed these ethnically-based regional parties[2] rather than those that operate at a national level, and this has given politics within the state a set of dynamics different to the rest of the country. With one major community (the Rohingyas) effectively disbarred from the electoral process, the stage is left clear for Rakhine extremists.[3]

The Arakan National Party (ANP) was formed in 2013 from a merger of the Rakhine Nationalities Development Party (RNDP) and the Arakan League for Democracy. By 2015 this alliance had broken apart due to the ambitions of senior politicians, and the RNDP is once more a separate party (although the bulk of the membership stayed in the ANP). However, regardless of the label they campaign under, these politicians have been heavily implicated in the 2012 and subsequent massacres and persecution of Rohingyas.[4]

Politics and administration in Rakhine

Geographically, Rakhine occupies the same area as Arakan did before the British conquest in 1826.[5] In ethnic violence in 1942, the previously mixed population of Rohingyas and Rakhine became separated. The bulk of the Rohingyas now live in the northern districts (Maungdaw, Buthidaung and Rathedaung) and around the major port of Sittwe, while the rest of the province is mostly populated by ethnic Rakhine (see Figure 10).

Unlike in the rest of Myanmar, local parties—the RNDP and the ANP—dominate Rakhine politics:[6] the USDP is represented where there is a significant military presence but lacks a substantial popular base. Another difference is that the move to democracy has been even more partial than in the rest of the country. The military remains completely in control of the civilian administration, as a Rohingya activist explained to me—'There's no democracy in this township'—and the administrators are those 'who were administrator[s] during the time of the military regime. They are re-appointed. ... So all people are under the administration of [the] military and their party administrator, township administrator. Where is the democracy?'[7]

Within Rakhine, many of the monasteries are also in close alliance with the RNDP and ANP.[8] This gives the Buddhist extremists a much closer hold over the political process here than they have elsewhere in Myanmar. When a charity wished to work with the monasteries to perform surgery to help local children with cleft lips, this was refused when they also wanted to treat children from the Rohingya community.[9]

In the period between 2008 and 2012 the persecution of the Rohingyas was continuous, and a US government report[10] noted that this had a particularly religious aspect. The period saw the destruction of many mosques which, it was claimed, had been built without proper permission, and saw the creation of 'Muslim Free Areas' in some parts of the state. In addition, Buddhist pagodas have been built in areas with no Buddhist population, often using Rohingya forced labour, and there is an ongoing campaign to entice conversion to Buddhism by lifting restrictions on travel, work and schooling for those who agree to do so.[11] In effect, those Rohingya prepared to change their religion received the same rights as other citizens.

This continuation of earlier policies of discrimination, including restrictions on family size and travel, reflects the RNDP's determination to force the Rohingyas out of Myanmar. On the most generous of interpretations, neither the NLD nor the military were prepared to challenge this policy; in reality they became complicit in allowing the RNDP to set the tone of debate within Rakhine. The continuous use of ethnic tensions as a political tool came to a head in 2012.

The 2012 massacres

The events of 2012 can only be described as an attempt at ethnic cleansing seeking to drive the Rohingyas either out of the country, or, at the least, from their homes and into internal refugee camps.[12] The initial violence started in June 2012 in four townships and spread to nine more in October, as initial acts of random violence was turned into a systematic attempt to force the Rohingyas to leave the state.[13]

The events in June commenced after the rape and murder of a Rakhine woman by three Muslims[14] in late May. On 3 June, a large group of Rakhine Buddhists stopped a bus and killed the ten Muslims who were travelling on board. Following this, the violence escalated to attacks on a number of villages and both communities were victims and aggressors in this phase, with armed mobs carrying out acts of murder and arson.

At the start, local security forces, especially the police (who are dominated by Rakhine Buddhists) stood to one side, but later some officials joined in the attacks to burn Muslim villages.[15] In contrast, at least in a few instances, the army tried to stop the violence or protect fleeing Muslims. But more often, they either stood aside, or actively joined in with the attacks.[16] After the June events had died down, the army dumped the bodies of some Rohingyas close to a refugee camp:

> None of the bodies were identified. Local residents took photographs showing some victims who had been 'hogtied' with string or plastic strips before being executed. By leaving the bodies near a camp for displaced Rohingya, the soldiers were sending a message—consistent with a policy of ethnic cleansing—that the Rohingya should leave permanently.[17]

Despite the evidence of military and police involvement in the riots, both the EU and the US praised the regime for its even-handed approach to containing the violence.[18] The EU Foreign Affairs Commissioner, Catherine Ashton, felt moved to claim, 'We believe that the security forces are handling this difficult intercommunal violence in an appropriate way. We welcome the priority which the Myanmar government is giving to dealing with all ethnic conflicts'.[19]

In reality, after the June violence the state refused to help those who had suffered or to investigate allegations of security forces' involvement.[20] Instead, President Thein Sein called for Rohingyas, once again described as 'illegal' non-citizens, to be transferred to other countries.[21] This statement effectively called for the forced deportation of an entire community. This demand has been repeated ever since and is now a regular part of the rhetoric of the extremists. As we will see, the desire to push the Rohingyas out of Myanmar has been one cause of the 2015 refugee crisis. The goal of expulsion is shared by most Rakhine community leaders and this pattern of blaming the Rohingyas for their own persecution has become the standard response of the Myanmar authorities.

By the end of June the first wave of spontaneous violence died down. In the meantime President Sein established a committee to investigate the June events and 'find solutions for communities with different religious groups to live together in harmony'.[22] In a speech at the end of August he suggested that the Rakhine bore responsibility for the June violence, stating that 'political parties, some monks, and some individuals are increasing the ethnic hatred'.[23] However, when his commission finally reported in July 2013 it blamed the Rohingyas for harming the good name of Myanmar with the international community[24] and said nothing about state complicity in the violence.

Unfortunately, the June events turned out to be simply a prelude to a larger wave of attacks in October. After the first wave of violence, Buddhist monks circulated pamphlets demanding that ethnic Rakhine cease all economic ties with the Rohingyas, ordering them not to sell them goods or associate with them. The pamphlets claimed that the Rohingyas were planning the 'extinction of the Arakanese'[25] as they were 'stealing our land, drinking our water, and killing our people. They are eating our rice and staying near our houses. So we will separate. We don't want any connection to the Muslim people at all'.[26] This campaign was widespread, seeking to isolate the Rohingyas economically and socially while at the same time claiming they represented a mortal threat to the Rakhine. In effect, there were twin demands that the Rohingyas go 'home' (that is, to Bangladesh) and that, if they stayed, they should be isolated within Rakhine province. One monk told the BBC that 'around the world there are many Muslim countries. They should go there. The Muslim countries will take care of them. They should go to countries with the same religion'.[27]

The monks organised in conjunction with the RNDP,[28] led by Aye Maung, and cooperated with other local political parties and community groups.[29] The RNDP seems to have been the driving force calling for the Rohingyas to be 'temporarily' relocated so that they would not live near the Rakhine, before being transferred to neighbouring countries. The RNDP even attacked those members of its own Rakhine community who continued to deal with the Rohingyas[30] and stoked fear that the Rohingyas, in league with Al-Qaeda, planned to massacre the Buddhist majority. These claims were supplemented with rumours that arms and ammunition were being stored in mosques and that the regime was too scared to protect the local community.[31] These arguments became widely believed among the Rakhine and were also broadcast on state-controlled radio.[32]

Social media has become important in Burma and forms a major source of information for many. Many stories start as social media reports and are then subsequently reported in the print media.[33] Thus hatred is stirred up online and then repeated by the press. One unedifying example of this comes directly from the top, from the director of President Sein's office, who posted on his Facebook page:

> It is heard that Rohingya Terrorists of the so-called Rohingya Solidarity Organization are crossing the border and getting into the country with the weapons. That is Rohingyas from other countries are coming into the country. Since our Military has got the news in advance, we will eradicate them until the end! I believe we are already doing it. ... We don't want to hear any humanitarian issues or human rights from others. Besides, we neither want to hear any talk of justice nor want anyone to teach us like a saint.[34]

The post has since been deleted but screenshots have been preserved of the original. What followed was not the type of response one would expect of a saint, of any religious denomination. One set of triggers for the October violence was widely believed reports that three Buddhists had been killed by Muslims and two Burmese soldiers injured by gunfire.[35] But mainly the violence was a consequence of the deliberate actions and planning of the extremist monks and political parties such as the RNDP,[36] which had worked to break any remaining links between the Rohingya and Rakhine communities.

This tends to support a belief that increasingly the violence in Rakhine is not directly under the control of the Myanmar authorities but is following local dynamics. This is not to absolve the regime, which has stoked up hatred over forty years and does little, if anything, to constrain the actions of Rakhine extremists.

The wave of violence started on 22 October and lasted a week. Many attacks started by burning the local community mosques and then burning houses forcing the local Rohingyas to flee. Some witnesses insisted that the initial attacks were not carried out by locals they recognised but by people who came into the community from outside.[37] On 23 October there were coordinated attacks in villages in Mrauk-U, Minbya, Kyauk Pyu, and Pauktaw districts. This time, however, the target was all Muslims, regardless of ethnicity, and the Kaman (who have legal citizenship) were also attacked in the coastal region of Kyauk Pyu.[38] The ensuing violence was not completely one-sided and, in some places, Rakhine Buddhists were killed as Rohingya and Kaman villagers defended their communities.

One of the worst incidents was at the village of Yan Thei on 23 October, where a massacre commenced at 6.30 AM. The attack was clearly prepared and followed on from the events of the previous day, when the local police (the Lon Thein) had disarmed the local Rohingyas of sticks and other crude weapons. One survivor presented evidence on the role of the police:

> [W]e went outside the village [when thousands of Arakanese approached], and then the Lon Thein told us to go back inside the village and then they took the sticks from our hands. First the [Lon Thein] security told us, 'Do not do anything, we will protect you, we will save you,' so we trusted them. But later they broke that promise. The Arakanese beat and killed us very easily. The security did not protect us from them.[39]

Other survivors have stated that the local police actually participated in the attack and opened fire on villagers. There is no independent evidence for this, but all the eyewitness reports support the claim that the villagers were promised protection from the Arakanese mob and then abandoned to their fates. Around 5 PM the army finally intervened, although by that stage most of the violence was over. Among the dead were twenty-eight children, thirteen of whom were aged under five, who had been hacked to death.[40]

Elsewhere it appears as if the security forces were definitely involved in the violence. There are several reports that in Kyauk Pyu on 23 October the army shot three young Muslims.[41] But the role of the army, as it had been in June, was not consistent. In places, the military did prevent violence or stepped in to end it as quickly as possible. There are also reports of Myanmar naval ships providing food and water to those who had fled by boat and were travelling to what they hoped was a safer part of Rakhine. However, when the refugees arrived near Sittwe (where there is a large refugee camp), the 'army arrived and pushed us back to the sea. We tried to force our way on the shore but they wouldn't let us come on shore'.[42] When they were finally allowed to land they were kept on the beaches, denied aid and beaten by the army.

Elsewhere the main contribution of the army was to urge the Rohingyas to flee the violence. A Kaman Muslim reported: 'I saw five or more army soldiers in front of my fish shop. The whole village was burning. When I saw the soldiers I thought they would help us, but they just shouted at us to get out quickly'.[43] This pattern of the military standing to one side was repeated elsewhere:

> The police and military came and told people to come out of their house, and they said if we didn't we'd all be killed. They said they couldn't provide us with security ... And in the presence of the military and police, [the Arakanese] entered our homes and took what they wanted.[44]

Violence by the state security forces carried on after the communal attacks had died down. They attacked those seeking help and continued to treat those displaced with great brutality.[45] The president's initial response was to deny any involvement of the state security forces in the violence.[46] However, the level of violence attracted too much international attention, and by mid-November he was forced to write to Ban Ki-moon to acknowledge that there had been communal violence and to pledge to address problems of forced resettlement and to grant citizenship to the Rohingyas.[47]

The timing of this promise was not accidental—it was released just prior to President Obama's visit to the country and was clearly designed to avoid any embarrassment for his important visitor. But the measure of the insincerity of these promises can be found in the UN Special Rapporteur's report to the UN Security Council in April 2014: he 'saw no improvements in the human rights situation. Instead, as time passes without clear action at the state and national level to address the widespread discrimination and human rights violations occurring there, the situation continues to worsen from an already dire state'.[48]

Despite promises, there has been no effort by the Myanmar authorities to investigate any of the alleged army or police involvement in the violence. The UN has noted that

> no credible investigation has taken place to uncover the human rights violations that have occurred there. The Government has prosecuted people from both communities accused of being involved in the violence. However, no State officials have been held to account and, in the absence of an independent and credible investigation, it remains unclear whether the main perpetrators have been prosecuted'.[49]

The UN has continued to raise concerns about the lack of progress in charging those responsible for organising the violence.[50]

This is where the voice of the opposition NLD could really have made a difference for the better. But as expected, they also stood idly by, apparently acquiescing to the extremists' demands that the Rohingyas leave the country.[51] One inevitable consequence of the violence was a substantial increase in the number of refugees. Again, the Buddhist extremists found a way to blame the Rohingyas for their plight. U Wirathu described the flight to refugee camps as being a result of 'Muslims deliberately razing their own houses to win a place at refugee camps run by aid agencies'.[52]

The result was a major displacement of the Rohingyas fleeing violence and persecution. Over 100,000 ended up in internal refugee camps in Myanmar, while the UNHCR estimated that 13,000 arrived in Malaysia and 6000 in Thailand between October 2012 and April 2013. In a foretelling of the events to unfold in 2015, hundreds were reported to have died at sea[53] and most of those arriving in neighbouring countries quickly disappeared into the unregulated migrant labour pools.

Massacres in 2013–14

Subsequent to the 2012 attacks, the level of direct violence declined. But it has by no means stopped. In more remote areas, such as the Maungdaw village of Duchiradan (Kila Dong), there have been occasional outbursts of violence where upwards of 4000 Rohingyas have been killed, raped, arrested, or taken to undisclosed places.[54] Their possessions have been looted, their homes destroyed in arson attacks. These events commenced after some murders were carried out by local officials, who, in order to cover up their crimes, sought to arrest witnesses and raped women related to them.[55] This provoked a reaction from the villagers and led to violence between Rohingya villagers and police, which ended when the military used live rounds to disperse the crowds.[56] Journalists and NGOs have been denied access to Maungdaw,[57] and the UN has only been allowed state-supervised access.[58]

The threat of violence continues to be pervasive in Rakhine,[59] and outbursts have continued to occur throughout 2013–15. There have also been attacks on non-Rohingya Muslims living elsewhere in Myanmar.[60] In March 2013, there were attacks led by Buddhist monks in Meiktila near Mandalay, where over 12,000 people were displaced. In advance of the violence, online Facebook postings described the local Muslim population as preparing

a Jihad. They are gathering in mosques in Mandalay under the guise of Ramadan but in reality they are recruiting and preparing for Jihad against us. The government of Myanmar must deal with these Islamic extremists and raid all suspicious mosques and homes. All Burmans must be ready and not falls into these Muslims' traps.[61]

What is striking is how closely this resembles the material circulated around Rakhine before the October 2012 riots.[62]

Meanwhile, the Myanmar regime remains convinced that the Rohingyas are deliberately, and successfully, manipulating international opinion, and has tried to cut off communication links between the Rohingyas and the outside world. Fortunately, due to social media and sympathetic external connections this has only been partially successful. In addition, there has also been a concerted pattern of excluding aid agencies from the country, the most notable example being when Medécins Sans Frontières (MSF) was ordered out of Rakhine and prevented from supporting the Rohingya community after events in 2014.[63] In effect, MSF have been banned for continuing to provide a minimal level of support and, specifically:

> the charity has been targeted for its stance on a massacre said to have taken place in Maungdaw township, a restricted area close to the Bangladesh border, where UN and human rights groups claim at least 40 Rohingya Muslims including children were killed by ethnic Rakhine Buddhists and Burmese security forces in January.[64]

The regime has come to see any critical mention of the conditions endured by the Rohingyas as an attack on the state, and will eagerly revoke access to NGOs if they speak out. This has also had a chilling effect on the way the situation in the area is being reported and is steadily eroding the last vestiges of support for the Rohingya community. A number of aid agencies are prepared to comply with government restrictions in order to carry on other work in the region.

Why did these events occur?

It is clear that while the Rohingyas were the main specific target in 2012–13, there has been widespread violence against other Muslim communities in Myanmar. The underlying dynamic driving these events has been the alliance between extremist Buddhist monks, elements of the old military regime, and the silence of the official opposition. In effect, a multi-cultural, multi-confessional state is being treated as a Buddhist state dominated by one 'Burmese' culture that only includes a specific set of ethnic groups and explicitly excludes others. This way of defining the Burmese national identity automatically leaves a group like the Rohingyas outside of the state and without legal rights to the protection that states normally afford their citizens. This is a significant precondition for further violence, and in the minds of the extremist Buddhist aggressors, a further rationalisation for their actions. In this conception of the state, it is certainly already the case that the Rohingyas have no place in the state of Myanmar. And from there, saying that they also have no place within the *territory* of the state follows quite naturally.

One solution favoured by the regime was to separate the Buddhist and Muslim communities in Rakhine, perhaps hoping that this would reduce friction between the groups. Taken to its extreme, this decision has led to the

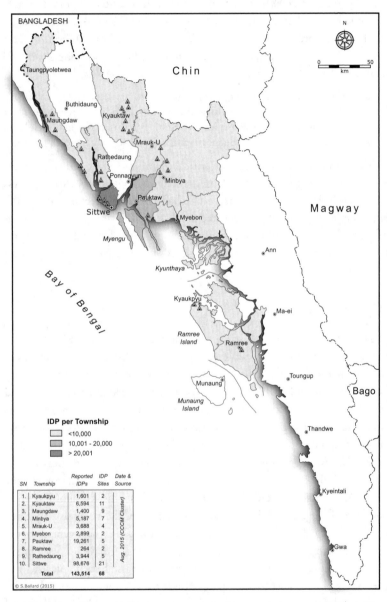

5. Map of Rakhine State Showing Locations of Internal Refugee Camps (2015)[65]

systematic creation of what are becoming permanent refugee camps within Rakhine. These are scattered across the areas where Rohingya villages and townships used to exist, but most are concentrated in the coastal area to the north of Sittwe.

For those still living in the towns, the situation keeps getting worse. The UN's Special Rapporteur noted that he had

> again visited Aung Mingalar, the only remaining Muslim neighbourhood in Sittwe, which he described as a ghetto. In Aung Mingalar ward, he heard from residents that the population had fallen by around 1,600 compared to his August visit. Many had left to risk their lives on rickety boats to reach neighbouring countries, where those who survived the journey were subjected to further human rights violations, including human trafficking.[66]

The isolation of the Rohingyas from the rest of Burmese society only fuels Buddhist suspicions—as such isolation often does. Traditionally, the Islamic community in Myanmar was open and active beyond its own members, for example running the Muslim Free Hospital in Rangoon.[67] But as they have become isolated, they are becoming more and more 'foreign' to the rest of the people of Myanmar. After all, the less contact you have with the Rohingyas, the less reason you have to disbelieve the extremist nationalist claims that they are 'preparing for Jihad' or any other such nonsense. You simply have no way of knowing any better. This separation of communities means a breakdown in empathy between the two groups, but also leads to ignorance on what each community needs and desires. Thus, you would never suspect a neighbour you know well of plotting for jihad. But one you never have the opportunity to speak to... who knows what he is plotting! Conversely, the Rohingyas have been given more than enough reasons to distrust their Rakhine neighbours. Unfortunately, such a cycle of distrust, once established, can take on a life of its own. And we have already seen some of the consequences of that. But things can still get a lot worse.

For those Rohingyas who stay in Rakhine, the reality is de facto imprisonment in the refugee camps, with no access to health or education.[68] Many Rakhine politicians are aiming to ensure that the refugee camps to which the Rohingyas fled in 2012 and 2013 remain their permanent homes,[69] if they cannot actually force them from Myanmar. More than this, they intend to force those Rohingyas still living in villages into the camps. Once there, they are denied the means to earn a living other than through the most precarious of work—a problem made worse as the extremists threaten anyone from the Rakhine community who deals with the Rohingyas.[70]

Such conditions of poverty, as is usually the case, hit women the hardest. Lacking healthcare, they tend to become pregnant[71] due to lack of access to any form of family planning, a situation which has become much worse since the expulsion of MSF from the country.[72] While many children die at an early age, perversely, the high birth rate in the Rohingya community is partly the fault of those extremists who then cite it as evidence of the threat to 'Buddhist' Myanmar (although note that the actual birth rate of the Rohingyas is hotly disputed). Even among the more moderate Buddhists there is now a fear that Muslims will 'outbreed' the Buddhists, diluting the Buddhist nature of Myanmar.[73]

The 2015 refugee crisis

If the level of outright violence in Rakhine dropped after 2013, persecution and exclusion continued unabated. There is now strong evidence that the Myanmar regime has decided to make the internal refugee camps permanent,[74] as the Rohingyas are to be displaced from the urban areas of Rakhine. The 2014 census, for example, is being used for this purpose: 'the authorities will construct temporary camps in required numbers for those who refuse to be registered and those without adequate documents and sequester them in closed camps in what amounts to arbitrary, indefinite detention with the possibility of deportation'.[75]

The 2014 census will be discussed in detail later on, as it had a major impact on the conduct of the 2015 elections. For the moment, it is sufficient to note that the Myanmar authorities simply refused to allow those Rohingyas who did not identify as 'Bengali' to complete the census. This has led to the removal of any remaining identification cards, and the resulting lack of adequate documentation is used as an excuse to force the Rohingyas into the refugee camps.

The systemic misery of the Rohingyas' lives is fuelling a massive refugee crisis with many seeking to escape by sea to neighbouring countries. This outflow of people has been a regular response to periods of systemic persecution and has become a regular feature of the spring post-monsoon period in recent years. This regular event briefly attracted international press attention in May 2015. Perhaps the most disturbing aspect of the refugee crisis from the point of view of ordinary observers was that in early summer 2015, when the crisis finally came fully to our attention, there was no obvious immediate trigger in the internal situation in Myanmar.[76] The 2015 refugee crisis was not a direct outcome of a particular policy decision, or even of a new outburst of violence.

It is quite simply what happens when human beings are expected to live in intolerable conditions.

Many Rohingyas seem to have themselves accepted that there is no place for them in Myanmar. To give just one example as to why they have done so, the level of persecution and exclusion has been normalised to the point where hospitals in Rahkine refuse to treat Rohingya people, especially if they have been beaten up by the police or army.[77] Steven Kiersons of the Sentinel Project for Genocide Prevention summarises: 'There is an utter loss of hope for the future, and people are risking their lives whether they stay in Burma or go abroad'.[78] What is more, not all the Rohingyas who leave do so voluntarily:

> There was a group of six men, they were Rakhine Buddhists from Bangladesh, they had knives and guns. They forced me to get on a boat, they told me I was leaving Myanmar [Burma]. They pushed me to the small boat, I fell into the water up to my shoulders. Fifteen other Rohingya were on that boat. All the people were forced onto the boat.[79]

There are other reports that among those paying to flee are many who are forced onto the refugee boats as part of the political goal of removing the Rohingyas. This makes former Australian prime minister Tony Abbott calling the boat people 'reckless' all the more unedifying. When asked if Australia would consider resettling any Rohingyas found to be refugees, he replied 'Nope, nope, nope'.[80] Fortunately, not all world leaders have been so indifferent. Pope Francis has described the persecution of the Rohingyas as a 'form of war':

> Let's think of those brothers of ours of the Rohingya, they were chased from one country and from another and from another, when they arrived at a port or a beach, they gave them a bit of water or a bit to eat and were there chased out to the sea. This is a conflict that has not resolved, and this is war, this is called violence, this is called killing![81]

The fate of the refugees

To understand the level of desperation, it is worth stressing just how awful the fate is that awaits those Rohingyas who do flee. In previous years, the people smugglers took most of them to Thailand, Indonesia or Malaysia, where they effectively worked as slave labourers or disappeared into the undocumented, unprotected labour force. Slave labour is commonly used in the regional prawn fishing industry, especially in Thailand, where it has become a significant part of the labour force.[82] Some estimates suggest that as many as 500,000 slaves work in Thailand,[83] and many are refugees from Myanmar. Some report that they had entered Thailand illegally, were caught by the police, and then handed over to the boat owners:

> 'One day I was stopped by the police and asked if I had a work permit,' says Ei Ei Lwin, 29, a Burmese migrant who was detained on the docks at Songkhla port. 'They wanted a 10,000 baht (£180) bribe to release me. I didn't have it, and I didn't know anyone else who would, so they took me to a secluded area, handed me over to a broker, and sent me to work on a trawler.'[84]

In Thailand slaves are now very cheap, in part due to the influx from Myanmar and in part due to the complicity of the Thai authorities. It has been estimated that the price of a human being is now 5 per cent of what it was in the nineteenth century. Modern-day slaves in the region are so cheap they are now seen as disposable.[85] Migrants quickly became aware of the threat of being sent to sea on the fishing boats: 'They told me I was going to work in a pineapple factory', recalls Kyaw, a broad-shouldered twenty-one-year-old from rural Burma. 'But when I saw the boats, I realised I'd been sold ... I was so depressed, I wanted to die.'[86]

Thailand has become the centre of this foul trade due to its lax regulations for its fishing industry and the extent of corruption between the police and people-smugglers. There is also emerging evidence that this collusion has involved senior military and police officials[87] who have not just been forcing those caught in Thailand into slavery but actually organising the trafficking of Rohingyas for the explicit purpose of selling them into slavery to create the economic basis of the Thai fishing industry.

Due to local over-fishing, Thai boats have started to operate off Indonesia, Malaysia and Myanmar, and cheap slave labour has become a crucial part of their economic model. Fuel for such long journeys is expensive, as is feeding and paying the crews. Slave labour is so cheap that if the slaves starve, are lost at sea or killed by the captains, it is easy to replace them.[88] Other Thai vessels have abandoned fishing altogether for the far more lucrative trade in trafficking Rohingyas into camps and then selling them on to other fishing captains.[89] Thailand's complicity with this business is so deep that it is in danger of being categorised, along with North Korea, as the world's worst abusers in the US State Department's Human Trafficking Index.[90] Recent evidence has implicated Thai officials directly in the trade, not just in turning a blind eye but in collecting Rohingyas from the traffickers when they arrive in Thailand and transporting them to jungle camps where they are held for ransom or sold to fishing boats.[91]

Of course, the problem is not just with Thailand. Western companies that source cheap prawns from the region, especially from Thailand, are complicit.[92] And though we may choose not to be aware of it, that part of our food supply chain is based on human misery in Myanmar too. In that sense at least, we are also complicit in this situation.

A lifetime of slavery in the Thai fishing industry, though, is not the only grim prospect that awaits Rohingya refugees who pay people-traffickers to escape Myanmar. Those who make it to land are no safer. If not sold into slavery, many are held in camps on the Thailand–Malaysia border, and recently mass graves have been uncovered of those who have died in captivity.[93] Individuals are held until their families can afford to pay a ransom.[94] Those who cannot pay are either killed or sold as slaves. Even if they escape this fate, many then work illegally with no protection.[95] Women and children are especially vulnerable to sexual exploitation[96] and there are regular reports of women starving themselves so their children can eat. There are also consistent reports of women being forced into prostitution or marriage as part of the price of being released by the smugglers,[97] and for some families selling a female member into marriage is a means to pay for their collective escape from Myanmar.

A Rohingya who survived has described their own ordeal:

> I spent 14 days on this ship. Three days after we were transferred, three smugglers arrived from Malaysia and boarded our ship. They carried mobile phones. They first asked who had phone numbers and, one by one, we started calling our relatives. Those [who did not provide] phone numbers were beaten ... The smugglers ordered passengers to beat them with engine chains wrapped in plastic and plastic pipes with something heavy inside. Even those with phone numbers were beaten. The abuses continued until families sent money, after which survivors were taken to shore by small fishing boats. ... Before I left, I witnessed three men who had become paralysed and one dead body was thrown overboard.[98]

Why has the crisis become visible?

In effect, the refugee crisis has become an annual event, especially since the 2012 violence, and happens in the May–July period, when the Andaman Sea is calm enough to allow safe passage.[99] It is fuelled by the utter desperation of people in Myanmar (and to a lesser extent in Bangladesh) and feeds into economies increasingly based on slave labour—or, at best, illegal and undocumented labour. Along the way, criminal gangs make substantial profits. The only real difference in 2015 was that the Malaysian and Indonesian governments closed their borders—in contravention of the UN Charter, but emulating the response of some European governments to the refugee crisis in the Mediterranean. Traditionally, boats would be abandoned by the traffickers close to the shore and people were expected to find their own way ashore, often helped by local fishermen. This year, when boats came close to the land they were pushed back out to sea by the local authorities.[100] However, by this point in the journey the trafficker crews were long gone, thus leaving those on board with no food and at the mercy of the sea.

In previous years all this had happened out of sight of the world's media. But in 2015 the sheer scale of the crisis and the response by Malaysia and Indonesia made it all too visible. Early coverage made no link to the situation in Myanmar and treated it as though these were migrants simply moving from one country to another in search of work. Fortunately, connections were eventually made.[101] In part, this was because of reporters' ignorance of the Rohingyas' situation, but it also reflects the success of the Myanmar regime in bullying independent organisations to the extent that some never even use the name 'Rohingyas', and never make an explicit link between their plight and Myanmar state policy.[102]

The response of the Myanmar regime

The regime has responded in a variety of ways to the migrant crisis, many of them depressingly predictable. To begin with, it refused to attend a regional ASEAN summit called to discuss the crisis.[103] When it finally relented, the authorities agreed to attend the Bangkok meeting only after being assured that the term 'Rohingya' would not be used. It was agreed that the term 'irregular migrant' would be used instead. A spokesman for the Myanmar government stated: 'They can't pressure us. We won't accept any pressure. We need the right approach to resolve the problem'.[104] After the conference, the Indonesian navy agreed to help any boats in danger of sinking and Myanmar agreed to close its borders to prevent any further refugees leaving. There is also some evidence of other regional powers, especially Malaysia, starting to lose patience with Myanmar over the refugee problem,[105] and being prepared to call for direct intervention to stop the core cause—the persecution of the Rohingyas.

But Myanmar closing its borders does not even begin to address the problems the Rohingyas face. Myanmar has no intention of stopping the persecution of the Rohingyas, and many in the regime would like to deport the entire population to Bangladesh. The basic attitude was summed up by U Zaw Htay, a deputy director general of the Myanmar president's office: 'There is no change in the government's policy toward the Bengalis'.[106] If this is so, the detention camps in Rakhine will simply become permanent prisons, and the international community will return to ignoring the problem. As could have been expected, another facet of some regime representatives' response has been to deny that the refugees are Rohingyas.

General Min Aung Hlaing, the Myanmar military's commander in chief, has said some 'boat people' landing in Malaysia and Indonesia are likely pretending to be Rohingya Muslims to receive UN aid. He suggested that 'most victims are expected to assume themselves to be Rohingya from Myanmar in the hope of receiving assistance from UNHCR'.[107] Other government spokesmen have made a similar argument, claiming that, as a government spokesman said, 'We cannot say the migrants are from Myanmar unless we can identify them ... Most victims of human trafficking claim they are from Myanmar; it is very easy and convenient for them'.[108] Of course, as the state refuses to grant them the basics of citizenship and has been known to seize even the identity cards they do have, it is exceptionally hard for any Rohingyas to prove they have come from Myanmar.

As discussed earlier, the flow of unbiased information within Myanmar has become very limited, and many ordinary people in the country have never even become aware of the refugee crisis, due to prejudice and a lack of information within the country.[109] Thus the regime's usual insensitivity to international criticism, and the lack of any real domestic pressure, allowed it to delay its response. Finally, in August, the local authorities in Rakhine agreed to bring twenty people to court for human trafficking.[110] This followed consistent denials by the regime that people smugglers were exploiting the misery of the estimated 150,000 Rohingya trapped in internally displaced persons camps. This limited shift of approach might be related to US concerns, documented in the 2015 *Trafficking in Persons Report*, which is particularly critical of the Myanmar authorities. The State Department's assessment is stark:

> Government officials are complicit in trafficking within Burma. Men, women, and children from ethnic areas, including the estimated 98,000 persons displaced by conflict in Kachin and northern Shan States and the estimated 146,000 displaced persons in Rakhine State, are particularly vulnerable to trafficking. Reports indicate some Rohingya women are subjected to sex trafficking in Rakhine State. Local traffickers use deceptive tactics to recruit men into forced labor on palm oil and rubber plantations or in jade and precious stone mines. Children are subjected to sex trafficking or to forced labor in teashops, the agricultural sector, and in begging.[111]

It is difficult to assess the extent to which the Myanmar authorities are active in forcing the Rohingyas to leave, rather than simply not intervening. While their usual first response is to try and ignore international criticism, adverse commentary, especially from powerful sources, does have some impact on their actions. The US Department of State's assessment that 'government continued law enforcement efforts to address cross-border sex trafficking, but did not make progress in holding significant numbers of traffickers, including public officials, criminally accountable for trafficking within the country'[112] perhaps sums up this ambiguity. On this basis the intended prosecution of twenty individuals may be little more than a necessary formal response to deflect external pressure, but it does support the view that external pressure can have some effect.

However, there is chilling evidence that Rakhine extremists may be involved at every stage in the process, not just in wanting to force the Rohingyas to leave. Reports suggest that some boats are crewed both by Thais and Rakhine Buddhists, as a recent Reuters article reported: 'They were guarded by 11 men with guns, he said. Most were Thai speakers but one was Rakhine, the majority Buddhist ethnic group in Rakhine State'.[113] If this is more widespread than an isolated incident, it indicates a very worrying trend. It would mean that Rakhine extremists are forcing the Rohingyas to flee, but not, as previously, as refugees, but as direct replacements for a growing fishing industry based on slavery—and, in turn, they are profiting from the fishing boats that function using slave labour.

Aftermath

By mid-June 2015 the worst of the crisis seemed to be over. Indonesia and Malaysia were allowing those at sea to land and Myanmar had effectively closed its borders. This, at least, avoided the risk of mass death at sea when the monsoon brought bad weather back to the Andaman Sea. But it did not offer any real solutions, and all the signs are that the ongoing persecution of the Rohingyas will continue to have major effects in the region.

Myanmar is clearly conflicted, unsure whether to force the Rohingyas out—a stance that has drawn US censure in the past—or to keep them in what are effectively concentration camps in the country. Since it has no intention of allowing the Rohingyas to live normal lives, it is hard not to see this as tantamount to slow murder—a kind of genocide by attrition. However, what 2015 has revealed is the linkage between the refugee outflow from Myanmar, people trafficking and other regional states, especially Thailand, which have allowed slave labour to become an important part of their economic system. As noted, slaves are now so cheap their lives have almost no value, even to the slave owners.

Of course, beyond the regional powers, there is yet another instance where other governments have opted to turn a blind eye. Abbot's statement about 'reckless' refugees sits badly with reports of individuals being forced onto the boats. Equally, the global food companies share some responsibility: they buy the products of the regional fishing industry and are clearly turning a blind eye to the conditions of the workers.[114] In effect, persecution in Myanmar now feeds people into an economic system largely based on slave labour, which would collapse if the refugees were no longer desperate to escape.

To add to the misery, some refugees who had escaped the country tried to return to Myanmar, fearing being trapped at sea in the monsoon season.[115] They had sold all their assets to pay for their escape and were left destitute when forced to return to Rakhine. In some cases, those who had stayed in the camps paid the smugglers to release those trapped on the ships. It is likely that each period of relative calm in the Andaman Sea will be marked by a refugee outflow. However, each year those trying to escape will be poorer, and more vulnerable to those looking to exploit their desperation and sell them into slavery.

If the fate of those who fled or were forced out of Rakhine has been grim, conditions for those left behind also worsened. The region subsequently had destructive monsoon rains connected with Cyclone Komen in mid-August, and this led to flooding of almost all the camps the Rohingyas are kept in and the destruction of what little goods and food they had stored.[116] Komen was not particularly destructive, and would normally have been seen as simply a particularly heavy storm within the normal weather patterns, but the non-existent infrastructure in the internal refugee camps left the Rohingyas very vulnerable to its effects. The authorities, naturally, continue to deny there is any problem:

> 'The camps are stable,' U Tin Maung Swe, a secretary for the Rakhine state government said. 'The people there are rich—they have land and they sell their crops on the market,' said the official, showing a booklet with projects such as an asphalt road and a school built with state money in the camps.[117]

The limited relief efforts of the provincial and state administration deliberately ignored the destruction of Rohingya villages and flooding in the camps.[118] Thus even as the political situation in Myanmar worsens and local politics in Rakhine falls into the hands of the Buddhist extremists, the Rohingyas are collectively losing what little communal wealth they have left.

5

GENOCIDE AND INTERNATIONAL LAW

If the primary driver for the abuse of the Rohingyas had simply been the repression by the military regime aimed at all the population of Burma, then there would be grounds for hope that the transition to a more democratic regime would mitigate the problems.[1] However, while in the past the worst of the violence has often been orchestrated by the regime, and has been linked to periods of wider political upheaval, animosity towards the Rohingyas has now become generalised and deep-seated across the Burmese political spectrum. The state has accepted no responsibility for the 2012–13 massacres and members of the opposition NLD also claim that the Rohingyas are in fact Bengalis and recent immigrants:

> [I]n an interview with GlobalPost, the Nobel Peace Laureate's spokesman and confidante, Nyan Win, confirmed that Aung San Suu Kyi has no plans to champion the Rohingya cause despite criticism swirling around her silence on the crisis. ... 'She believes, in Burma, there is no Rohingya ethnic group. It is a made-up name of the Bengali. So she can't say anything about Rohingya. But there is international pressure for her to speak about Rohingya. It's a problem.'[2]

In addition, as identified earlier, Buddhist extremists are becoming more influential, not least by offering basic education and social services for the poor of Myanmar. Many people will accept their version of Buddhist teachings, and their emphasis on the incompatibility of allowing Muslims to be part of the country, simply due to a lack of alternative sources of information.

Overall, there is now a real risk that a very vulnerable group, with no international diaspora to speak up for it (except the hundreds of thousands of refugees in Bangladesh, Thailand and other countries in the region, who are often themselves in conditions that are little better than those of the Rohingyas interred in Myanmar's internal refugee camps), now face a serious human rights crisis. Yet, at this time many Western states would rather choose to believe that Myanmar is finally on course to become a full member of the international order and that the apparent moves towards democracy in recent years are going to solve everything.[3] In fact, however, the latest outbursts of violence have happened against the background of increasing democratisation, and even in the new democratic order, there are no political checks to curtail the anti-Rohingya rhetoric or violence. As in other instances, little thought is given to what the transition from an authoritarian regime to a conventional democracy might mean in a nation state that was constructed out of arbitrary colonial borders, with significant ethnic and religious differences.[4]

However, while there is no doubt that what is happening in Rakhine now is a form of ethnic cleansing involving sustained human rights abuses, aided, if not orchestrated, by the state, the charge in this book is that Myanmar now stands on the brink of genocide.[5] This is a serious assertion and the next chapter will consider what could possibly trigger the shift from systemic oppression to genocide. For almost seventy years the Rohingyas have been stateless in their own country, their economic livelihood has been dismantled and restrictions have been placed on their ability to marry and have children. At the moment, all the preconditions for genocide are in place and, so far, the world is choosing to ignore the warning signs.

Here we need first to understand just how international law defines the crime of genocide, and then consider the dynamics of previous genocides in the twentieth century. The term genocide has a very specific meaning in international law. It is defined in the UN Convention on the Prevention and Punishment of the Crime of Genocide, in force since 1951.[6] A key element of the convention is that genocide includes the 'intent to destroy, in whole or in part, a national, ethnical, racial or religious group'. This can include killing, inflicting serious bodily or mental harm, or imposing a regime of constraints designed to eliminate the group over time, such as forcible prevention of births or transfer of children to another ethnic group. Finally, culpability is established not just on the basis of the act of genocide, but also on conspiracy to commit the act, incitement of it, attempts to commit it, and complicity in it.

The argument in this book is that the first test is now met in Rakhine and that the leadership of the Rakhine ethnic parties is culpable. At the very least, the regime in the detention camps is such that it is designed 'to eliminate the group over time' and it is clear that Rakhine politicians are aiming at the forced removal of the Rohingyas from the country of their birth.[7]

That said, crimes by a state against its entire people (such as those of the Khmer Rouge in Cambodia) are not genocide, even if they are clearly a major breach of human rights and can be tried under other UN laws.[8] A definition of genocide requires a clear targeting of a defined group, in a manner that can include systemic persecution and exclusion. This is the case in Myanmar today. Equally, those who incite or are complicit in such crimes are judged to be as guilty as those who actually carry out the crime. This speaks directly to those Buddhist monks who claim that they bear no responsibility if others commit violence, having been inspired to so by what they say.

Recent scholarship has indicated that there are seven characteristics that will determine if a given instance of ethnic tension is likely to turn into an act of genocide.[9] These are:

• Previous instances of severe ethnic tension;
• Political upheaval;
• The governing elite is drawn overwhelmingly or entirely from a particular ethnic group;
• That elite has an ideology that believes it is right to persecute a particular ethnic group;
• The regime is autocratic;
• The regime is closed to the wider international order;
• A minority is targeted for severe political or economic discrimination.

The simple reality is that all these apply in Rakhine, even if there has been some opening up to the outside world in recent years. Furthermore, genocide is never the first step, but always follows from less severe forms of repression. The usual precursor is the creation of a racist culture that rationalises or encourages discrimination, systemic legal discrimination, and abuse of the historical record to construct a narrative in which mass murder becomes desirable or even imperative. The world has often failed when faced with incipient genocides,[10] sometimes because of the context of a wider conflict, and at other times because intervention is simply seen as being inconvenient and becomes caught up in international political paralysis.[11]

Evidence from elsewhere

Genocide and mass murder stem from a complex set of circumstances which collectively are used to legitimise violence against a specific group. Despite the claims of ethnic or religious ideologues, inter-group harmony is perfectly possible and in fact has been the norm for most of human history. Yes, group differences on the grounds of ethnicity or religious belief can and often do lead to tensions. And, if they are sufficiently serious and no higher authority intervenes, these tensions can often spill over into localised acts of violence. But in many cases, even when such local acts of violence flare up, they never produce something that could be defined as genocide. A good example comes from nearby northern India. This area sees regular acts of communal violence on religious grounds,[12] but these acts are highly localised. And even though there are quite a number of pockets of violence, other very similar areas nearby remain perfectly peaceful.[13]

One reason for this difference is the actions of local politicians. Thus Mumbai has seen regular violence, mostly stoked by politicians seeking to control the votes of particular ethnic groups, while Kolkata, which actually is even more mixed in terms of ethnicity and confessional communities, has rarely seen any ethnic or religious violence.[14] Of course, that's not all there is to the story. As Ashutosh Varshney argues, the difference is not just the malign actions of political leaders but the extent to which inter-communal interaction exists. Where society is organised so that different groups share many aspects of their communal life with each other (such as sports clubs, the educational system and access to the local state bureaucracy), it is hard to create the conditions for excessive violence. But where all these social and political institutions are also segregated (or one group is denied access) along political, ethnic or religious lines, it is easier to create the basis for inter-communal violence. In this respect, the exclusion of the Rohingyas from daily life in Rakhine is worrying, especially as fracturing the links between them and the Buddhist majority has become the deliberate policy of some extremist parties and is amplified by holding many Rohingyas within internal refugee camps.

Sustained ethnic or religious violence is hardly ever accidental, and even in situations where inter-ethnic distrust is common, it needs to be constructed by politicians and powerful groups who see it as a means to gain or retain power.[15] The shift to outright genocide in turn requires the careful construction of a supporting narrative.[16] However, once a culture of violence is established, it becomes easier to escalate from discrimination to direct violence against individuals, and from there to large-scale attacks and murder.[17] In these circumstances, group differences don't just become more entrenched over time, but a situation can be created in which active conflict with the 'Other' becomes a key part of the identity of each ethnic or religious group.

For example, can you be a true (Sunni) Muslim if you accept that the Shi'a also have a legitimate system of beliefs? Or, in our case, can you be a true Burmese if you are perfectly happy for Muslims to live in Myanmar?

If the answer to either question is no, then the only remaining debate is over how you should go about resolving the problem. While some would argue that there is still a need for dialogue (after all, these examples are differences related to chosen beliefs, not fundamental ethnicity), the reality is that exclusion of the 'Other' or even their complete destruction become 'acceptable' solutions, at least to some—and support for this sort of response can be increased by deliberate actions.

A key act in producing the conditions for genocide is slow legitimation and normalisation of the framework used to justify discrimination and murder on the basis of identity, and testing the limits of what is acceptable. Genocide requires the long-term development of the cultural and institutional conditions we have highlighted in order to organise and sustain such violence.[18] This takes real effort by those with power, and the development of the required conditions is unlikely in most settings. In reality, genocide has been rare, and one reason for this is that most situations cannot sustain the necessary ideological conditions for it to happen. People revert to living with their neighbours with some degree of give and take, and find out through interaction that those deemed to be 'Other' are actually not that fundamentally different from themselves.

In other instances, external powers may be able to intervene in localised communities to prevent a situation slipping out of control. Regional powers have often historically intervened to protect the interests of oppressed minorities in countries around them, as for example Iran often does today to further the interests of Shi'a groups all over the Muslim world. This logic has a long tradition of alleviating potentially genocidal situations, even if it can be destabilising in other respects.[19] And it also underpins the UN's approach, developed since World War II,[20] in which intervention to prevent genocide is actually mandatory under international law.

When we have a situation of violence against a particular ethnic and religious group that is becoming slowly normalised, combined with a failure by the international community to intervene on behalf of that group, genocide becomes increasingly likely. This trajectory can be usefully explored in the contexts of four different genocides that have scarred the twentieth century. Each had their own logic, but in each we can see the same pattern of normalising violence, the importance of a trigger event, and international silence (or inability to interfere).

For our purposes, we can look at the Ottoman massacres of the Armenians in 1915–16, the Soviet crimes against the Muslim minority groups in Ukraine and Southern Russia in 1941–3, the Nazi-led holocaust against the Jews from 1933–45, and the genocide in Rwanda in 1994–5.

The normalisation of violence

In the case of the Armenian massacres of 1915–16, a new Ottoman regime, established by the Young Turks in 1908, had turned against the multi-cultural norms of the old monarchy and had started to stress the 'threat' posed by various non-Turkish groups (Slavs in southeastern Europe, Arabs and Armenians) to the Turkish people. Up to the final years of the Ottoman Empire, the regime was multi-cultural and usually broadly tolerant of the various ethnic groups within its borders. There were periods of active repression, but state violence against identifiable ethnic or religious groups was usually connected to wars or external threats, as for example were the massacres in the Balkans in 1877–8[21] and 1912–13,[22] when there were major revolts against Ottoman rule, combined with wars with external powers who backed those ethnic groups.

As such, there was no systemic denigration of the Armenians for most of the Ottoman Empire era. After the Young Turk Revolution in 1908[23] the new regime took a stance that was more aggressively Turkish in its identity, and also, by 1914, it had lost most of its Balkan provinces in the 1912–13 war. The advent of World War I brought nationalist revolts by the Arabs in the south and, to a lesser extent, by the Armenians in the north-east. Turkey's entry into World War I also brought it into conflict with Tsarist Russia and caused a repetition of the clashes between the two powers that had occurred over the previous century.

Russia had historically liked to present itself as a protector of the Christian Armenians and when the Russian army invaded eastern Turkey in 1915 it found itself welcomed by many. The Armenian genocide was mainly carried out by the Turkish army rather than reflecting wider communal violence, but it was a situation in which violence against the 'out-group' was regarded as perfectly sensible in the circumstances, and also fitted with the long history of Ottoman armies taking revenge on civilian populations whom they believed to be in rebellion.

A similar pattern can be seen in Soviet violence against Muslims, as this again was more state-directed violence than inter-communal violence. However, as with the Ottomans, violence had been normalised by the Soviet state and the 1941–3 events can be seen as an extension of the mass murder and starvation inflicted on the wider population in the 1930s.[24] Equally, the Turkic groups who lived in the Crimea, Caucasus and to the north of the Caspian Sea had long been regarded with deep suspicion by the Russian state. As late as the 1600s they had posed a serious threat to a Russian state[25] that was still recovering from the Mongol invasions, and in the 1760s the Crimean Khans had made an alliance with Prussia to attack Russia.[26] In this case, long standing fears about the loyalty of a defined group (similar to Ottoman distrust of the Armenians) combined with a regime that had no limits in terms of the violence it wreaked on its own citizens.

Rwanda shows some similarities and some differences to these two instances. Here the violence was a mixture of communal antagonism and state intervention. The colonial region of Rwanda brought together two different ethnic groups—the Hutus and the Tutsis. Anti-Tutsi sentiment had been built up by the Hutu regime ever since Rwanda became independent.[27] Under Belgian colonial rule (after the region was transferred from German rule at the end of World War I), the minority Tutsi population (some 14 per cent of the total population) had had a privileged role in helping to administer the colony. After independence, some politicians from the Hutu majority claimed that the Tutsis were unreliable and still owed their primary loyalty to a foreign power. Both the Germans and Belgians had played on existing ethnic divisions to ease their own control over the territory, and to that purpose both colonial powers arbitrarily declared the Tutsis as being 'racially superior' to the Hutus.

As we have seen, Buddhist extremists paint a similar picture of the Rohingyas. It is claimed that they owe their loyalty to a foreign power (Saudi Arabia is the usual nominated state) and it is true that the British favoured various ethnic and religious groups. In particular, the colonial civil service included many Muslims.

The unfortunate long-term consequence of European favouritism in Rwanda was that the independence movement after World War II took on an overtly ethnic aspect, as Hutus targeted the Tutsis due to their alleged support for Belgian rule. Independence consequently brought with it ongoing ethnic violence, and as many as 300,000 Tutsis had been forced to flee the country by the mid-1960s.

This exile community formed what was to become the Rwandan Patriotic Front, which commenced a limited invasion of Rwanda in the late 1980s. The advent of a multi-party government in early 1992 heralded a ceasefire. However, the political process of reconciliation was opposed by Hutu hardliners who started to make detailed plans for widespread massacres of Tutsis.[28] The actual genocide commenced in April 1994, after the president's plane was shot down by the army.

Perhaps the best example of how critical is the creation of the background for genocide is that of the Nazi genocide against Europe's Jews. It is the most studied of recent genocides, and offers clear examples of the importance of slow escalation of inter-group antagonism and the creation of a culture of violence as preconditions for genocide. Such a gradual development of the conditions of genocide both creates a feeling of normality towards violence across society, and also enables a gradual testing of the likely reaction of the international community.

The Nazis drew on the long-standing European narratives of anti-Semitism and the late-nineteenth-century political concept of racial purity.[29] This enabled them to identify the Jewish community as alien and a fundamental threat to their vision of a racially pure Germany. However, while they came to power determined to remove Jewish influence from Germany (and Europe) it is certainly not apparent that they started with a clear plan for mass murder. The initial racial laws were designed to ban Jews from defined professions and to ensure they were second-class citizens. The goal seemed to be to bring about the forced migration of Jews from Germany through a combination of discrimination, legal pressure and controlled acts of violence. At points in the 1930s, the pressure on the Jews was even reduced (such as in the period of the 1936 Olympics) as they sought to limit negative international publicity.

What became known as the Holocaust commenced in mid-1941 and progressed in two different phases. To begin with, there were distinctions in how Jews were treated in different occupied territories. Within the occupied territories of the USSR, mass murder became the norm within days of the invasion and fused with the war against the Soviet partisans. This was mass killing of civilians as soon as possible after the German army had occupied a region. In Poland, the Jewish community was increasingly imprisoned in ghettos where starvation and brutality exacted a steady death toll. In Germany and Western Europe, the norm was increasingly exclusion from society and deportation to the east. However, even in Germany, the Nazis faced some constraints from public attitudes in terms of what was acceptable.

These relative distinctions broke down in early 1942 for several related reasons. The entry of the US into the war had removed any remaining fear of adverse international reaction. Civil and religious pressure had forced the suspension of a campaign of murder against Germans deemed to be mentally or physically unfit, thus freeing up 'specialists', who had already experimented with mass killing using poison gas, for other tasks. Finally, the regime was facing food shortages and was desperate to eliminate those it saw as surplus and undesirable.[30] This effectively removed the last constraints and led to the construction of the extermination camps in Poland and, by late 1944, the massacre of over 6 million European Jews.

In effect, the Nazi genocide actually progressed in stages and needed to test the degree of tolerance in wider society. Open mass murder only became the norm with the invasion of the Soviet Union. With that final barrier crossed, by 1942 sufficient sections of German society and the state were prepared to engage in the mass murder of Europe's Jewish population. However, even at this stage it progressed unevenly. Satellite regimes such as Mussolini's Italy and Horthy's Hungary were anti-Semitic but not prepared to engage in the mass murder of their own citizens. In these two countries mass deportation and murder only started once these regimes fell. Equally, in some occupied countries, civil society continued to function as a brake on the Nazis.

The existence of a trigger event

In each of the four instances above, there was a very identifiable (at least with hindsight) trigger event, when existing prejudice spilled over into genocide. For the Ottomans in 1915 and the Soviets in 1941, the trigger was war and invasion. Both feared that a particular ethnic group would side with their invader and carried out massacres and forced deportation to reduce the risk of this happening. In Rwanda, the immediate trigger was the very suspicious air crash that killed President Habyarimana[31] (who had been seen by the Hutu hardliners as too keen on national reconciliation). The day after his death, the massacres commenced, showing a mixture of state organisation and inter-communal violence.

For the Nazis, there were two triggers that meant they shifted from systemic persecution (and limited murder) to mass murder. One was the invasion of the USSR, where German troops organised the mass killing of the Jewish population as soon as they occupied a region. The second was the US entry into the war at the end of 1941 as, up to this stage, Hitler had been keen to keep the United States out of the war and described the Jews as 'hostages' whose lives would be at risk if the war spread.[32]

We need to bear this in mind when considering contemporary events in Myanmar. The preconditions are in place, but so far there have been neither universal killings nor total expulsion. However, as we will explore in the next chapter, there are plenty of potential trigger points, ranging from the aftermath of the 2015 elections to a major natural disaster.

International impotence

The role of the wider international community is of importance in preventing genocides. Even authoritarian, insular states have some degree of international links and a need to maintain at least some good relations. As we saw previously, the Myanmar regime is keen to ensure it can make money and buy weapons, and, despite its reservations, has developed substantial international links to assist in these goals. This potentially gives the international community considerable leverage—if it is prepared to use it.

The four instances discussed above show the importance of international partners in restraining, or providing a free hand to, a state on the verge of genocide. In the case of the Ottomans, their nominal allies in the war (Imperial Germany and the Austro-Hungarian Empire) had no interest in restraining their actions. There are some reports of German liaison officers intervening in isolated incidents,[33] but there was no official attempt to restrain the Ottoman regime. The Soviet attacks on the Turkic minorities were similarly uncontested by their American and British allies. In each incident it is unlikely that co-belligerent allies could have made any difference to the outcome, but what is clear is that in neither instance was there an attempt at restraint. The Nazi Holocaust, as argued above, was actually allowed to go ahead in its full horror precisely as the regime no longer had any conventional goals in terms of international relations. By the end of 1941 it was already embroiled in total war with most of the world, an event that could only end in complete defeat or absolute victory.

However, the Rwandan situation was one in which the international community could indeed have stepped in. It was also unusual in that it is the only one of our chosen instances that did not occur in the context of a full blown wider war. Key to allowing the violence to escalate to genocide was international silence. For different reasons, Belgium and France had links to the existing government yet were not prepared to criticise its actions. And the US was desperate to avoid being forced to intervene,[34] which would have been required if the UN Security Council designated the situation as constituting genocide. This silence was fundamental to enabling the genocide. Here, international inaction allowed the violence to escalate when states either with influence over the Hutu government (Belgium and France) or the capacity to intervene (the US) opted instead to stand aside. In planning and carrying out genocide, the Hutu regime did not have to fear an immediate international response. This has direct relevance to the situation in Myanmar as it is unlikely that any final step to genocide will be within the framework of a wider, global, conflict. Instead it will be the choice of the Myanmar regime, perhaps responding to domestic dynamics.[35]

The definition of genocide in international law

We have seen that the UN defines genocide as the 'intent to destroy, in whole or in part, a national, ethnical, racial or religious group'.[36] This is an exacting test, and the International Court of Justice (ICJ) has recently deemed the ethnic violence in Croatia in the early 1990s not to be genocide on the grounds that there was 'a lack of a systematic or general plan to destroy a group and to prevent births from occurring within that group'.[37] In effect, crimes of violence, even full blown war crimes, do not necessarily constitute genocide. But in the case of the Rohingyas these extra requirements are beginning to be met. As an example, for the Rohingyas, marriage is strictly regulated, and the number of children they can have is limited to two by law, which is below the rate needed for demographic replacement (that is, fewer than are necessary to ensure the population does not decline).

And it is hugely important that we call a genocide a 'genocide' for practical reasons as well: not just the act of genocide itself, but the fear that such an act is imminent triggers a requirement for the UN Security Council to take direct action.[38] Indeed, reports by UN officials suggest that the treatment of the Rohingyas warrants referral to the International Court.[39]

The ICJ judgement for Croatia defines genocide in terms of aiming to destroy an identified group in sufficient numbers that it no longer has a significant presence in a particular region. Thus the genocides affecting Armenians, Jews and Tutsis in the twentieth century all fit this definition about the intended scale of the killing. In addition, systematic attempts to deny a group the means to sustain itself or to prevent births are also part of genocide, and both of these tests can be applied to the Rohingyas' case. This is why it warrants referral to the International Criminal Court.

In this respect it is worth quoting at length what the UN Rapporteur has to say about the situation in Myanmar:

[T]he pattern of widespread and systematic human rights violations in Rakhine State may constitute crimes against humanity as defined under the Rome Statute of the International Criminal Court. He believes that extrajudicial killing, rape and other forms of sexual violence, arbitrary detention, torture and ill-treatment in detention, denial of due process and fair trial rights, and the forcible transfer and severe deprivation of liberty of populations has taken place on a large scale and has been directed against the Rohingya Muslim population in Rakhine State. He believes that the deprivation of health care is deliberately targeting the Rohingya population, and that the increasingly permanent segregation of that population is taking place. Furthermore, he believes that those human rights violations are connected to discriminatory and persecutory policies against the Rohingya Muslim population, which also include ongoing official and unofficial practices from both local and central authorities restricting rights to nationality, movement, marriage, family, health and privacy.[40]

Further reports by UN officials stress that they are denied access to the Rohingyas and that the community is facing systemic persecution and denial of civil and human rights.[41] The regime has shown itself to be unwilling to properly investigate ethnic attacks against the Rohingyas,[42] especially in instances where the military was involved. This in itself removes one of the barriers for the case of genocide to be heard at the International Criminal Court,[43] as the host nation can be seen as incapable of taking action within its own jurisdiction.

At the moment, the situation in Rakhine can be described as almost a textbook case of pre-genocide.[44] All that is missing is a final trigger which could come from conflict, economic crisis, natural disaster or political events. This is likely to start a massacre of those Rohingyas still living in urban areas (such as around Sittwe) and villages and then those held in the various prison camps dotted around the state.

Summary

Organising a genocide is not easy. Even people who are prejudiced against other ethnic or religious groups are often not prepared to engage in violence or to sanction mass murder. Thus regimes or other actors who would pursue such a policy need to move relatively slowly, building a consensus for their plans by drawing on existing narratives and testing the limits of acceptable behaviour. This involves both domestic opinion and the likely reaction of other governments. Even once hatred and social exclusion has become acceptable, there is a large step left to take towards genocide. For that, there is a need to fuse the capacity of the state with the indifference or active support of the population, and add silence or complicity from the international community.

In the end, every genocide (as opposed to instances of ethnic conflict) has happened due to state policy, and only when that state believes it can get away with it in the face of domestic and international opinion.

6

CURRENT SITUATION

In Myanmar the preconditions for genocide are now firmly in place. Racism has been normalised among the ethnically Burman population and the Rohingyas have already been subject to communal violence, state oppression and have been forced into both internal and external exile. Anti-Rohingya sentiment has been deliberately stoked up by a series of regimes since Burma gained independence. And most of the waves of anti-Rohingya violence have either been orchestrated by the state or have seen the officials of the state acting in close cooperation with other ethnic or religious groups.

A powerless minority is the victim of effective ethnic cleansing, in an environment where they are hated by their neighbours and actively discriminated against by state authorities. The situation is stark. Rohingya human rights activist Tun Khin has said, 'We fear we will be wiped out'. Given the importance of preparing the ground for genocide, in terms of creating a particular set of social attitudes, his conclusion should be a warning to the world: 'in the case of inhumanity and injustice, no one should be silent. What's happening to us requires a serious kind of humanity—this is a very important moment for Rohingya'.[1]

There has been no improvement since 2004 when Barbara Harff argued that Myanmar was the state in the world most at risk of genocide.[2] Indeed, with the recent waves of violence, the situation has palpably worsened. According to United to End Genocide, 'nowhere in the world are there more known precursors to genocide than in Burma today'.[3] The Early Warning Project identified Myanmar in 2015 as the state in the world most at risk,[4] above countries such as Sudan, Nigeria and the Democratic Republic of the Congo, which all receive more international attention.

The attitude of the Myanmar state towards its Rohingya minority has already crossed many of the lines from ethnic conflict towards genocide. The way the state thinks about this minority is also fundamentally racist, and more than that, the Rohingyas are now seen to be an existential threat to the chosen religious identity of the state. The events since 2012 can be seen as testing the limits of what is deemed acceptable both by Myanmar's society and the wider international community, and are comparable to the build up to genocide we have seen in the other examples discussed. As such, it seems the only thing missing is a trigger for outright genocide.

Potential triggers

The situation could escalate for any number of reasons, some even apparently unrelated. One could be an unexpected natural disaster, leaving the regime under pressure and desperate to find a scapegoat. Equally, there will be repeats of the 2015 exodus by sea of both willing refugees and those forced to flee. It is not impossible that neighbouring states could close their borders,[5] partly in an attempt to force Myanmar to face up to its responsibilities towards its own population. The situation for the Rohingyas is now so bad that anything from natural disaster to loss of food supplies to the regime lashing out at external pressure could set off a genocide.

What is clear is that the return of limited democracy since 2010 has done nothing to reduce the risks. This section starts with the dynamics around the 2015 election. In part, this allows us to explore just how marginal the position of the Rohingyas now is and thus the extent to which almost any political, environmental or economic shock could act as the trigger for genocide.

Build up to the 2015 elections

As we have seen, each electoral cycle in Myanmar since 1990 has seen a further reduction in the rights of the Rohingyas. They were able to participate in the elections between independence and military rule, with some limits, and ethnic Rohingyas were elected to parliament (and continued to serve in parliament even after the imposition of military rule in 1962). In 1990, despite the loss of many rights in the intervening period, a number of Rohingyas were still allowed to vote and stand for elections, and even won seats. Disgracefully, the

NLD and its Rakhine allies then cooperated with the military to have these victories annulled. Even in 2010, some Rohingyas had the right to vote and three were elected from Rakhine.[6] One of these, Shwe Maung, stood for the USDP. To properly understand the risks of the 2015 electoral cycle we need first to look at how the lead up was used to complete the exclusion of the Rohingyas from civic life in Myanmar, then consider the wider political dynamics in Myanmar as a whole, and then move on to consider the very specific dynamics within Rakhine. There is a risk that tensions at either national or regional level could be the final trigger; however, the complete exclusion of the Rohingyas in effect means that either the authorities reverse their recent decisions or the situation will escalate into forced deportation and/or mass murder.[7] In effect, this has created a situation in which anything can be the final trigger, since any safety nets or alternative power structures have been destroyed.

Exclusion of the Rohingyas

The lead up to the 2015 elections was marked by an escalation of the exclusion of the Rohingyas. As a group, they have been left with no place in civic Myanmar, many have been forced into internal camps, their last vestige of official documentation has been stripped away and there were, for the first time ever, almost no Muslim candidates from any ethnic group,[8] including those outside Rakhine, standing for parliament in 2015.[9]

A key step in bringing this situation about was the census conducted in 2014, when the Rohingya ethnic group was not included, and was expected to self-identify as foreigners. David Mathieson of Human Rights Watch has expressed severe concerns not just about the conduct of the census but also the complicity of the UN and other donors:

> The exclusion of the Rohingya from the census was a betrayal of the very principles and purpose of conducting the census, and the international donors and UN agencies who were involved are complicit in this exclusion. The Rohingya have the right to self-identify and should be accorded the rights of citizens. The census [in] refusing to do so doesn't solve the problem of stateless Rohingya, it exacerbates it and the government shouldn't be caving to extremists and their racist agendas.[10]

The 2014 census[11] saw the deliberate exclusion of the Rohingyas, as they were forced to choose to register either as 'Bengalis' or be excluded. Even the official version of the census report shows the reality in Rakhine. One third of the population were declared as 'not enumerated' and nowhere in the glossy state publications can the casual reader find an explanation for this remarkable outcome. The relatively small numbers excluded in Kachin and Kayin States reflects ongoing armed conflict in those areas, something that clearly is not the case in Rakhine.

6. 2014 Census Results[12]

State/Region	Total	Male	Female
Union	51,419420	24,821,176	26,598,244
Union (enumerated)	50,213,067	24,225,304	25,987,763
Union (not enumerated)	1,206,353	595,872	610,481
Kachin	*1,689,654*	*877,664*	*811,990*
Kachin (enumerated)	1,643,054	854,633	788,421
Kachin (not enumerated)	46,600	23,031	23,569
Kayah	286,738	143,461	143,277
Kayin	*1,572,657*	*775,375*	*797,282*
Kayin (enumerated)	1,502,904	739,234	763,670
Kayin (not enumerated)	69,753	36,141	33,612
Chin	478,690	230,005	248,685
Sagaing	5,320,229	2,518,155	2,802,144
Tanintharyi	1,406,434	700,403	706,031
Bago	4,863,455	2,324,214	2,539,241
Magmay	3,912,711	1,814,993	2,097,718
Mandalay	6,145,588	2,919,725	3,225,863
Mon	2,050,282	986,454	1,063,828
Rakhine	*3,188,963*	*1,529,606*	*1,659,357*
Rakhine (enumerated)	2,098,963	992,906	1,106,057
Rakhine (not enumerated)	1,090,000	536,700	553,300
Yangon	7,355,075	3,517,486	3,837,589
Shan	5,815,384	2,908,259	2,907,125
Ayeyawady	6,175,123	3,010,195	3,164,928
Nay Pyi Taw	1,158,367	565,181	593,186

The Rohingyas were removed from the electoral register whether they accepted the state-imposed designation of 'Bengali' or refused to answer.[13] Accepting the state designation as 'Bengali' was tantamount to accepting the loss of any right to live in the country of their birth. Refusing to accept this designation meant the regime confiscated any remaining identity cards and tried to force all those who now lack identification into the internal refugee camps. A recent report has noted that this has 'led many Rohingya to believe that there is little hope for their future in Myanmar'.[14] An ASEAN report[15] believes that this complete exclusion from the civic life of their own country has led many Rohingyas to conclude they are being forced out of Myanmar. Naturally, a government spokesman managed to justify this exclusion: 'They are holding household cards stating that they are Bengali even though they self-identified themselves to be Rohingya, which is not allowed, so we did not accept that and instead classified them as "unidentified"'.[16]

However, the destruction of the last vestiges of their participation in civil life has not just been a product of the census. The persecution of the Rohingyas continues to be a factor in the interaction between the USDP, the NLD and the extremist Buddhist organisations. For example, in late 2013 the USDP had supported the idea that the holders of so-called 'white cards' (that is, Rohingyas who lack normal citizenship) would be able to vote on constitutional reforms, but Buddhist nationalists immediately protested the move and the USDP was forced to back down. Thein Sein later declared that all white cards would expire in March 2015 and armed groups of security personnel carried out the removal of the last official documents from the possession of the Rohingyas. The loss of the last identity documents is critical as it means the Rohingyas are no longer entitled to travel or work outside the designated refugee camps.

In addition, Muslims in general have been removed from the electoral process by a re-interpretation of electoral law. In particular, the MaBaTha and 969 Movement have forced the regime to pass further discriminatory laws about citizenship and civil rights, for example restricting marriage between Buddhists and other religious groups.[17] Not only do the new laws add to the wider repression of the Rohingyas but, under pressure, the government has removed more than 100 possible Muslim candidates[18] from the electoral list. Among them was Shwe Maung, on the grounds that his parents were not citizens. This effectively eliminated the last Rohingya voice in parliament. Tun Min Soe, who was planning to run for the NLD, has also been rejected, a decision that provoked a mild rebuke from the NLD, with their spokesman Nyan Win stating, 'the rejection of candidates based on the citizenship of their parents is in my opinion an infringement upon the equal rights of citizens'.[19]

However, the electoral commission has cited two related laws in justification of its decisions: one barring people from running for office if their parents were not Myanmar citizens at the time of their birth; and another requiring candidates to have lived in the country for the past ten consecutive years.[20]

Of course, the NLD's protests would carry more weight if Aung San Suu Kyi could bring herself to speak out. Even in late June 2015, she was still ducking this issue, arguing that 'the protection of rights of minorities is an issue which should be addressed very, very carefully and as quickly and effectively as possible, and I'm not sure the government is doing enough about it'.[21] In some ways, that may count as progress, given her previous statements, but it treats the situation of the Rohingyas as if it were a technical academic exercise, a problem of the same type as that created by their exclusion from the designated list of ethnic groups in the 1947 Constitution. Furthermore, the electoral commission is not just removing Rohingyas from the list but any Muslim candidates regardless of their ethnicity. The 2015 elections were unique in Burma's post-colonial history. For the first time, there were no Rohingya candidates and no Rohingya members of parliament, and very few Muslims from other ethnic groups. Even under the worst of the military rule this did not happen.

The forced displacement of the Rohingyas into internal camps, and the removal of their last vestige of democratic rights[22] has led some observers to call Myanmar an 'apartheid state'.[23] In consequence, the Rohingyas are now excluded both as electors and in terms of representation[24] and they are an easy (and shared) target for all the represented political camps. The implication is clear: failure to gain any political voice to speak for their interests in the 2015 elections means that, as a Rohingya activist put it, 'the whole Rohingya will be a sort of degraded or persecuted community, and that cannot continue for long'.[25] The inevitable result is that 'the Rohingyas will disappear from Rakhine State. It is sure Rohingya will disappear'.[26]

2015 elections: wider issues

In terms of electoral politics, the NLD also faces significant challenges even after its 2015 victory. It needs to retain support among the Burman ethnic majority and this carries a price in terms of the policies it can put forward. Some observers suggest that its 'move to the right has been a pragmatic step to try to gain a majority, by promising everything to everyone and making sure to bow to popular anti-Muslim sentiment'.[27] Indeed the MaBaTha has openly backed the USDP[28] on the grounds that the NLD opposed some of the recent anti-Muslim laws (in particular the ban on inter-communal marriages). Before the 2015 election, the NLD failed to break with its old allies despite this shift of allegiance, for fear of undermining its electoral appeal. This has led to the situation identified by Mark Farmaner of the Burma Campaign UK:

I think [Aung San Suu Kyi] has seriously miscalculated her response to anti-Muslim violence in Burma, She has ended up with the worst of both worlds. On the one hand, she hasn't spoken up for an oppressed and endangered minority, on the other hand, she's still being attacked by the 969 Movement and losing support because there remains a perception that she's friendly to Muslims. Because she didn't take a firm moral stance against anti-Muslim feeling from the start, using her moral authority, she has opened the way for people like Wirathu to act with absolute impunity.[29]

There is strong evidence to suggest that Aung San Suu Kyi personally shares some of the views of the Buddhist hierarchy, which indicates that while she may be a prisoner of her allies she may not be so unhappy with the consequences. She wrote a short paper in 1985 praising the Burmese 'racial psyche' and claiming that Buddhism 'represents the perfected philosophy. It therefore follows that there [is] no need either to develop it further or to consider other philosophies'.[30] If those remain her views, then her silence over the persecution of the Rohingyas is not just a reflection of the pressures she faces, but an indication that there is at least some ambiguity in her position over the right of the Rohingyas to live in Myanmar.

This has affected the NLD's approach in two ways. In a sense it has joined in the consensus that the Rohingyas have no place in Myanmar. The NLD calculates that there is no political benefit to standing up for the Rohingyas, and it has not done so. Aung San Suu Kyi's spokesperson has even used the word 'Bengalis' to refer to Rohingyas, which indicates her public position. In addition, after the white card declaration in 2015 (which removed the final form of state identification held by the Rohingyas), the NLD, in compliance with a legal requirement, expelled about 20,000 members from the party in order to comply with the new law.[31] Many of these had joined the NLD in 2000 and held membership cards with 'Rohingya' as their ethnic identity.[32] In addition, the NLD has accepted the banning of individual candidates from the wider Muslim community.

So far the NLD has found it convenient to remain silent on the question of the Rohingyas and anti-Muslim violence. Even when it has met with civil society groups to oppose the recent ban on marriages between Burmese women and Muslim men,[33] this has been presented as an issue around women's rights rather than religious discrimination—an accurate and valid response but one that deliberately misses the reason why the laws were introduced. Other than this, the NLD seems unprepared to do much beyond vaguely condemning inter-communal violence and discrimination.

Despite this, many Rohingyas still hope that the NLD's electoral success in 2015 might change their situation for the better.[34] There is some evidence that many plan to flee if the situation in the camps does not improve (as is discussed further below). But the NLD's victory provides some hope, with some Rohingyas believing that the party might try to reduce current levels of persecution. This attitude of limited hope has been summed up by Kyaw Min (who was the leader of the mainly Rohingya Democracy and Human Rights Party before being banned from standing): 'I would not say that I am disappointed with her because she has to operate in this country with the mood here now. I am sure that things will be better for us if the NLD wins the elections'.[35] Whether or not, without external pressure, the NLD either can or wants to make changes is an issue discussed in the next chapter.

It is not just the Muslim community that the NLD abandoned in the 2015 electoral cycle. Their list of candidates included only one prominent representative of the generation who took part in the 1988 uprising.[36] In addition to the low number of female candidates, this supports a fear that the NLD is seeking to ensure its parliamentary ranks include very few who would oppose a post-election deal with the USDP.[37] This may be pragmatic: Aung San Suu Kyi is desperate to have the bar on her being president lifted, and the NLD's policies may be designed to lessen the risk of a post-election coup. However, they increase the chances that the post-election government in Myanmar will be unable to deepen the democratic process and amend those parts of the 2008 Constitution that embeds the power of the military, as they have lost some key voices who would have pressed for more radical change.

As well as the systematic discrimination that stripped the Rohingyas of their last voting rights during the run up to the 2015 elections, the complex political interaction discussed above, between the USDP, the NLD and the Buddhist extremists, has the capacity to destabilise the entire regime. As we have seen, the USDP courts the MaBaTha, and even the actions of the NLD are sometimes influenced by extremists' sectarian interpretation of what it means to be Burmese. If this does lead to even more violence in Rakhine, it is possible that the international community may be forced to take note. The USDP has continued to pass even more discriminatory legislation and Thein Sein has boasted about his role in removing the Rohingyas from civic life and in passing the new laws.[38]

The final risk is what the USDP and the military will do given their decisive electoral defeat, since every time they have contested relatively fair elections (1990, 2012, and now 2015) they have lost badly. It would appear that some factions in the USDP have been preparing for life after the election by looking for a compromise with the NLD[39] (in this respect it is worth recalling that since 2008 the USDP has been guaranteed a large block of seats regardless of votes gained).[40] An alternative, as some have suggested, is a grand alliance of Thein Sein, Shwe Mann (in effect leaders of the two factions in the USDP) and Aung San Suu Kyi. This is not so implausible, as part of such a deal could be the lifting of the legislation that currently prevents Aung San Suu Kyi from becoming president.[41]

An alternative of course is that the military decides on a coup in order to cling to power[42] and safeguard its control over the economy.[43] If so, and if it wishes to retain its current international links,[44] it will need an excuse that is more than just sour grapes at losing an election.[45] Its real motive will be to retain its economic status and this means it may only need a reason that is acceptable to those whose sole concern is their own investments in Myanmar.[46] Also, as we have seen, the military are often quite content with a degree of civil unrest, as that in turn creates a need for them to step in as 'the only real guarantors of the nation'.[47]

Therefore unrest in Rakhine may well suit their plans.[48] A renewed outbreak of violence, perhaps triggering a major refugee crisis, could easily be presented as a situation needing an urgent and unconstitutional response. In this respect it is worth noting that the 2008 Constitution is relatively unusual—it actually contains clauses that specify when it can be suspended.[49] Thus, triggering violence in Rakhine might present an ideal opportunity for the military to retain power. If numerous Rohingyas die or flee as a result, that, to the military, would be a price well worth paying.

This brings us back to the specific dynamics within Rakhine.

2015 elections: dynamics in Rakhine

As noted earlier in this book, the political dynamics in Rakhine are different from the rest of the country. In part, there is a greater degree of direct military rule, and the notional opposition to the USDP is not the NLD but regional and ethnically-based parties. The Rakhine confessional parties have regularly divided. In 1988 they were the Arakan League for Democracy (ALD) but by 2008 most members had left to form the Rakhine Nationalities Development Party (RNDP). The name was subsequently changed to the Rakhine National Party (RNP) and is currently the Arakan National Party[50] (ANP). These transitions have been complicated as at each stage some members have opted to retain the old name, reflecting different geographical and economic power bases within Rakhine. In particular, a party calling itself the RNDP contested the 2015 elections—this effectively split the ethnic Rakhine vote, significantly reducing the parliamentary representation of the Rakhine ethnic parties.

The ANP is proving to have volatile internal politics, as leaders of the previous incarnations of the party all push for power and influence.[51] Its predecessor, the RNDP, was heavily implicated in the 2012 and 2013 massacres[52] and regularly called for the expulsion of the Rohingyas (a platform the original ALD promoted during the 1990 elections). The stated platform of the ANP is to 'represent the interests of Rakhine people in Rakhine (Arakan) state and the Yangon region'.[53] In other words, it is a self-declared ethno-centric party.

At the time of the 2012 violence, the ANP demanded that 'Bengalis must be segregated and settled in separate, temporary places so that the Rakhines and Bengalis are not able to mix together in villages and towns in Rakhine state'.[54]

The ANP has produced electoral leaflets with the slogan 'Love your nationality, keep pure blood, be Rakhine and vote ANP'.[55] The elimination of the Rohingyas from the electoral roll potentially increased the number of seats the ANP could have won.[56] In effect this reduced the electoral contest in the Rakhine to a fight for the ethnic Rakhine vote between the ANP, the RNDP and the NLD. The ANP makes much both of its Buddhist heritage and of the fact that Rakhine has been left as a poor and impoverished province by the ethnic Burmese governments that have ruled since independence. The NLD is described by the ANP as being 'pro-Muslim' and sympathetic to the Rohingyas while the USDP is seen to embody years of state neglect.[57] In this sense the NLD is suffering for standing up to the Buddhists extremists over the recent laws banning inter-marriage between Muslims and Buddhists.[58] As a result, when she visited Rakhine as part of the campaign, Aung San Suu Kyi deliberately avoided the regions where the Rohingyas lived and, of course, avoided any mention of their plight.

Despite its advantages, infighting within the ANP, combined with an electoral challenge from the rump of the RNDP, seems likely to reduce its influence in the next parliament, as many Rakhine will probably opt to vote for the USDP or NLD instead.[59] Whether or not this is good news for the Rohingyas is less clear. It is quite likely that, in an attempt to shore up waning support, the party will become even more extreme, as Aye Maung seeks to achieve his goal of becoming minister of Rakhine State.[60] In advance of the 2015 elections it was hard to know whether him succeeding in this aim (and thus having no constraint on his actions by the state administration) or failing (and perhaps seeking to create support by agitating for further violence and forced deportations) would have been the worse outcome for the Rohingyas. In the event, he lost his seat in parliament, making the future stability of Rakhine even less certain. One possibility is that, having been defeated electorally, the extremists will seek to bolster their support by further attacks on the Rohingyas.

Alternatively, this defeat may indicate that many Rakhine have turned their backs on the extremists. At the moment, the chief minister of Rakhine State, Maung Maung Ohn, is not an ethnic Rakhine (something that has annoyed the extremists) and has played a small but important role in controlling the Rakhine extremists.[61] Again, this points to the complexities of the situation, but also to just how much the current persecution of the Rohingyas is a political construct. They are still, as they have been since the late 1960s, a target of convenience.

This is reflected in how the NLD presents the violence in Rakhine. Sometimes it argues that it is an unfortunate side effect of the move to democracy, in which long-suppressed tensions can come to the surface. In other instances they are willing to declare, 'The Rohingyas are not our citizens'.[62] Equally, while the NLD has a long history of collaboration with the ALD/RNDP/ANP within Rakhine, in 2015 it found itself in electoral competition with them as it sought to maximise its vote outside Burman ethnic areas. Perhaps to its frustration, it found that its old allies in the RNDP/ANP were now seeking to portray the NLD as pro-Muslim simply because it stood up to some of the worst of the recent legislation (and that on the basis of women's rights, not discrimination against non-Buddhist communities). Equally, as noted earlier, the NLD has lost the backing of the MaBaTha over this stance.

Other risks

Even if the 2015 electoral cycle passes without significant violence against the Rohingyas, the simple reality is they have been pushed to the margins of life in Myanmar. The last vestiges of civic engagement have been stripped away in the course of the 2015 election campaign at a national level, and powerful regional politicians vie with each other as to who can produce the most extreme statements.

The most likely risk after the electoral cycle is complete is of a renewed refugee crisis,[63] but there are other potential triggers for further violence. One is the possibility of acts of terrorism and another is the impact of a new major natural or health-based disaster.

A new refugee crisis

At the moment, it is clear that only two things are preventing a renewal of the outpouring of refugees from earlier in 2015. Some Rohingyas are still hoping for positive changes in the aftermath of the elections, but for many it is a case of waiting until the seas are calm enough to cross.[64] In October 2014, it was estimated that some 13,000 Rohingyas fled by way of the sea, and there is every reason to believe that this time the number will be much higher. Many are now determined to join relatives who fled in earlier periods, but for others the calculation is simple. The risk of death or enslavement at sea is now no worse than the prospects of staying in Myanmar.[65] Quite simply, there are plenty of Rohingyas who share the view that 'I will take a risky boat journey again as I consider that dying in a boat journey is better than staying in miserable conditions in the camps with no access to health care and employment opportunities'.[66]

Since many Rohingyas are now effectively confined to the camps, they can no longer even travel to make arrangements with the people-smuggling gangs. However, this has been resolved by the simple expedient of the smugglers setting up 'offices' in the refugee camps. A report for Human Rights Watch, which documents the appalling levels of poverty and lack of services in the camps, noted:

> In the midst of these appalling conditions, we encountered—rather incongruously—a tent filled with high tech phone and video equipment. A young mother was sitting inside and calling a relative in Malaysia, asking him to send money so that she could care for her sick mother. He had apparently left by boat some years previously. We asked about these boats leaving Burma, and whether others in the camp were keen to go too. Some nodded. But others, seemingly in charge of the tent, were evasive and hostile, and we judged that we should not stay long. We later heard from UN officials that people smugglers are very active in the camps.[77]

Effectively, it makes no difference if the next major refugee crisis is triggered by post-election violence, deliberate expulsion organised either by the military or the Rakhine extremists, or as the final response of people driven beyond despair by the denial of every reasonable expectation of a citizen of a state. It will happen unless the persecution of the Rohingyas is stopped.[68] As even some in the NLD have noticed, the series of steps taken in the run up to the elections—including the removal of the white cards, the deeply flawed census and the discriminatory election laws—leave the Rohingyas with no place in their own country.[69] This is a defining indictment of the claims that Myanmar is making a transition to being a normal democratic country, and indicates both the government's contempt for its obligations under international law and the failure of the international community in promoting serious reform.

When the next refugee crisis occurs, the regional ASEAN states will bear its brunt.[70] The traditional movement of refugees in May and June 2015 only came to international attention because Indonesia and Malaysia closed their borders. Historically ASEAN, as with many regional collections of post-colonial states, has stressed the importance of non-interference in the internal affairs of its member states. But this time there is growing awareness that a problem that has the capacity to destabilise the region is the deliberate result of Myanmar's domestic policies. In early 2015 ASEAN parliamentarians have concluded that there is 'a high risk of genocide, war crimes, and crimes against humanity' in Rakhine, and later added that 'The situation ... has only deteriorated since. Disenfranchisement, combined with economic depression, lack of access to livelihoods, and dire humanitarian conditions, will drive increasing numbers of Rohingya to flee the country'.[71]

It is now quite clear that there will be further refugee crises unless Myanmar reduces the persecution of the Rohingyas. Such crises will be marked by significant payments to people smugglers, violence, death and slave labour (or at best unprotected labour) in the wider region. Neighbouring states can mitigate the worst of this by abiding by the UN conventions on protection of refugees, but the blame lies squarely with the policies of the Myanmar government. But meeting obligations under the UN conventions is not just a matter for the ASEAN nations. Australia persists in refusing to accept any refugees from Myanmar[72] either directly or as part of a wider programme of resettlement.

Terrorism

A regular motif in the extremist Buddhist narrative is the alleged close links between the Rohingyas and states such as Saudi Arabia, or armed jihadist groups such as Al-Qaeda or ISIS.[73] So far, there is no evidence that such links, if they exist, have led to jihadist violence within Myanmar. A local Rohingya group, the Unity for Peace Network, has taken the step of issuing a strict interpretation of what is meant by jihad, the role of mosques and certain Koranic verses.[74] This might be seen as a deliberate attempt to remove the justifications often used by violent jihadist movements that their acts are justified by the Koran and Hadith.

However, the plight of the Rohingyas is now desperate and there has to be a serious question as to how much longer the Rohingyas will wait for intervention on their behalf before they decide that any intervention on their behalf will do—even one from Al-Qaeda or ISIS. So far, any such interventions, even if they are truly linked to Islamist extremism, have been very rare. But the potential for further violence and the intrusion of forces with no interest in compromise is very real, and this is starting to worry some neighbouring states who have substantial numbers of Rohingya refugees.[75]

This of course relates to the regular outflow of refugees from Myanmar, as many Rohingyas who have escaped live in appalling conditions in their new countries.[76] This creates a further set of risks. Left to make a living as best they can, some Rohingyas have become involved in running illegal businesses and criminal networks.[77] For those who have fled to India, they are also vulnerable to being targeted by a number of Islamist terrorist groups seeking to exploit any Muslim grievance, including Lashkar-e-Taiba (LeT), Jama'atul Mujahideen Bangladesh (JMB), and the Harkat-ul-Jihad al-Islami (HuJI). It should be noted that some of these groups quite deliberately offer humanitarian aid in circumstances where state or international bodies have failed, thus building up a client network.

Any Rohingyas who are radicalised by these groups pose a risk to their host country, which further undermines the limited status of Rohingyas who have fled as refugees. In addition, even though there is no evidence this has happened, there is a risk they might return to Myanmar. Given widespread suspicion of the Rohingyas, and widespread belief that they are funded by Saudi-backed extremists, any sustained terrorist campaign would inevitably set off a new round of inter-communal violence. Unlike in 2012, this time the Rohingyas are mostly isolated from the rest of society and are already held in camps. The likelihood of mass murder is all too obvious.

A natural disaster

Other possible triggers include a national crisis with its roots in an environmental or health problem.[78] Such a crisis is perfectly possible, especially given the pressures that climate change has already put on the region. We have seen how Cyclone Nargis may have played a part in encouraging the military regime to allow a return to limited democracy in 2008. A similarly destructive cyclone could badly undermine Myanmar's economy and leave the regime looking for scapegoats to divert popular anger.

The impact of Cyclone Komen in the summer of 2015 points to the risks.[79] This was a major storm but not particularly unusual in either its strength or its storm track (unlike Cyclone Nargis, which fortunately appears to have been a once-in-a-generation storm). Komen led to widespread flooding and around fifty deaths across Myanmar. However, given the poor construction of the refugee camps, the Rohingyas were particularly affected both in terms of loss of life and destruction of their few remaining items of property. The practical issue is that each storm threatens to further destabilise the situation, and each time the Rohingyas suffer due to being held in poorly built refugee camps.

7

WHAT CAN BE DONE?

The previous chapter argued that the build up to the 2015 elections excluded the Rohingyas from any vestige of civic or political life in Myanmar, leaving them without any official documents and increasingly held in what are becoming permanent refugee camps. Unless something happens to reverse this trend, it is highly likely that the mass refugee flows of previous years will be repeated whenever the weather systems allow safe passage on the Andaman Sea.

As we saw in Chapter 5, peace-time genocides are exceptionally rare. Rwanda is the most recent and, crucially, in that case the outside world ignored all the warnings and only reacted after the events. This forces a practical question: just what can the outside world do to prevent genocide in Myanmar?

The ideal response is clear. Stand up to the regime; demand they abide by the UN Charter on citizenship and nationality; insist that those directly implicated in the 2012 and 2013 violence in Rakhine face charges of preparing for and inciting genocide at the International Criminal Court. Rohingyas living in the camps have indicated far more modest demands: citizenship; the right to return to their homes; and freedom of movement.[1]

Few observers are so confident as to identify a single simple solution to a problem that has been allowed to escalate over more than forty years. Some have proposed steps that a given organisation might be able to undertake. So ASEAN parliamentarians have proposed that the issue of Myanmar's persecution of the Rohingyas be a permanent item on the agenda of future meetings,[2] not least since the refugee crises now present a problem for all states in the region. Linked to this, they suggest offering practical help to build better community relations in Rakhine and to ensure that all ASEAN members abide by their international duties towards refugees.

One solution that has some support among those concerned for the fate of the Rohingyas is the de facto partition of Rakhine, with the northern region created as a semi-autonomous region with its own governance.[3] To assist in this, and to make it easier for the Myanmar authorities to agree, there would be a need to offer substantive economic aid. This might also enable Myanmar to return to the essentially federal structure envisaged by General Aung San in the period immediately after independence.[4]

In effect, arguments for a degree of internal partition are based on the logic that it is more feasible to target the Rakhine local politicians than to directly challenge the Myanmar regime. As we have seen, the charge of inciting genocide is probably much easier to apply to them than to the state authorities.[5] If such individuals were to be charged and threatened with financial embargos and travel bans, this might have two desirable outcomes. First, those who may have been involved in the 2012 violence[6] would face justice. Second, it might help both the NLD and the USDP if the extremist leadership of the ANP was to be directly charged by the international community. Removing such individuals might help create the basis for a gradual return to some normality in Rakhine.

A further strand of action proposed by a number of observers[7] is to improve the level of external monitoring in Rakhine. Not only might it help reduce violence if the current culture of impunity was broken, but the ability to counteract rumours has been found to be critical in other situations with substantial ethnic tension. As we have seen in earlier chapters, many of the more violent episodes have followed on from rumours being spread and believed. The effective separation of the Rohingyas from the wider community makes this more likely. After all, if you never encounter a Rohingya in the course of your normal life it is easier to believe they are rich, funded by the Saudis, buying Buddhist women as wives and, of course, stock-piling arms.[8] In this context, the ability of external voices to challenge rumours may just be the key step that prevents an outbreak of localised violence becoming a more generalised massacre.

This argument broadly suggests the outline of a possible solution. In effect: target the Rakhine extremists and ignore the complicity of the regime in, and the silence of the NLD over, the persecution of the Rohingyas. Use the removal of some of those stoking the violence to pursue practical steps such as the gradual return of the Rohingyas to their original villages. If aid is delivered to Rakhine to offset the under-development that has harmed both communities, relative prosperity may also help to reduce the risk of inter-communal violence. In effect, it is an argument for pragmatism over fundamental rights, but the current situation is so dangerous that something needs to be done to reduce the level of persecution. However, even pragmatism must have its limits and a key measure is the acceptance that the Rohingyas, like everyone else in the world, are entitled to citizenship in the country of their birth.[9]

Broadly, this line of thought identifies three key actors who can help to bring about these changes. One is the international community, the second is the International Criminal Court and the third is Myanmar's fractured civic society. The rest of this chapter discusses how each can contribute to helping find a solution. It is easy to be pessimistic, and many observers are,[10] but the world has to take note and needs to use what pressure it can to force the regime to accept that all its citizens are entitled to fundamental human rights.

The importance of external pressure

This book has challenged the myth that the Myanmar regime is isolated and cannot be influenced by external pressure. It is clear the generals would prefer for their international partners to refrain from critical comment and are acutely suspicious of anything that looks like direct foreign intervention; but that is not the same as saying they are immune to pressure. A regular theme, as we have noted, is that they have often had links with multiple regimes which have slightly conflicting interests in Myanmar. Their ability to balance their competing external suitors has proved useful in allowing them to trade, earn money and buy weapons with a minimum of interference.

In the period when Burma was notionally a socialist state, the regime was adept at avoiding close links with either the Soviet Union or China while at the same time building its relations with North Korea and remaining an active member of the Non-Aligned Movement. Since the return to partial democracy it appears as if it is trying to balance the US, China, India and its ASEAN partners[11] while still keeping its North Korean links intact. However, its ability to effectively threaten any one of its partners with favouring the others does not amount to completely ignoring international influence.

We have some evidence that it set up the inquiry into the violence in Rakhine in order to ensure that President Obama's visit went ahead. A recent US State Department report on ethnic Rakhine involvement in organising the exodus of Rohingya refugees has led to the arrest and trial of a few low-level smugglers.[12] Equally, although the regime attempted to defy its ASEAN partners over the May–June 2015 refugee crisis, in the end it took steps to meet their demands.[13]

Thus there is scope for international leverage on Myanmar. The state needs foreign investment and even though its first instinct will often be to reject any such pressure as foreign intervention in domestic affairs, it will eventually respond to it. International opinion is critical,[14] should we be willing, but it is important to choose the right issues. Each of the genocides considered in Chapter 5 happened when either the few states with leverage simply did not care (Turkey in 1915, the USSR in 1941–3), the state had become so isolated that such pressure no longer had any effect (Nazi Germany after 1942), or the wider international community did not want to face up to its responsibilities (Rwanda). We must not repeat the mistakes of the past.

My suggestion is that the wider world needs to focus on two key issues. The first is to ensure that the Rohingyas regain proper citizenship. This simple step is going to be fundamental to proving to the world that the Myanmar regime is no longer complicit in planning genocide.[15] Secondly, external powers must stop treating the persecution of the Rohingyas as a secondary concern. Unless Myanmar's rulers change policy, there is a serious risk of destabilising the entire region as well as of outright genocide. As has been repeated throughout this book, the potential influence of external powers is critical in defusing the current situation. It is, in the short-term, unlikely that any foreign state or international body will force Myanmar to grant citizenship to the Rohingyas, but pressure must be maintained.

An interview with a senior Rohingya politician (barred from standing in the 2015 elections) speaking under conditions of anonymity, indicated that some in Myanmar are clear as to both importance of international pressure and its limits:

> It's very crystal clear Myanmar government is harassing, and it's very clear international community is giving pressure consistently … And it's very clear, as well, Myanmar government is not caring. And finally, it's very crystal clear that Rohingyas are suffering more and more, more and more each day. Finally, Myanmar government created such an environment, so that Rohingya will not enjoy—Rohingya could not stay over there, because their social, economic life was damaged. They are not allowed to move freely.
>
> …
>
> US government should give a warning to them. This diplomatic warning; it's not like war. They say, 'You have to do these things—enough is enough—within a time frame.' Very simple. We are not demanding anything. We are just demanding—

what we need is not new thing, just to restore our previous rights. We just simply want to enjoy normal rights. And ethnic name is totally blocked for us. It's nothing concerned with the government. That's it. We want to be part of the union, we want to be the good citizen, and we want to have our better socioeconomic life, with simple living, with—starting with our own land. If Myanmar government deny, please make sanction, start with economic sanction again, which was lifted before by blah, blah, blah, because of this Aung San Suu Kyi.[16]

In this respect, it is clear that some Rohingyas believe that Western indulgence of Aung San Suu Kyi is feeding into the regime's overall belief that it will face no real pressure, and is thus steadily preparing the ground for the day when an attempt at mass expulsion of the Rohingyas may occur. Those who support the Rohingyas believe that in 1978 and 1994 there was a reduction in the level of persecution due to the economic weakness of the regime and some external pressure, specifically from the Organisation of Islamic Cooperation (OIC). This grouping has continued to support the Rohingyas and to call on the international community to meet its responsibilities.[17] But the regime now feels much stronger, with potentially tragic consequences: 'if the international community keeps supporting Myanmar country, if they become a bit stronger, my gosh, they will kill us like in Rwanda'.[18]

Past pressure from the OIC and other bodies is credited with forcing Myanmar to accept a partial return of refugees in 1978 and 1994 from Bangladesh and Malaysia. We have seen that pressure from the US and ASEAN has led Myanmar to take limited conciliatory steps. The evidence is that to the extent to which it has been attempted, international pressure has worked to alleviate conditions for the Rohingyas. This surely is a strong argument in favour of stepping up this pressure.

There are four main external players in Myanmar: the UN, the US, China and the ASEAN group. Each offers something different.

The UN has been warned repeatedly as to how bad the situation is[19] and indeed it has continued to publish highly critical reports.[20] But, as ever, its impact is limited, in part by the enduring politics of the Security Council (in this case it is most likely that China and Russia would back the Myanmar military), and also by the fact that it has multiple roles in Myanmar. Some observers were afraid that the UN's criticism of the conduct of the census was muted due to fear that its other humanitarian efforts would be evicted from Rakhine[21]—as happened to MSF recently.[22] However, consistent pressure matters and while criticism annoys the Myanmar authorities[23] it is clear that they do take some steps to avoid overt criticism.

The US, and to a much lesser extent the EU, are important influences. Both have been generally tolerant of the regime[24] (especially the EU), and both seem to hope that in some way the military are allies of the move towards democracy,[25] which they seem to think will alleviate the situation of the Rohingyas. So far, the Western powers have sometimes scolded,[26] sometimes chided[27] Myanmar but the pressure is inconsistent. Both the US and their allies have found it easier to talk about relaxing sanctions so as to reward progress[28]—to the extent that the only sanctions the EU retains are related to direct arms sales—rather than consider just what progress has actually occurred. But simply ignoring the plight of the Rohingyas and emphasising trade links is a deeply flawed approach. If, or perhaps more accurately when, Rakhine descends into extreme violence, many firms that have invested substantively will be deeply embarrassed and may well lose their new assets.[29] Economic progress is not an alternative to human rights; it fundamentally depends on the acceptance of human rights.

China is often presented as being indifferent to the governance of the states where it invests and where it has, in its terms, strategic interests. It seems that it prefers authoritarian partners[30] and that it can be ruthless in its pursuit of its self-interests.[31] But it is also a pragmatic regime. It has recently started a dialogue with the NLD,[32] presumably in the expectation that the latter will take a role in the government after the 2015 elections. It is unlikely that China would pressure Myanmar over the wider issue of democratic reforms, but it might be less tolerant if unrest in Rakhine threatened its vital infrastructure projects.

Finally, ASEAN has reversed its usual posture of non-interference. The refugee crises provoked by persecution in Rakhine have become serious problems, especially for Malaysia and Indonesia. Senior members of ASEAN are effectively now calling for permanent external monitors to be based in Rakhine in order to minimise the level of violence and exclusion suffered by the Rohingyas.

In addition to those states with influence, a number of important individuals have called for action, including the Pope,[33] the Dalai Lama[34] and Ban Ki moon.[35] Words are of course cheap, and action much harder, but no one can claim the world has not been warned about the realities of modern day Myanmar. And the regime is very aware of the negative impact of external comment, and worried enough to want to find ways to stem the flow of information.[36] Indeed, large sections of the recommendations from the official report on the 2012 massacres in Rakhine are focused on the need for better news management to reduce the amount of international criticism.[37]

Reference to the International Criminal Court

A related issue is the need to deal with what has happened so far. Many observers argue that what has been done in Rakhine since 2012 already constitutes genocide.[38] There have been several failed attempts to bring a case at the International Criminal Court (ICC) at The Hague.[39] At the moment, there is no means of justice, or even access to the justice system, for the Rohingyas in Myanmar. The ICC is the court of last resort for the prosecution of crimes against humanity[40] and its jurisdiction includes both the crime of genocide and more general 'crimes against humanity'.[41] Although Myanmar is not a signatory to the 2002 Rome Statute,[42] which means it cannot (even if it wished) refer itself (this usually happens when a new regime is dealing with past abuses), and though the ICC is unlikely to receive a referral from the UN Security Council acting under Chapter VII of the Charter of the United Nations, it can still commence its own investigation if it is made aware of a possible case.[43]

The importance of using the ICC cannot be over-emphasised. So far, known powerful individuals have been responsible for the steady build up of hatred against the Rohingyas and the increasing incarceration of an entire ethnic group inside what are effectively prison camps. The threat of legal action, not on the basis of future actions, but in terms of what has already been done, would be a powerful statement that these individuals are not immune from being held accountable for their actions. In this respect, it is essential that the ICC calls for the prosecution of named Rakhine leaders.

Domestic pressure

Finally, groups and individuals are active in Myanmar who reject the logic and claims of the extremists. While the regime fears a US-inspired 'colour revolution',[44] acknowledging the existence of these dissenting groups is important. Sometimes such challenges will happen over a specific issue for reasons not immediately connected with the Rohingyas. For example, the opposition of many Buddhist women's groups to the recent marriage bill was framed in terms of women's rights and freedom, rather than particularly in terms of the clear attempt to break some of the few remaining links between Myanmar's Muslim minorities and the rest of the population. In consequence, these activist groups forced Aung San Suu Kyi to oppose the legislation limiting the rights of Buddhists and Muslims to marry—on the grounds that this was a direct attack on women's rights.[45] This in turn has led to the Buddhist and Rakhine extremists claiming that the NLD is now a pro-Muslim party.

While it is clear that both the USDP and the NLD have links to the Buddhist extremists, there is evidence that the regime, the USDP and the NLD sometimes feel they are being pushed too far by the MaBaTha, the 969 Movement and the Rakhine ethnic extremists. Sometimes this is due to a fear of provoking an international response, but at other times it is connected with simple human decency. During the worst of this spring's refugee crisis, Nyam Min, an NLD spokesman, published a bold and strongly-worded statement: 'If they are not accepted (as citizens), they cannot just be sent onto rivers. Can't be pushed out to sea. They are humans. I just see them as humans who are entitled to human rights'.[46] Given the studied ambiguity, if not actual indifference, of most NLD comments about the Rohingyas, this is remarkable. Subsequent events, in terms of voter registration and candidate selection for the elections,[47] suggest this is not indicative of a fundamental shift. However, at least some in senior positions in the NLD have worked out that the only possible end point to the complete separation of the Rohingyas from civil society is mass murder or forced removal. If the party cannot support this then it may have to accept that the current level of persecution needs to be eased. Again, international pressure may be important in this regard.

The more those who do not share the extremists' ideology are forced to think about its inevitable consequences, the more likely it is they will have to stop being complicit. This is important, because as we have discussed earlier, there is an authoritarian and discriminatory element to Theravada Buddhism. This is not unique to that belief system, and is a significant problem for many of the world's contemporary religions. However, other faiths are having to find ways to challenge their own extremists, and it is important this also takes place within Myanmar.

Conclusions

Despite the grim situation there is much that can be done, both domestically and internationally, to help the Rohingyas and hopefully avoid a genocide—but a real will to take action is needed, rather than the continuation of 'business as usual' in the hope that nothing actually happens in Rakhine to make us complicit through inaction in a repeat of the genocide in Rwanda. Practically, this involves creating a minimum set of demands and seeking to hold the Myanmar authorities to them. Some international bodies, such as ASEAN, are already creating pressure, as they are suffering directly from the consequences of the persecution of the Rohingyas. It is not enough for foreign powers to hide behind the ready belief that nothing they can say or do will influence the regime. In this, the lesson from Rwanda is clear: international silence will be interpreted as international disinterest—removing one of the few barriers now standing between the Rohingyas and genocide.

CONCLUSION

This book has argued that Myanmar stands on the edge of genocide and that the persecution of the Rohingyas has been quite deliberately constructed by the state since the early 1960s. The return to relative democracy has seen the Rohingyas' situation deteriorate rather than improve, and again this reflects the deliberate policy of the Myanmar elite.[1] In order to understand why this has happened it is useful to summarise some of the key arguments advanced in the previous chapters.

First, the NLD and the USDP/military share, at an elite level, the same background. Their differences can be traced back to the debates before and after independence about whether, and to what extent, the new country should be inclusive of all who lived there or should only be for ethnic Burmans, or, slightly more generously, for those who accepted Buddhism. Senior leaders of the NLD share the background of their notional opponents. Aung San Suu Kyi's father was one of the leaders of the independence movement and her mother was a minister in the post-independence civilian governments. The NLD's vice-chairman was in charge of the army until he was sacked after leading a failed coup. Others have similar personal backgrounds.

Second, the NLD claims to sit in the Burmese (and indeed Indian) political tradition of being both a mass movement and an elite organisation. In the period before independence this saw nationalists in both Burma and India try to fuse together a combination of an educated elite, armed revolt and mass street protests. After 1988 the elite in the NLD effectively joined up with the students and the Buddhist monks who were leading protests. However, they made little direct connection with the peasantry or the small Burmese working class and gained almost no support among Burma's many ethnic minorities.

The USDP is clearly an artificial political force designed to give the generals an electoral vehicle. It has real power due to its control over the army and the country's main economic resources, but it lacks popular appeal. Every time the generals have allowed a relatively open election, they have gained very few votes. A practical problem is that they too are reliant on the Buddhist hierarchy if they wish to shore up their economic and military power with some degree of popular appeal. Equally, as with the NLD, they have little or no popular support outside the Burman ethnic group. However, it is now clear that they are using the extremists in the MaBaTha in an attempt to channel popular support away from the NLD and towards the USDP.

Third, the two main parties have effectively become Burman ethnic parties. In most ethnically-dominated areas of Myanmar local groups have their own electoral vehicles, whatever level of discrimination they face. In Rakhine, the ethnically Rakhine, who are also all Buddhist, have followed this pattern and this creates a basis of support for the RNDP/ANP. One threat to the RNDP's electoral dominance there has come from the splits within the Rakhine political elite over the share of the spoils.[2] There is one ethnic group in Myanmar not only lacking its own political party but, due to all the changes put in place for the 2015 elections, now completely denied both the vote and the possibility of members of its community being elected as part of the other political parties.[3] For the first time since independence, the parliament in Myanmar has no Muslim members, from any ethnic group.

Practical politics in Rakhine has been reduced to the dispute between the RNDP and ANP, with the NLD[4] and the USDP seeking to gain their own electoral base in the province. In fighting for the votes of the Buddhist Rakhine community, none of these parties will gain if they publicly moderate their views about the Rohingyas.[5] The result is that none will do so: having rigged the electoral system to exclude the Rohingyas, all the parties can compete about is being most likely to be the most brutal.

Fourth, this leads on to a consideration of the nature of Buddhism in Myanmar. Since the 1990s, the monks, monasteries and religious schools have become increasingly important in the lives of many Burmese. They provide a social security network and offer education for those unable to afford formal schooling. This, combined with their role in the 1988 and 2007 uprisings, has given the monks a great deal of moral authority. It also meant that as a political force they were able to act as the link between the NLD, with its elite and student base, and the mass of Burmese people.

One major problem in Western responses to Buddhism is to see it as an essentially benign religion and as a uniform confessional group. Thus, to many, Buddhism is the Dalai Lama speaking out about oppression and for peace, and representing Tibet against Chinese domination. Equally, it has connotations of yoga, meditation and the modern psychological technique of 'mindfulness'. All these images are valid but they are not the complete story.

Theravada Buddhism had split from Indian–Tibetan Mahayana Buddhism by the fifth century AD and took root in three states—today's Sri Lanka, Myanmar and Thailand. Buddhism places emphasis on religion's role in the wider polity, besides individual devotion. The state should support Buddhist institutions and the Buddhist hierarchy and seek to drive out or minimise non-Buddhist influences. It was partly this mindset that led the Burmese kings to conquer Arakan in the 1780s.

In effect, the Theravada tradition has potentially a very exclusive model of the acceptable social structure. At the least, any non-Buddhists are accorded less value, and quite often this can lead to ethnic tensions (where ethnicity and religion overlap). It is no accident that Buddhism is closely associated with violent inter-ethnic tensions in Sri Lanka and Thailand as well as in Myanmar. This creates several major problems for resolving the situation in Myanmar. First, several prominent Buddhist groups are actively driving the anti-Muslim violence, and second, if for slightly different reasons, both the NLD and the USDP are dependent on the approval of the Buddhist hierarchies. Within Rakhine the situation is made more extreme by the disenfranchisement of the Rohingyas and the extent to which both the NLD and the USDP are competing with ethnic and Buddhist confessional parties for the votes of the Rakhine.

Add on over forty years of telling the majority of people who live in Myanmar that the Rohingyas are really citizens of another country and have no place in Myanmar, and this leads to a significant problem. In effect, as some in the NLD have finally acknowledged,[6] the situation is now so bad that the only outcomes are to ease the level of persecution or for it to slip into outright genocide.

This presents a worrying picture. There are few internal factors that will enable Myanmar to step back from the now complete exclusion of the Rohingyas from civil life. If genocide is to be averted, this exclusion must be reversed, and for this to happen there has to be systemic international pressure on the regime.

EPILOGUE
November 2017

On 19 September 2017 Nobel Peace Prize laureate and democratically elected leader of Myanmar, Aung San Suu Kyi finally bowed to pressure from the international community and addressed perhaps the biggest political development in her country's post-independence history. At the time of writing, the Myanmar military's crackdown on the Rohingya Muslim ethnic group has displaced some 580,000 people, or well over a third of the entire Rohingya population, and driven them across the border into Bangladesh.

Ms Suu Kyi's speech was not what the international community would have expected from a Nobel Peace Prize winner. Her first stated priority was to 'find out why this is happening'. This was odd because in late 2016 she commissioned an enquiry into the Rohingya 'problem' after decades of their being persecuted. This enquiry was led by the globally respected diplomat Kofi Annan, the former UN Secretary-General, and had already produced a full analysis and a list of recommendations a month prior to Ms Suu Kyi's speech.

Then Ms Suu Kyi bemoaned the fact that this violence was ongoing 'despite all [her government's] efforts'. Another odd thing to say, given that her government had taken no measures to alleviate the Rohingya situation in Rakhine state since the earlier violence in 2016. Moreover it should be reiterated that the current violence is being carried out by Myanmar's army.

Next, she claimed that there had been 'no clearing operations since 5 September' by the army in Rakhine state, even as Western journalists based in Bangladesh reported seeing fresh fires in villages across the border in Myanmar. To assure her audience that there had not been sustained violence against the Rohingyas, she argued that more than 50 per cent of Muslim villages remained intact.

The first edition of this book was completed during the run up to the 2015 elections in Myanmar and its immediate aftermath. These elections were the first free polls in the country in decades and were widely seen as fair. They were won by Aung San Suu Kyi's National League for Democracy (NLD) by a landslide. This despite the fact that a number of seats in the Parliament were reserved for the Union Solidarity and Development Party (USDP), the party created by the erstwhile military junta in 2009 to represent their interests in the new civilian system of government.

The Rohingyas have been the enemy within of choice for the succession of dictatorships which have ruled Myanmar since 1962. Arbitrary state violence had been a way of life for them for decades. But the new political dispensation after the 2015 elections allowed the Rohingyas to hope that there might be better times ahead for them. Those hopes and dreams were shared by all the international observers with an interest in the humanitarian record of Myanmar. It was hoped that these elections would change everything.

Yet, even then, most informed observers remained sceptical that the situation would indeed change for the better. For example, one of the things that was airbrushed out of Ms Suu Kyi's international profile, and from the reporting of her pro-democracy movement and party, was that just before the 2015 elections the NLD had removed all Muslims from its candidate lists.

There could have been two explanations for this. One was that the party regarded it as a tactical necessity. The political complexities of Myanmar's slow transition to democracy required even a progressive party to tow the line on most of the issues the military still cared about. Buddhism is one of those those. Until the NLD was actually in power and had had the time to consolidate its position and that of the civilian government against any return to military rule, it would simply have to go along with certain things. Democratic representation of Muslims in parliament and the government would have to wait.

The Rohingyas seem to have pinned their hopes on this possibility. The annual refugee numbers flowing out of Myanmar slowed markedly from the end of 2015 and in the first half of 2016, as the new NLD government took over the reins of power.

The other possibility was that the NLD, and Ms Suu Kyi herself, were just as hostile to the Rohingyas as the former military governments. Hints of this attitude were already abundant. Since its formation in the late 1980s, the NLD had always echoed the conventional sectarian narrative about the Rohingyas: that they are 'Bengalis' who had no innate right to live in

Myanmar. The NLD casually parroted the ultra-nationalist line that the Rohingyas were illegitimately transplanted from British India during the colonial period after 1824.

'Burmese identity' is a fraught concept. The borders the state inherited from the British bore little relationship to the distribution of the various ethnic groups in the region, or to history. At best, the history of the region gives us a Burmese cultural core along the Irrawaddy River and its main tributaries. But the territory the country found itself with in 1948 extended well beyond that cultural core and included groups who straddled the borders with China or Thailand, and could identify more readily with those foreign powers, or indeed, who might want their own independent states. In 1948, the newly independent federal state of Burma represented no nation at all. But it was politically dominated by the Burmese ethnic nation.

Out of that difficult and complex cultural reality the Army had tried to build a coherent nation to correspond to the state ever since they first took power in 1962. The pillars of that new national identity had to be those traits that are common to all the residents in the country: adherence to Buddhism, and being light-skinned Indo-Chinese. Both of those traits apply to roughly 90 per cent of the population. The Rohingyas uniquely fall foul of both of those.

The question then is what are the positions of the NLD and Ms Suu Kyi herself on this approach to national identity in Myanmar? One of my arguments in this book is that the NLD's leadership, and especially Aung San Suu Kyi, have always believed that the Rohingyas are an 'alien' population with no natural place in their Buddhist state, primarily because they are a Muslim community.

Even if Ms Suu Kyi and her government are still Buddhist nationalists, we could have reasonably expected them to be less hardline than the old military establishment. And in any case, they should be less inclined to violence. After all, one of the most remarkable aspects of Ms Suu Kyi's career as a democracy advocate was that her movement was successful precisely because it was a peaceful movement. The peaceful character of her movement is precisely what won her the Nobel Prize.

The Rohingyas had every reason to hope that active persecution by the state would ease, and perhaps even that constraints would be placed on the Buddhist Rakhine extremists who perpetrated the recent 2012 and 2013 massacres against them.

Some actions by the NLD in 2015 and 2016 justified such hopes. The NLD had been allied with the Rakhine nationalist party associated with the

2012 and 2013 massacres, but the latter broke the alliance with the NLD on the grounds that the NLD was too tolerant of Muslims. For example, one consequence of this falling out was that the NLD only won 8 out of the 35 constituencies in Rakhine state in 2015. What is more, after the election, the NLD government moved to limit the influence of the sectarian, ultra-nationalist Buddhist monks allied with the Rakhine nationalists in particular over Myanmar's education system.

But these actions were not, in fact, signals that the NLD was taking the side of the oppressed Muslim minority over the ultra-nationalists. Rather, the motivation for the change in education policy in particular was more about the problems raised by the old legislation on women's rights in Myanmar. Even so, the fact that the NLD made a progressive move that went beyond what they had promised during the election campaign did feed into the emerging hope that in government the NLD might move the country in the right direction on all fronts.

It is no longer necessary to second-guess Ms Suu Kyi's and her government's motives and predilections. The faith the international community and the Rohingyas wanted to place in them can no longer be sustained. Hope has given way to despair, and sober realisation should be the order of the day. Under the patient eye of the Nobel Peace Prize winner, the Myanmar armed forces have already pushed over the border over half of the Rohingya population. Since 24 August 2017, some 500,000 Rohingyas have fled to refuge in Bangladesh out of a remaining population of less than 1 million. Ms Suu Kyi's September speech to the international community could not be more jarring in the circumstances.

Aung San Suu Kyi, however, is much more emblematic of this humanitarian crisis than one might expect just from her failure to live up to our hopes and expectations. If we dig beneath the surface, we discover just what views and ideologies make ethnic cleansing and genocide possible. Ms Suu Kyi does not seem like a bad person to those who have met her and who know her personally. And it would be too facile to reduce her response to the Rohingya crisis to mere craven politicking. So how can a reasonably decent person who has a life-long history of self-sacrifice in the service of the rights of others look on the plight of the Rohingyas with such sang-froid? Why is it that an entire country that has suffered decades of oppression under military rule alongside the Rohingyas remains so unmoved by their suffering now, or in many cases are even supportive of the actions against them?

As far as we can tell Aung San Suu Kyi and most of her countrymen have certain anti-Muslim views and attitudes that inure them against empathising with the suffering of their neighbours. Her writings, which I discuss at length in the main text, show that she subscribes to the common Theravada Buddhist position that the state must protect the state religion and that religious diversity is a threat to the Buddhist sasana. Muslims cannot properly be part of the body politic in Ms Suu Kyi's ideal vision for Myanmar. The majority of her countrymen share that opinion.

Both Ms Suu Kyi and her fellow Burmese seem to have a deep and visceral aversion to Muslim individuals in person too. She recently complained publicly about the BBC after an interview because she had not been given prior notice that her interviewer would be Muslim. The Muslim in question, the BBC's Mishal Hussain, is one of the corporation's most respected journalists and had no political axe to grind with Ms Suu Kyi. Her 'offence' was to ask about Ms Suu Kyi about her response to the humanitarian problems that were already widely reported by the Western press.

Aung San Suu Kyi's stance on the issue of the Rohingyas is emblematic of the situation in the country, not because she leads the pack on discriminatory views, but rather because she echoes perfectly the attitudes of an entire society. Her voice, when she issues measured defences of the military operations in Rakhine state, or her deafening silence when prompted to consider the situation from the position of the Rohingya victims, mirrors that exactly of 90 per cent of her country's population.

And that is precisely why the genocide in Rakhine state is happening, and why it will not stop until all the Rohingyas are pushed over the border to Bangladesh, while stragglers will continue to be hunted down by the military. Nobody likes violence. Some, the nationalist extremists, condone and encourage the attacks against the Rohingyas, not out of blind bloodlust, but because they deem it 'necessary'. But the majority of Burmese do not even condone the violence. Yet they also do not especially mind the violence because the victims are Muslims. And they also agree that everything would be better if the Rohingyas had already been moved to Bangladesh. So really it is the Rohingyas' fault that they are being attacked, because they are still hanging around in the country of their birth. Those are the social attitudes which will enable a genocide. And from those attitudes, it takes little to push it past the point of no return.

After the 2012–13 assaults on the Rohingya community, the great majority found themselves in internal refugee camps. Here they were denied the means to work or to travel, access to health care or education. This clustering of an already vulnerable community into large camps has been a source of concern as it would make it easier for any future ethnic violence to become an act of genocide. By mid-2016, it was becoming increasingly clear that the persecution of the Rohingyas was being renewed, and the threat of a full-fledged genocidal frenzy looked as imminent as ever.

Still, the renewed violence followed a pattern already established since 2012. The Burmese army and its local Rakhine allies started to burn the homes of those Rohingyas living outside the refugee camps. This period saw killings and a renewed refugee exodus but came to an end in October 2016. The violence led to a more robust international response, and the involvement of Kofi Annan. The NLD has responded in the same way that the old military regime had to brief periods of international pressure. It has tried to prevent any external oversight by the UN or by journalists. It has also steadily banned all aid agencies from Rakhine, insisting that all aid be channelled through the Myanmar regime—and thus denied to the Rohingyas.

But what looked like a familiar cycle masked some fundamental changes in the underlying dynamic between the Rohingyas and their oppressors. This time around, the NLD were in government. And that made no difference. Hope is one of the most powerful forces in politics. So long as the NLD had been in opposition and had a viable way to power, the Rohingyas maintained hope. That hope held the community together and kept them tied to Myanmar and to the project of reconciliation with the Myanmar federal state. But now, those hopes have proved entirely forlorn.

This new state of affairs has led to a step-change in Rakhine state. Over the past year, a new actor emerged on the scene in this already complex and intractable conflict: the Arakan Rohingya Salvation Army (ARSA). They first appeared on the scene in October 2016 when they attacked three police outposts in the Maungdaw and Rathedaung townships, killing nine police officers. Since then, they have carried out more attacks in August 2017 and their actions have been the trigger for the recent wave of ethnic cleansing by the Myanmar military. While the group is small, probably no more than a few hundred fighters, it has already acted as a catalyst for more localised acts of resistance, as some Rohingya men try to defend their communities. In turn, of course, the emergence of such a group has led to predictable claims by the NLD and the Myanmar military that they are facing attacks by people with links to Al-Qaeda or Islamic State.

While the claims that Muslims in Myanmar have a 'jihadist' agenda have been a common part of the military and extremist Buddhist narrative about the Rohingyas, the reality is that apart from a brief uprising in 1946–7, the

Rohingyas have been entirely peaceful in the face of persecution. While most other ethnic minority groups have had a long history of armed resistance to the Burmese state, the Rohingyas have opted to remain peaceful. They have fought back on a localised basis, such as during the ethnic conflicts of 2012, but this has not coalesced into a structured resistance.

But now, in the wake of the most brutal crackdown the military has ever undertaken against the Rohingyas and the rise of ARSA, there is a genuine worry that Al-Qaeda or IS might manage to insert themselves into the situation. For example, IS has recently started to mention the Rohingyas in its propaganda broadcasts and Indonesian authorities report they have thwarted two plots to blow up the Myanmar embassy in Jakarta.

This concern also extends beyond the Rohingyas in Myanmar. The treatment of the Rohingya refugees who fled to India and to Bangladesh is also hugely problematic. There has been some evidence of terrorist groups linked to the conflict in Kashmir trying to make connections with the Rohingyas in India. Some quarters in the Indian government, led by the Hindu-nationalist Bharatiya Janata Party (BJP), have called for an end to sanctuary for Rohingya refugees, and for the deportation of those Rohingyas already in the country back into the hands of the Myanmar army. Denied official status even as refugees, and therefore any of the protections mandated by international law, the Rohingyas are likely to become highly susceptible to any radical group prepared to offer humanitarian aid, education and health care. There are already instances of individual Rohingya men joining groups such as Lashkar-e-Taiba in Pakistan. How long before the lack of friendship from the government of India translates into friendships with its enemies?

For obvious reasons of geography and poverty, most Rohingyas have tried to flee into Bangladesh. Unfortunately, Bangladesh has a long history of ignoring the plight of the Rohingyas and of forcing refugees back into Myanmar. This started in the 1970s and continues to this day. At the moment, Bangladesh is trying to force the new arrivals to stay in large camps on the border and has forbidden them from travelling into the rest of the country. A positive interpretation is that this is, as claimed by the Bangladeshi authorities, a means to organise relief efforts. However, such camps are squalid and overcrowded and the Rohingyas have the lessons of recent history as a reason to mistrust Bangladesh's intentions. The Rohingyas are thus far from salvation even once they manage to escape the clutches of the Myanmar military.

What we have in the Rohingyas is an extremely precarious population, divided into densely populated and under-provisioned refugee camps, spread across three countries, with some tentative connections to radical groups especially in Pakistan and Saudi Arabia, and with a new, developing inclination towards insurgency, led by ARSA. This is a recipe for absolute disaster not just for the Rohingyas themselves, but for the entire region.

The emergence of a group like ARSA is predictable and depressing. Predictable because sooner or later an ethnic group left with no hope will strike back at its persecutors. Depressing, because the attacks by ARSA certainly triggered the violence in August and September 2017 against the Rohingyas. The emergence of ARSA also fits neatly into the preferred narrative of the Myanmar state that it is facing a sustained terrorist threat to its very existence.

In addition, if conditions for refugees do not improve, and ethnic cleansing continues within Rakhine, the likelihood is that ARSA will not lack for recruits. Thus a situation that till recently was marked by peaceful resistance by the Rohingyas is likely to shift to a low-level insurgency, at the very least. In that situation, there are plenty of extremists—both Buddhist and Islamist—who will wish to exploit the conflict for their wider goals.

The first edition of this book argued that Myanmar was on the edge of a genocide aimed at the Rohingyas. By 2015, they had been marginalised within the country of their birth and denied all normal human and civic rights. I argued then that 'the situation is now so bad that the only outcomes are to ease the level of persecution or for it to slip into outright genocide'. The NLD did nothing to address the persecution of the Rohingya, and we are now seeing an unstable situation escalate into the ethnic cleansing of an entire community—or, to give it its proper name: genocide. And the troubles for the Rohingyas, and for the wider region, are only just beginning.

APPENDIX 1

H. G. BELL ON THE ETHNIC GROUPS OF ARAKAN, 1852[1]

AN ACCOUNT

OF THE

BURMAN EMPIRE,

COMPILED FROM THE WORKS OF COLONEL SYMES, MAJOR
CANNING, CAPTAIN COX, DR. LEYDEN, DR.
BUCHANAN, &c, &c. &c. ;

A DESCRIPTION OF

DIFFERENT TRIBES

INHABITING IN AND AROUND THAT DOMINION ;

AND

A NARRATIVE

OF THE

LATE MILITARY AND POLITICAL OPERATIONS

IN THE

BURMESE EMPIRE,

WITH SOME ACCOUNT OF THE PRESENT CONDITION OF
THE COUNTRY, ITS MANNERS, CUSTOMS AND
INHABITANTS.

BY

HENRY G. BELL, Esq.

WITH A COLOURED MAP.

CALCUTTA:

PRINTED FOR THE PUBLISHER BY D'ROZARIO AND CO.

151

APPENDIX 2

EXCERPT FROM PATON'S REPORT[1]

The population of Arracan and its dependencies Ramree, Cheduba & Sandaway does not at present exceed 100,000 souls, may be classed as follow-

- Mughs six tenths
- Mussalman three tenths
- Burmese One tenth

Total 100,000 Souls

The Mussalaman Sirdars generally speak good Hindoostanee, but the lower orders of that class, who speak a broken sort of Hindoostanee, are quite unintelligible to those who are not thoroughly acquainted with the jargon of the southern parts of the Chittagong District. The universal language of the provinces is the Mugh, which although differing in some respects from the Burmah, particularly in pronunciation, is written and spelt in the same way and with the same character; almost everyone is able to write and as females are not precluded from receiving instruction, they are often shrewd and intelligent. The Mughs being particularly found of hunting and fishing, do not make such good farmers as the Mussalman. However as Bunneahs and shop keepers they surpass the Bengollee in cunning and on all occasion try, and very often successfully, to overreach their customers; stealing is a predominant evil amongst them, yet they are not given to lying, when detected after the commission of any felonious act, however serious, they almost invariably, and with the utmost frankness confess the crime, and detail with the greatest minuteness the manner in which it had been perpetrated.

152

APPENDIX 3

STATEMENT OF CITIZENSHIP[1]

Judicial Department No.C.4A/ ctxx/ dated the 2 December 1949

From U Tha Zan,   To
    Subordinate Judge,   Abdul Jolil,
    Buthidaung,   Retd. Process-server,
Citizenship Election Officer.   Buthidaung.

Subject:- Burma Citizenship.

Reference:- His application dated the 18th December 1949.

It is to inform you that, according to your affidavit, you need not apply for the Citizenship Certificate as you belong to one of the indigenous races of the Union of Burma as defined in section 3 (1) of the Union Citizenship Act, 1948. (Burma Act No. 66 of 1948).

                                    (Tha Zan)
                                Subordinate Judge,
                                    Buthidaung.
                            (Citizenship Election Officer).

APPENDIX 4

ROHINGYA STUDENT ASSOCIATION, RANGOON UNIVERSITY

APPENDIX 5

PRO-MILITARY SLOGAN[1]

GLOSSARY

969 Movement	A loose organisation of extremist Buddhist monks, which grew out of the 1988 popular revolt and is now responsible for much of the anti-Muslim violence
Arakan	The traditional name for Rakhine, the region that now forms the westernmost province of Myanmar. Excepting spells when it was ruled by Muslim kingdoms, it was an independent kingdom until the 1780s
Arakan League for Democracy (ALD)	Ethnic Rakhine party formed to contest the 1990 elections. Called for the expulsion of the Rohingyas and were close allies of the NLD
Arakan National Party (ANP)	Latest incarnation of the Rakhine ethnic party, formed in 2013 from a merger of existing parties
Burmese Independence Army	Main armed force of the anti-British nationalist movement. Originally funded and trained by the Japanese
Burmese Road to Socialism	Official ideology of the military regime between 1962 and 1988
Burma Socialist Programme Party (BSPP)	Formal (civilian) governing party from 1974–88
Committee Representing the People's Parliament	Shadow parliament created by the NLD and other opposition parties after the 1990 elections

Cyclone Nargis	Highly destructive storm that struck Burma in 2008. Some have argued it helped provoke unrest which in turn forced the military to concede a new round of democratic elections
Democracy and Human Rights Party	A mainly Rohingya party formed to contest the 2011 and 2015 elections. All its candidates were banned from standing in 2015
Kaman	A Muslim confessional ethnic group from Afghanistan who settled in Arakan after 1600 AD
Kuomintang	Chinese army opposed to Mao, active in northern Burma in the period from 1948–56
MaBaTha (The Patriotic Association of Myanmar)	Important extremist Buddhist organisation formed officially in 2014, perhaps with the active support of the military. Very influential in Myanmar's religious education; active in demanding laws to limit the rights of Muslims; often, along with the 969 Movement, implicated in anti-Muslim violence
Mahayana Buddhism	One of the major strands within Buddhism, common in Tibet, Nepal and India. The Dalai Lama belongs to this tradition
Mayu	The northernmost district within the province of Rakhine
Mon	A Khmer ethnic group living in southern Burma. Important for bringing Theravada Buddhism to the region
Mrauk-U Dynasty	Rulers of Arakan from 1300–1800 AD
Myanmar	The name given to Burma in 1989
National League for Democracy (NLD)	Main democratic opposition movement to the regime
National Unity Party (NUP)	Replaced the BSPP. Formed to contest the 1990 elections by the generals
Pagan Kingdom	An important Tibetan–Burmese dynasty

	which unified the Irrawaddy Valley region from 1000–1300 AD
Pan Zagar	A civil society movement that is challenging the narrative of the Buddhist extremists
Rakhine	Either refers to (a) a mostly Buddhist ethnic group that moved to the province of Arakan after 1000 AD; or (b) the modern-day name given to the old province of Arakan after Burma became independent in 1948
Rakhine Nationalities Development Party (RNDP)	Successor to the ALD, heavily implicated in the 2012 massacres of Rohingyas and has called for the expulsion of the Rohingyas from Myanmar
Saffron Revolution	Name given to the 2007 popular uprisings
Shan	A largely Buddhist ethnic group, have been in revolt against the Burmese regime since at least the early 1960s
Tatmadaw	Name used by the military to describe itself
Theravada Buddhism	One of the main strands of Buddhism, also popular in Sri Lanka and Thailand, where it is also often associated with inter-confessional and inter-ethnic strife
Union Solidarity and Development Party (USDP)	Political party formed by the military to contest elections since 2010
White Cards	The last form of official documentation held by the Rohingyas. These were confiscated by the regime in 2015

NOTES

INTRODUCTION

1. Holmes, R. A. 1967. 'Burmese domestic policy: the politics of Burmanization'. *Asian Survey*, pp. 188–197, see especially pp. 191–2.
2. Coclanis, P. A. 2013. 'Terror in Burma: Buddhists vs. Muslims' [Online]. Washington, D.C.: World Affairs. Available: http://www.worldaffairsjournal.org/article/terror-burma-buddhists-vs-muslims [Accessed 29 June 2015].
3. Akins, H. 2013. 'No place for Islam? Buddhist nationalism in Myanmar' [Online]. Al Jazeera. Available: http://www.aljazeera.com/indepth/opinion/2013/10/no-place-islam-buddhist-nationalism-myanmar-2013101710411233906.html [Accessed 26 February 2014].
4. Tharoor, I. 2015. 'Why does this Buddhist-majority nation hate these Muslims so much?' [Online]. *Washington Post*. Available: http://www.washingtonpost.com/blogs/worldviews/wp/2015/02/13/why-does-this-buddhist-majority-nation-hate-these-muslims-so-much/ [Accessed 18 February 2015].
5. Zan, U. S. and Chan, A. 2005. *Influx Viruses: The Illegal Muslims in Arakan*, New York: Arakanese in United States.
6. A complication in writing this book is whether to use modern names for provinces, regions and political parties, or the names by which they were known at the time. Mostly the approach has been to use whichever term was in use during the period under discussion. Thus Arakan, the westernmost province of modern-day Myanmar, became known as Rakhine when Burma gained independence from the British in 1948.
7. Luce, G. H. 1986. *Phases of Pre-Pagan Burma*. Oxford: Oxford University Press.
8. Aung Thwin, M. 1985a. 'Burma Before Pagan: The Status of Archaeology Today'. *Asian Perspectives*, 25:2, 1–22.
9. Luce, *Phases of Pre-Pagan Burma*.
10. Aung Thwin, M. 1985b. *Pagan: the Origins of Modern Burma*. Honolulu: University of Hawaii Press.

11. Gutman, P. 1976. 'Ancient Arakan', PhD thesis. Australian National University: Department of Asian Civilisations, pp. 16–17; Gutman, P. 2001. *Burma's Lost Kingdoms: Splendors Of Arakan*. Boulder, CO: Weatherhill, p. 14.

12. Smith, M. & Allsebrook, A. 1994. *Ethnic Groups in Burma: Development, Democracy and Human Rights*. London: Anti-Slavery International, p. 1; cf. Luce, G. H. 1986, *Phases of Pre-Pagan Burma*, p. 51.

13. James, H. 2000. 'The Fall of Ayutthaya: A Re-assessment'. *The Journal of Burma Studies*, Vol 5, 75–108.

14. Baxter, J. 1941. *Report on Indian Immigration*. Rangoon: India Office.

15. See Myanmar 2008. Constitution of the Republic of the Union of Myanmar. See also UNHCR. 2010. *Burma Citizenship Law 1982* [Online]. UNHCR. Available: http://www.refworld.org/cgi-bin/texis/vtx/rwmain?page=printdoc&docid=3a e6b4f71b [Accessed 28 February 2014].

16. United Nations 2013. 'Situation of human rights in Myanmar'. New York: UN.

17. SIL 2015. *Languages of Myanmar: An Ethnologue Country Report*, Dallas, TX: SIL.

18. Buchanan, F. 1799. 'A Comparative Vocabulary of Some of the Languages spoken in the Burma Empire'. *Asiatic Researches*, 5, 219–240.

19. Ibid; and *Classical Journal* 1811. 'Numbers in 200 Tongues', London, 535; and Vateri, J. S. 1815. *Linguarum totius orbis Index*, Berlin.

20. Paton, C. 1826. *A Short Report on Arakan*. London: Colonial Office.

21. Colonial Office 1911. *Census of India: Burma*. Rangoon.

22. Baxter, *Report on Indian Immigration*.

23. Charney, M. W. 2009. *A History of Modern Burma*, Cambridge: Cambridge University Press.

24. Lintner, B. 1990. *The Rise and Fall of the Communist Party of Burma*, Ithaca: Cornell University Press.

25. Foley, M. 2010. *The Cold War and National Assertion in Southeast Asia: Britain, the United States and Burma, 1948–1962*, London: Routledge.

26. Lee, J. 2013. 'A History of Broken Promises' [Online]. Alders Ledge. Available: http://aldersledge.blogspot.co.uk/2013/04/a-history-of-broken-promises.html [Accessed 4 March 2014].

27. Christie, C. J. 1997. *A Modern History of Southeast Asia: Decolonization, Nationalism and Separatism*, London: IB Tauris, p.166; Yegar, M. 1972. *The Muslims of Burma: The Study of a Minority Group*, Wiesbaden: Otto Harrossowitz, p. 96; Gibson, T., James, H. & Falvey, L. 2016. *Rohingyas: Insecurity and Citizenship in Myanmar*, Songkhla: Thaksin University Press, p. 65.

28. Human Rights Watch. 2000. 'Malaysia/Burma: Living in Limbo' [Online]. Available: http://www.hrw.org/reports/2000/malaysia/maybr008–01.htm [Accessed 28 February 2014].

29. Ibid.

30. Yegar, *The Muslims of Burma*.

31. Constituent Assembly 1947. 'The Constitution of the Union of Burma'. Rangoon: Foreign Office; and FIDH 2000. 'Burma: repression, discrimination and ethnic cleansing in Arakan'. Paris: International Federation of Human Rights Leagues.

32. Lwin, N. S. 2012. *Making Rohingya Stateless* [Online]. Rangoon: New Mandala. Available: http://asiapacific.anu.edu.au/newmandala/2012/10/29/making-rohingya-statelessness/ [Accessed 8 July 2015].

33. Pugh, C. L. 2013. *Is Citizenship the Answer? Constructions of belonging and exclusion for the stateless Rohingya of Burma*. Oxford: International Migration Institute.

34. Citizenship Election Officer 1948. 'Indigenous Race Recognition'.

35. Lwin, *Making Rohingya Stateless* [Online].

36. Min, U. K. 2012. *An Assessment of the Question of Rohingya's Nationality: Legal Nexus between Rohingya and the State*. Rangoon.

37. Busczynski, L. 1986. *Soviet Foreign Policy and Southeast Asia*, London: Routledge.

38. Government of the Union of Burma 1974. 'The Constitution of the Socialist Republic of the Union of Burma'. Rangoon.

39. Refworld. 1982. *Burma Citizenship Law* [Online]. UNHCR. Available: http://www.refworld.org/docid/3ae6b4f71b.html [Accessed 28 February 2014].

40. Interviews conducted with journalists from *Myanmar Times*, *Burma Times*, and *The Guardian*. Anonymity preserved for their safety.

41. Venkateswaran, K. S. 1996. 'Burma: Beyond the Law'. Article 19. Available: https://www.article19.org/data/files/pdfs/publications/burma-beyond-law.pdf [Accessed 23 November 2015].

42. Interview with U Kyaw Min, former Rohingya MP and now president of the Democracy and Human Rights Party, interviewed in Yangon on 30 June 2015.

43. Interview with Rohingya politician, then sitting in parliament, 2015 (left anonymous for safety).

44. Interview with U Kyaw Min, Yangon, 30 June 2015.

45. Médecins Sans Frontières 2002. '10 Years for the Rohingyas Refugees in Bangladesh: Past, Present and Future'.

46. Seekins, D. M. 2008. 'The Social, Political and Humanitarian Impact of Burma's Cyclone Nargis'. *Asia-Pacific Journal*, 6:5.

47. Myanmar 2008. 'Constitution of the Republic of the Union of Myanmar'.

48. Williams, D. C. 2014. 'What's so Bad about Burma's 2008 Constitution?' In Crouch, M. & Lindsey, T. (eds.) *Law Society and Transition In Myanmar*. Oxford: Hart Publishing.

49. Burma Centrum Nederlands 2014. 'Ethnicity without Meaning, Data without Context: The 2014 Census, Identity and Citizenship' in *Burma/Myanmar*. Burma Policy Briefing. Amsterdam: Burma Centrum Nederlands; and Heijmans, P. 2014. 'Myanmar's Controversial Census' [Online]. The Diplomat. Available: http://thediplomat.com/2014/09/myanmars-controversial-census/ [Accessed 20 February 2015].

50. ASEAN Parliamentarians for Human Rights 2015. 'Disenfranchisement and Desperation in Myanmar's Rakhine State: Drivers of a Regional Crisis'. APHR.

51. *Burma Times*. 2015. 'In Burma's historic elections, a Muslim minority is banned from voting but still the focus of the campaign' [Online]. Available: http://burmatimes.net/in-burmas-historic-elections-a-muslim-minority-is-banned-from-voting-but-still-the-focus-of-the-campaign/ [Accessed 19 October 2015].

52. Sheridan, M. 2015. 'Myanmar "effectively a state of apartheid" for Muslims' [Online]. *The Australian*. Available: http://www.theaustralian.com.au/news/world/myanmar-effectively-a-state-of-apartheid-for-muslims/story-fnb64oi6–1227537589783 [Accessed 22 September 2015].

53. Myintzu, S. Y., Ei, K. K., Thu, K. & Kyaw, N. R. 2015. 'Myanmar Election Body Rejects Muslim Parliamentary Candidates' [Online]. *Radio Free Asia*. Available: http://www.rfa.org/english/news/myanmar/election-body-rejects-muslim-parliamentary-candidates-09012015161036.html [Accessed 22 September 2015].

54. *The Irrawaddy*. 2007. 'Heroes and Villains' [Online]. Rangoon: The Irrawaddy. Available: http://www2.irrawaddy.org/article.php?art_id=6883 [Accessed 27 June 2015].

55. BBC. 2015a. 'Dalai Lama presses Aung San Suu Kyi over Rohingya migrants' [Online]. BBC: London. Available: http://www.bbc.co.uk/news/world-asia-32925805 [Accessed 15 June 2015]; and Caralucci, T. 2015. 'Myanmar's Aung San Suu Kyi Dodging or Driving the Rohingyas Crisis?' [Online]. *New Eastern Outlook*. Available: http://journal-neo.org/2015/06/20/myanmar-s-aung-san-suu-kyi-dodging-or-driving-the-rohingya-crisis/ [Accessed 22 September 2015]; and Doyle, D. 2015. 'Burma elections: Aung San Suu Kyi steers clear of 'stateless' minority the Rohingyas' [Online]. *The Independent*. Available: http://www.independent.co.uk/news/world/asia/burma-elections-aung-san-suu-kyi-steers-clear-of-stateless-minority-the-rohingya-a6697341.html [Accessed 20 October 2015]; and Smith, M. 2014. *Politics of Persecution*. Fortify Rights International; and Winn, P. 2013. 'Suu Kyi spokesman: "There is no Rohingya"' [Online]. *Global Post*. Available: http://www.globalpost.com/dispatch/news/regions/asia-pacific/myanmar/130501/suu-kyi-no-rohingya [Accessed 26 February 2014].

56. BBC. 2012. 'Suu Kyi gives historic Parliament address' [Online]. Available: http://www.bbc.co.uk/news/uk-18543045 [Accessed 2 November 2014]; and Woolacott, M. 2015. 'Why Burma still needs Aung San Suu Kyi' [Online]. *The Guardian*. Available: http://www.theguardian.com/commentisfree/2015/apr/06/burma-aung-san-suu-kyi-democracy-election [Accessed 1 July 2015].

57. Interview with Rohingya politician, then sitting in parliament, 2015 (left anonymous for safety).

58. Win, T. L. 2014a. 'Burmese journalist beseeches brethren: Stop with the Muslim hate speech' [Online]. Thomson Reuters. Available: http://www.trust.org/item/20140313074529–3vfw4/ [Accessed 20 July 2015]; Win, T. L. 2014b.

'Myanmar activists launch anti-'hate speech' campaign' [Online]. Thomson Reuters. Available: http://www.trust.org/item/20140403131148–4mqvg/ [Accessed 20 July 2015].

59. Michaels, S. 2014. 'Suu Kyi Meets Critics of 'Protection of Race and Religion' Bills' [Online]. Rangoon: *The Irrawaddy*. Available: http://www.irrawaddy.org/ burma/suu-kyi-meets-critics-protection-race-religion-bills.html [Accessed 16 July 2015].

60. *The Irrawaddy*. 1997b. 'Who Killed Aung San?' [Online]. Available: http://www2. irrawaddy.org/article.php?art_id=719 [Accessed 17 September 2015].

61. Charney, M. W. 2009. *A History of Modern Burma*. Cambridge: Cambridge University Press.

62. Venkateswaran, 'Burma: Beyond the Law'.

63. Han, K. K. 2003. *1990 Multi Party Democracy: General Elections* [Online]. Rangoon: National League for Democracy. Available: http://www.ibiblio.org/ obl/docs/1990_elections.htm [Accessed 2 July 2015].

64. Zin, M. 2014. 'Return of the Myanmar Military?' [Online]. New York: *New York Times*. Available: http://www.nytimes.com/2014/11/18/opinion/return-of-the-myanmar-military.html?partner=rss&emc=rss&_r=1 [Accessed 27 June 2015].

65. Macdonald, A. P. 2015. 'Time to engage Myanmar's military' [Online]. *Asia Times*. Available: http://www.atimes.com/atimes/Southeast_Asia/SEA-01–040215. html [Accessed 27 June 2015].

66. Lewis, S. & Doherty, B. 2015. 'Turmoil in Burma's military-backed ruling party as leaders are deposed' [Online]. London: *The Guardian*. Available: http://www. theguardian.com/world/2015/aug/13/burmese-forces-surround-ruling-party-headquarters-and-confine-mps-report [Accessed 13 August 2015].

67. Stoakes, E. 2015. 'Monks, PowerPoint Presentations, and Ethnic Cleansing' [Online]. Washington, D.C.: Foreign Policy. Available: http://foreignpolicy.com/ 2015/10/26/evidence-links-myanmar-government-monks-ethnic-cleansing-ro-hingya/ [Accessed 28 October 2015]; Al Jazeera. 2015. '"Strong evidence" of geno-cide in Myanmar' [Online]. See documentary video. Available: http://www. aljazeera.com/news/2015/10/exclusive-strong-evidence-genocide-myan-mar-151024190547465.html [Accessed 1 November 2015].

68. Han, *1990 Multi Party Democracy: General Elections*.

69. Zin, M. 2010. 'Opposition Movements in Burma: The Question of Relevancy' in Levenstein, S.L. (ed.) *Finding Dollars, Sense and Legitimacy in Burma*. Washington, D.C.: Woodrow Wilson International Centre for Scholars.

70. World Elections. 2012. *Burma (Myanmar) by-elections 2012* [Online]. Available: http://welections.wordpress.com/2012/04/06/burma-by-elections-2012/ [Acces-sed 8 March 2014].

71. Jagan, L. 2014. 'Suu Kyi shifts pre-election tack in Myanmar' [Online]. *Asia Times*. Available: http://www.atimes.com/atimes/Southeast_Asia/SEA-01–120614. html [Accessed 30 June 2015].

72. Reuters. 2015b. 'Myanmar's ousted ruling party leader Shwe Mann meets Aung San Suu Kyi' [Online]. Available: http://www.rohingyablogger.com/2015/08/myanmars-ousted-ruling-party-leader.html [Accessed 18 August 2015].

73. Simonson, T. 2015. 'The taming of the NLD... by the NLD' [Online]. New Mandala. Available: http://asiapacific.anu.edu.au/newmandala/2015/08/12/the-taming-of-the-nld-by-the-nld/ [Accessed 11 October 2015].

74. Han, *1990 Multi Party Democracy: General Elections.*

75. Interview with U Kyaw Min, Yangon, 30 June 2015.

76. McLaughlin, T. 2015b. 'Rising Arakanese Party could further marginalize Rohingya' [Online]. Reuters. Available: http://www.thestateless.com/2015/10/03/rising-arakanese-party-could-further-marginalize-rohingya/ [Accessed 13 October 2015].

77. Human Rights Council. 2014. 'Hear our Screams'.

78. CSIS. 2012. 'The Leaderboard: Aye Maung' [Online]. Center for Strategic and International Studies. Available: http://cogitasia.com/the-leaderboard-aye-maung/ [Accessed 22 September 2015].

79. Ibrahim, A. 2015. 'Who Is Instigating the Violence Against the Rohingyas in Myanmar?' [Online]. New York: *Huffington Post.* Available: http://www.huffingtonpost.com/azeem-ibrahim/who-is-instigating-the-vi_b_7810972.html [Accessed 17 July 2015].

80. Walton, M. & Hayward, S. 2014. *Contesting Buddhist Narratives: Democratization, Nationalism, and Communal Violence in Myanmar.* Honolulu: East-West Center, p. 22.

81. Marshall, A. R. C. 'Myanmar gives official blessing to anti-Muslim monks' [Online]. Reuters, 27 June 2013. Available: http://uk.reuters.com/article/2013/06/27/us-myanmar-969-specialreport-idUSBRE95Q04720130627 [Accessed 26 January 2016]. Cf. BBC. 'Myanmar's Radical Monk and the Rohingya Crisis' [Online]. 28 May 2015. Available: http://www.bbc.co.uk/monitoring/myanmars-radical-monk-and-the-rohingya-crisis [Accessed 26 January 2016].

82. Caralucci, T. 2015. 'Myanmar's Aung San Suu Kyi Dodging or Driving the Rohingyas Crisis?' [Online]. New Eastern Outlook. Available: http://journal-neo.org/2015/06/20/myanmar-s-aung-san-suu-kyi-dodging-or-driving-the-rohingya-crisis/ [Accessed 22 September 2015].

83. *Sydney Morning Herald.* 2015. '"They are Humans": Myanmar Opposition says Rohingya People Have Rights' [Online]. *Sydney: Sydney Morning Herald.* Available: http://www.smh.com.au/world/they-are-humans-myanmar-opposition-says-rohingya-people-have-rights-20150519-gh4q8m.html [Accessed 23 September 2015].

84. Walton, M. 2014. 'What are Myanmar's Buddhist Sunday Schools Teaching?' [Online]. East Asia Forum. Available: http://www.eastasiaforum.org/2014/12/16/what-are-myanmars-buddhist-sunday-schools-teaching/ [Accessed 16 July 2015].

85. Win, S. 2015. 'Special Report—With Official Help, Myanmar's Radical Buddhists Target Muslim-owned Businesses' [Online]. Rangoon: *Myanmar Now*. Available: http://www.myanmar-now.org/news/i/?id=9ba61afc-285d-49bd-8f73-8b9efaf 941c0 [Accessed 21 September 2015].

86. Akins, H. 2013. 'No place for Islam? Buddhist nationalism in Myanmar' [Online]. Al Jazeera. Available: http://www.aljazeera.com/indepth/opinion/2013/10/no-place-islam-buddhist-nationalism-myanmar-2013101710411233906.html [Accessed 26 February 2014]; Human Rights Watch 2013a. '"All You Can Do is Pray"': Crimes Against Humanity and Ethnic Cleansing of Rohingya Muslims in Burma's Arakan State'. Washington, D.C.: Human Rights Watch; Smith, 'Politics of Persecution'. Fortify Rights International.

87. Stoakes, 'Monks, PowerPoint Presentations, and Ethnic Cleansing' [Online]. Washington, D.C.: Foreign Policy. Available: http://foreignpolicy.com/2015/10/26/evidence-links-myanmar-government-monks-ethnic-cleansing-rohingya/ [Accessed 28 October 2015].

88. Heinemann, T. 2015. 'Misunderstanding Myanmar's Military' [Online]. *Asia Times*. Available: http://www.atimes.com/atimes/Southeast_Asia/SEA-01–110215.html [Accessed 27 June 2015], International Crisis Group 2001. 'Myanmar: The Military Regime's View of the World'. Bangkok: International Crisis Group; Khin, T. 2015. 'Risk of Mass Atrocities and Policies of Persecution in Burma' [Online]. Washington, D.C.: Early Warning Project. Available: http://www.earlywarningproject.com/2015/07/16/policies-of-persecution-in-burma [Accessed 22 September 2015]; Zin, M. 2014. 'Return of the Myanmar Military?' [Online]. New York: *New York Times*. Available: http://www.nytimes.com/2014/11/18/opinion/return-of-the-myanmar-military. html?partner=rss&emc=rss&_r=1 [Accessed 27 June 2015].

89. Kyaw, K. 2012. 'Analysis of Myanmar's NLD landslide' [Online]. New Mandala. Available: http://asiapacific.anu.edu.au/newmandala/2012/05/01/analysis-of-myanmars-nld-landslide/ [Accessed 21 October 2015].

90. Dosch, J. & Sidhu, J. S. 2015. 'The European Union's Myanmar Policy: Focused or Directionless?' *Journal of Current Southeast Asian Affairs*, 34:2, 85–112; Pedersen, M. B. 2014. 'Myanmar's Democratic Opening'. *In:* Cheesman, N., Farrelly, N. & Wilson, T. (eds.) *Debating Democratization in Myanmar*. Singapore: ISEAS Publishing; Woolacott, M. 2015. 'Why Burma still needs Aung San Suu Kyi' [Online]. London: *The Guardian*. Available: http://www.theguardian.com/commentisfree/2015/apr/06/burma-aung-san-suu-kyi-democracy-election [Accessed 1 July 2015].

91. Win, T. L. 2014b. 'Myanmar activists launch anti-"hate speech" campaign' [Online]. Thomson Reuters. Available: http://www.trust.org/item/20140 403131148–4mqvg/ [Accessed 20 July 2015].

92. Associated Press. 2013. 'Buddhist monks offer shelter to persecuted Burma

Muslims' [Online]. Washington, D.C.: CBS News. Available: http://www.cbsnews.com/news/buddhist-monks-offer-shelter-to-persecuted-burma-muslims/ [Accessed 16 September 2015].

93. Walton, M. 2013a. 'Myanmar needs a new nationalism' [Online]. *Asia Times*. Available: http://www.atimes.com/atimes/Southeast_Asia/SEA-02–200513. html [Accessed 16 July 2015].

94. Michaels, S. 2014. 'Suu Kyi Meets Critics of 'Protection of Race and Religion' Bills' [Online]. Rangoon: *The Irrawaddy*. Available: http://www.irrawaddy.org/burma/suu-kyi-meets-critics-protection-race-religion-bills.html [Accessed 16 July 2015].

95. United Nations Human Rights. 2015. 'Myanmar: UN rights experts express alarm at adoption of first of four 'protection of race and religion' bills' [Online]. New York: Office of the High Commissioner for Human Rights. Available: http://www.ohchr.org/EN/NewsEvents/Pages/DisplayNews.aspx?NewsID=16015&LangID=E [Accessed 28 June 2015].

96. Human Rights Council 2014. 'Hear our Screams'.

97. ASEAN Parliamentarians for Human Rights 2015. 'Disenfranchisement and Desperation in Myanmar's Rakhine State: Drivers of a Regional Crisis'. APHR, Kin, T. 2015. 'Risk of Mass Atrocities and Policies of Persecution in Burma' [Online]. Early Warning Project. Available: http://www.earlywarningproject.com/2015/07/16/policies-of-persecution-in-burma [Accessed 15 October 2015].

98. Lefevre, A. S. & Marshall, A. R. C. 2014. 'Special Report: Traffickers use abductions, prison ships to feed Asian slave trade' [Online]. Reuters. Available: http://www.reuters.com/article/2014/10/22/us-thailand-trafficking-specialreport-idUSKCN0IB0A320141022http://www.reuters.com/article/2014/10/22/us-thailand-trafficking-specialreport-idUSKCN0IB0A320141022 [Accessed 20 September 2015]; UCANEWS. 2015. 'Refugee boats set sail as monsoon season ends' [Online]. UCANEWS. Available: http://www.ucanews.com/news/refugee-boats-set-sail-as-monsoon-season-ends/74455 [Accessed 21 October 2015].

99. Dosch, J. & Sidhu, J. S. 2015. 'The European Union's Myanmar Policy: Focused or Directionless?' *Journal of Current Southeast Asian Affairs*, 34:2, 85–112.

100. Interview by author with Rohingya elders in Sittwe IDP camp, 26 October 2015; Cockett, R. 2015. *Blood, Dreams and Gold: The Changing Face of Burma*, New Haven: Yale University Press.

101. Bünte, M. & Dosch, J. 2015. 'Myanmar: Political Reforms and the Recalibration of External Relations'. *Journal of Current Southeast Asian Affairs*, 34:2, 3–19.

102. Chachavalpongpun, P. 2012. 'The Vexing Strategic Tug-of-War over Naypyidaw: ASEAN's View of the Sino-Burmese Ties'. Ibid.31:1, 97–114.

103. ASEAN Parliamentarians for Human Rights 2015. 'Disenfranchisement and

Desperation in Myanmar's Rakhine State: Drivers of a Regional Crisis'. APHR,
Yee, T. H. 2015. 'Expect further Rohingya exodus, report warns' [Online].
Singapore: *The Straits Times*. Available: http://www.straitstimes.com/asia/se-
asia/expect-further-rohingya-exodus-report-warns [Accessed 19 October 2015].

104. ASEAN Parliamentarians for Human Rights, 'Disenfranchisement'.

105. Win, T. L. 2014b. 'Myanmar activists launch anti-'hate speech' campaign'
     [Online].

106. Harff, B. 2005. 'Assessing Risks of Genocide and Politicide'. *In:* Marshall, M. G. &
     Gurr, T. R. (eds.) *Peace and Conflict*. College Park, MD: Center for International
     Development and Conflict Management; Tharoor, I. 2015. 'The risk of geno-
     cide around the world' [Online]. Washington, D.C.: *Washington Post*. Available:
     https://www.washingtonpost.com/news/worldviews/wp/2015/09/21/map-
     the-risk-of-genocide-around-the-world/ [Accessed 22 September 2015].

107. Win, T. L. 2014d. 'Will the Rohingya, driven from their homes, spend the rest
     of their lives segregated in ghettoes?' [Online]. Thomson Reuters. Available:
     http://www.trust.org/item/20140827082155-p627d/ [Accessed 20 July 2015].

108. UCANEWS, 'Refugee boats set sail as monsoon season ends' [Online].

109. Andrews, T. & Sullivan, D. 2014. 'Marching to Genocide in Burma'. Washington,
     D.C.: United to End Genocide; International Court of Justice 2015. 'Case
     Concerning Application of the Convention on the Prevention and Punishment
     of the Crime of Genocide (Croatia v Serbia)'. The Hague: International Court
     of Justice; Jones, A. 2008. 'Genocide and Mass Killing'. *In:* Williams, P. D. (ed.)
     Security Studies: An Introduction. London: Routledge; United Nations 1951.
     'Convention on the Prevention and Punishment of the Crime of Genocide'.
     Geneva: United Nations.

1. A SHORT HISTORY OF BURMA TO 1948

1. Smith, M. & Allsebrook, A. 1994. *Ethnic Groups in Burma: Development, Democracy
   and Human Rights*. London: Anti-Slavery International.

2. Aung Thwin, M. 1985a. 'Burma Before Pagan: The Status of Archaeology Today,'
   Asian Perspectives, 25:2, 1–22.

3. Galloway, C. K. 2007. *Burmese Buddhist Imagery of the Early Bagan Period (1044–
   1113)*. Canberra: Australian National University; Moore, E. 2011. The Early
   Buddhist Archaeology of Myanmar: Tagaung, Thagara, and the Mon-Pyu
   Dichotomy. *In:* McCormick, P., Jenny, M. & Baker, C. (eds.) *The Mon over Two
   Millennia: Monuments, Manuscripts, Movements*. Bangkok: Institute of Asian
   Studies, Chulalongkorn University.

4. Drabble, J. H. 2000. *An economic history of Malaysia, c. 1800–1990: The transition
   to modern economic growth*, New York: St Martin's Press.

5. Chan, A. 2005. 'The Development of a Muslim Enclave in Arakan (Rakhine) State

of Burma (Myanmar)'. *SOAS Bulletin of Burma Research*, 3:2, 396–420; James, H. 2000. 'The Fall of Ayutthaya: A Re-assessment'. *The Journal of Burma Studies*, 575–108.

6. Bell, H. G. 1852. *An Account of the Burman Empire, Compiled from the Works of Colonel Symes, Major Canning, Captain Cox, Dr. Leyden, Dr. Buchanan*, Calcutta: D'Rozario and Co; and Gutman, P. 2001. *Burma's Lost Kingdoms: Splendors of Arakan*, Boulder, CO: Weatherhill.

7. Maw, B. 1995. 'Research on Early Man in Myanmar'. *Myanmar Historical Research Journal*, 1, 1213–220.

8. Luce, G. H. 1986. *Phases of Pre-Pagan Burma*, Oxford: Oxford University Press.

9. Aung Thwin, M. 1985a. Burma Before Pagan: The Status of Archaeology Today.

10. Luce, *Phases of Pre-Pagan Burma*.

11. Moore, E. 2004. 'Interpreting Pyu material culture: Royal chronologies and finger-marked bricks'. *Myanmar Historical Research Journal*, 13:1, 1–57.

12. Ibid.

13. Aung Thwin, 'Burma Before Pagan'.

14. Mathias, J. 2015. 'Foreign Influences on the Burmese Language'. *International Conference on Burma/Myanmar Studies: Burma/Myanmar in Transition: Connectivity, Changes and Challenges*. University Academic Service Centre (UNISERV), Chiang Mai University:Thailand, 24–26 July 2015.

15. Aung, S. T. 1979. *The Buddhist art of ancient Arakan: An eastern border state beyond ancient India, east of Vanga and Samatata*, Rangoon: Daw Saw Saw.

16. Shah, I. 2015. 'Rohingyas' demand Burmese Gov't: either historically disprove "the ethnical term Rohingya" or pay back their indigenous rights' [Online]. Rangoon: *Burma Times*. Available: http://burmatimes.net/rohingyas-demand-burmese-govt-either-historically-disprove-the-ethnical-term-rohingya-or-pay-back-their-indigenous-rights/ [Accessed 8 July 2015].

17. Gutman, P. 2001. *Burma's Lost Kingdoms: Splendors Of Arakan*.

18. Wilson, H. H. 1817. *The History of British India*, London: Baldwin, Cradock and Joy.

19. Gutman, P. 2001. *Burma's Lost Kingdoms: Splendors Of Arakan*.

20. SIL 2015. *Languages of Myanmar: An Ethnologue Country Report*, Dallas, TX: SIL.

21. Buchanan, F. 1799. 'A Comparative Vocabulary of Some of the Languages spoken in the Burma Empire'. *Asiatic Researches*, 5 219–40.

22. Collis, M. 1937. *Trials in Burma*, London: Faber and Faber.

23. Min, U. K. 2012. 'An Assessment of the Question of Rohingya's Nationality: Legal Nexus between Rohingya and the State'. Rangoon.

24. Aung Thwin, M. 1985b. *Pagan: the origins of modern Burma*, Honolulu: University of Hawaii.

25. Houtman, G. 1999. 'Remaking Myanmar and Human Origins'. *Anthropology Today*, 15:4, 13–19.

26. Luce, G. H. 1986. *Phases of Pre-Pagan Burma*, Oxford: Oxford University Press.

27. Tun, T. 1959. 'Religious Buildings of Burma AD 1000–1300'. *Journal of Burma Research Society*, 42:2, 71–81.

28. Aung Thwin, 'Burma Before Pagan'. Though this argument is rejected by Luce, who argues that the Mongol invasion was the sole cause of the decline, pointing to the cultural continuity of the successor city states and kingdoms (see Luce, *Phases of Pre-Pagan Burma*).

29. Bischoff, R. 1996. *Buddhism in Myanmar: A short history*, Kandy, Sri Lanka: Buddhist Publication Society.

30. Ibid.

31. SOAS 2003. 'Burmese Buddhism in Colonial Burma'. *Bulletin of Burma Research*, 1:2, 42–47.

32. Bischoff, R. 1996. *Buddhism in Myanmar: A short history*.

33. Walton, M. & Hayward, S. 2014. *Contesting Buddhist Narratives*.

34. Yeni. 2005. 'An Enduring Legacy Written in Blood' [Online]. Rangoon: *The Irrawaddy*. Available: http://www2.irrawaddy.org/article.php?art_id=4498&page=2 [Accessed 27 June 2015].

35. Walton, M. & Hayward, S. 2014. *Contesting Buddhist Narratives*.

36. Bischoff, R. 1996. *Buddhism in Myanmar: A short history*,

37. Walton, M. 2013b. *A Primer on the Roots of Buddhist/Muslim Conflict in Myanmar and a Way Forward*.

38. Gutman, P. 2001. *Burma's Lost Kingdoms: Splendors Of Arakan*.

39. Shin, B. 1998. *From early Bama (Myanmar) up to the present Myanmar nation. Myanmar before Anawrahta*. Yangon: Innwa Publishing House.

40. Bell, *An Account of the Burman Empire*, pp. 33–46.

41. Ibid., p. 66.

42. Buchanan, F. 1799. A Comparative Vocabularly of Some of the Languages spoken in the Burma Empire. *Asiatic Researches*, 5219–240, p. 55.

43. Ibid.

44. Ibid.

45. Vateri, J. S. 1815. *Linguarum totius orbis*, Index: Berlin.

46. Baxter, J. 1941. 'Report on Indian Immigration'. Rangoon: India Office.

47. Aung Thwin, M. 1985a. 'Burma Before Pagan: The Status of Archaeology Today', *Asian Perspectives*, 25:2, 1–22; Charney, M. W. 2009. *A History of Modern Burma*, Cambridge: Cambridge University Press; James, H. 2000. 'The Fall of Ayutthaya: A Re-assessment'. *The Journal of Burma Studies*, 5, 75–108.

48. Pearn, B. 1944. 'Arakan and the First Anglo-Burmese War, 1824–1825'. *The Far Eastern Quarterly*, 4:1, 27–40.

49. Smith, M. & Allsebrook, A. 1994. *Ethnic Groups in Burma: Development, Democracy and Human Rights*.

50. Bischoff, R. 1996. *Buddhism in Myanmar: A short history*.

51. Ibid.

52. Zin, M. 2010. *Opposition Movements in Burma: The Question of Relevancy. Finding Dollars, Sense and Legitimacy in Burma.*

53. Walton, M. 2013b. 'A Primer on the Roots of Buddhist/Muslim Conflict in Myanmar and a Way Forward'.

54. Seekins, D. M. 2008. 'The Social, Political and Humanitarian Impact of Burma's Cyclone Nargis'. *Asia-Pacific Journal,* 6:5.

55. Tha, B. 2013. 'Massacre of 1942' [Online]. *Arakan Bumiputra.* Available: http://www.arakanbumiputra.com/2013/04/massacre-of-1942-by-ba-tha-buthidaung.html [Accessed 4 March 2014].

56. Ibid.

57. Jilani, A. 2006. 'The Muslim massacre of 1942' [Online]. Arakan Rohingya National Organisation (ARNO). Available: http://www.rohingya.org/portal/index.php/rohingya-library/26-rohingya-history/55-the-muslim-massacre-of-1942.html [Accessed 4 March 2014].

58. Lee, J. 2013. 'A History of Broken Promises' [Online]. Alders Ledge. Available: http://aldersledge.blogspot.co.uk/2013/04/a-history-of-broken-promises.html [Accessed 4 March 2014].

59. Ibid. And see Christie, C. J. 1997. *A Modern History of Southeast Asia: Decolonization, Nationalism and Separatism,* London: IB Tauris, p. 166; Yegar, M. 1972. *The Muslims of Burma: The Study of a Minority Group,* Wiesbaden: Otto Harrossowitz, p. 96; Gibson, T., James, H. & Falvey, L. 2016. *Rohingyas: Insecurity and Citizenship in Myanmar,* Songkhla: Thaksin University Press, p. 65.

60. Human Rights Watch. 2000. 'Malaysia/Burma: Living in Limbo' [Online]. Available: http://www.hrw.org/reports/2000/malaysia/maybr008–01.htm [Accessed 28 February 2014].

61. Ibid.

62. Yegar, M. 1972. *The Muslims of Burma: A Study of a Minority Group,* Wiesbaden: Otto Harrassowitz.

63. *The Irrawaddy.* 2007. 'Heroes and Villains' [Online]. Rangoon: The Irrawaddy. Available: http://www2.irrawaddy.org/article.php?art_id=6883 [Accessed 27 June 2015].

64. Slim, W. J. 1956. *Defeat into Victory: Battling Japan in Burma and India 1942–1945,* New York: Cooper Square.

65. Lintner, B. 1990. *The Rise and Fall of the Communist Party of Burma,* Ithaca, NY: Cornell University.

66. Slim, W. J. 1956. *Defeat into Victory: Battling Japan in Burma and India 1942–1945,* New York: Cooper Square.

67. Mathieson, D. S. 2004. 'The Enemy Within' [Online]. Rangoon: *The Irrawaddy.* Available: http://www2.irrawaddy.org/article.php?art_id=963 [Accessed 27 June 2015].

68. Callahan, M. P. 2005. *Making Enemies: War and State Building in Burma,* Ithaca, NY: Cornell University Press.

69. Tonkin, D. 2014b. 'The "Rohingya" Identity: British experience in Arakan 1826–1948', Rangoon: Network Myanmar.

70. Leider, J. P. 2012. '"Rohingya", Rakhaing and the Recent Outbreak of Violence—A Note'. *Burma Studies*, 8–12.

71. Paton, C. 1826. *A Short Report on Arakan*. London: Colonial Office.

72. Ibid.

73. Ibid., p. 4. My emphasis.

74. Tonkin, D. 2014a. 'Political Myths' [Online]. Network Myanmar. Available: http://www.networkmyanmar.org/index.php/political-myths [Accessed 28 February 2014].

75. Ibid.

76. Zan, U. S. & Chan, A. 2005. *Influx Viruses: The Illegal Muslims in Arakan*, New York: Arakanese in United States, p. 21.

77. Tonkin, D. 2014a. 'Political Myths'.

78. Leider, J. P. 2012. '"Rohingya", Rakhaing and the Recent Outbreak of Violence—A Note'.

79. Ibid. p. 8.

80. Leider, J. P. 2014. 'Rohingya: The name, the movement, the quest for identity'. *Nation Building in Myanmar*, Yangon: Myanmar Egress & Myanmar Peace Center.

81. Leider, J. P. 2012. '"Rohingya", Rakhaing and the Recent Outbreak of Violence—A Note', p. 9.

82. Ibid. p. 10.

83. Leider, J. P. 2014. 'Rohingya: The name, the movement, the quest for identity'.

84. Leider, J. P. 2012. '"Rohingya", Rakhaing and the Recent Outbreak of Violence—A Note'; Leider, J. P. 2014. 'Rohingya: The name, the movement, the quest for identity'.

85. Zan and Chan, *Influx Viruses*.

86. Ibid. Quotation is from the Foreword.

87. Colonial Office 1875. *The Census of British Burma*. Rangoon: Colonial Office, p. 30.

88. United Nations 2013. 'Situation of human rights in Myanmar'. New York: UN.

2. FROM INDEPENDENCE TO DEMOCRACY (1948–2010)

1. Charney, M. W. 2009. *A History of Modern Burma*, Cambridge: Cambridge University Press. Apparently the precise date was chosen as it was deemed propitious by (animist) astrologers: Coclanis, P. A. 2013. 'Terror in Burma: Buddhists vs. Muslims' [Online]. Washington, D.C.: World Affairs. Available: http://www.worldaffairsjournal.org/article/terror-burma-buddhists-vs-muslims [Accessed 29 June 2015].

2. Steinberg, D. I. 2001. *Burma: The State of Myanmar*, Washington, D.C.: Georgetown University Press.

3. Goldston, J. 1990. *Human Rights in Burma (Myanmar)*, New York: Human Rights Watch.

4. Confusingly, it is still referred to by both titles to this day.

5. Taylor, R. H. 1987. *The State in Burma*, London: C. Hurst & Co., see in particular discussion in Chapter 2.

6. Yeni. 2005. 'An Enduring Legacy Written in Blood' [Online]. Rangoon: *The Irrawaddy*. Available: http://www2.irrawaddy.org/article.php?art_id=4498&page=2 [Accessed 27 June 2015].

7. *The Irrawaddy*. 2007. 'Heroes and Villains' [Online]. Rangoon: *The Irrawaddy*. Available: http://www2.irrawaddy.org/article.php?art_id=6883 [Accessed 27 June 2015].

8. *The Irrawaddy*. 1997b. 'Who Killed Aung San?' [Online]. *The Irrawaddy*. Available: http://www2.irrawaddy.org/article.php?art_id=719 [Accessed 17 September 2015]. Who actually carried out the murder and who ordered it are contested issues. To the NLD, Aung San would have set Burma on a non-military democratic road, and he represented a threat to British plans to retain influence over Burma after independence. Others point to the factional fight within the '30 Comrades' and that Ne Win (who came to power in 1962) had much to gain from the removal of a charismatic rival.

9. Yeni. 2005. 'An Enduring Legacy Written in Blood'.

10. Han, K. K. 2003. '1990 Multi Party Democracy: General Elections' [Online]. Rangoon: National League for Democracy. Available: http://www.ibiblio.org/obl/docs/1990_elections.htm [Accessed 2 July 2015].

11. Callahan, M. P. 2005. *Making Enemies: War and State Building in Burma*, Ithaca, NY: Cornell University Press.

12. Lintner, B. 1990. *The Rise and Fall of the Communist Party of Burma*, Ithaca, NY: Cornell University.

13. It is worth noting that the pro-NLD *Irrawaddy* newspaper actually blames the British for fermenting this civil war as they were trying to bring their Shan allies to power. See, for example: *The Irrawaddy*. 1997b. 'Who Killed Aung San?'

14. Smith, M. & Allsebrook, A. 1994. *Ethnic Groups in Burma: Development, Democracy and Human Rights*, London: Anti-Slavery International.

15. These were troops who had been loyal to Chiang Kai Shek. When he fled to Taiwan in 1949 they escaped the Communists by crossing the border into Burma. Many of the Kuomingtang troops had fought alongside the British and Americans against the Japanese (and the local allies of the Japanese in the Burmese Independence Army). This meant they were trying to invade China from a region also occupied by the pro-Chinese Burmese Communist Party and were being pressed by their former enemies, who now made up the Burmese army.

16. Callahan, M. P. 2005. *Making Enemies: War and State Building in Burma*, p. 157.

17. Mathieson, D. S. 2004. 'The Enemy Within' [Online]. Rangoon: *The Irrawaddy*.

Available: http://www2.irrawaddy.org/article.php?art_id=963 [Accessed 27 June 2015].

18. Callahan, M. P. 2005. *Making Enemies: War and State Building in Burma.*

19. Ibid.

20. Charney, M. W. 2009. *A History of Modern Burma*, Cambridge: Cambridge University Press.

21. Walton, M. & Hayward, S. 2014. *Contesting Buddhist Narratives*, p. 10.

22. Htwe, R. 1990. 'Monthly Report: December'. Karen Refugee Council.

23. Goldston, J. 1990. *Human Rights in Burma (Myanmar)*, New York: Human Rights Watch.

24. Rangoon Suspense 2002. 'Report Card, Burma'. Bangkok: Alternative ASEAN Network on Burma.

25. *The Irrawaddy.* 1997a. 'Slaughter of the Innocent Soldiers' [Online]. Rangoon: *The Irrawaddy.* Available: http://www2.irrawaddy.org/article.php?art_id=847 [Accessed 27 June 2015].

26. Images Asia 1997. 'No Childhood at all: A Report about Child Soldiers in Burma'. Geneva: UN Quaker Office.

27. Win, T. L. 2014a. 'Burmese journalist beseeches brethren: Stop with the Muslim hate speech' [Online]. Thomson Reuters. Available: http://www.trust.org/item/20140313074529–3vfw4/ [Accessed 20 July 2015].

28. Venkateswaran, K. S. 1996. 'Burma: Beyond the Law'. Article 19. Available: https://www.article19.org/data/files/pdfs/publications/burma-beyond-law.pdf [Accessed 23 November 2015].

29. Mathieson, D. S. 2004. 'The Enemy Within'.

30. Venkateswaran, 'Burma: Beyond the Law'.

31. International Labour Organisation. 1998. 'Forced labour in Myanmar (Burma)' [Online]. Geneva: ILO. Available: http://www.ilo.org/public/english/standards/relm/gb/docs/gb273/myanmar3.htm [Accessed 1 March 2014].

32. BBC. 2007. 'Burma's 1988 protests' [Online]. London: BBC. Available: http://news.bbc.co.uk/1/hi/world/asia-pacific/7012158.stm [Accessed 28 June 2015].

33. Ibid.

34. Ibid.

35. Goldston, J. 1990. 'Human Rights in Burma (Myanmar)', New York: Human Rights Watch.

36. *The Irrawaddy.* 2007. 'Heroes and Villains'.

37. Case, W. 2002. *Politics in Southeast Asia: Democracy or Less*, Oxford: Routledge.

38. Zin, M. 2010. *Opposition Movements in Burma: The Question of Relevancy. Finding Dollars, Sense and Legitimacy in Burma.* Washington, D.C.: Woodrow Wilson International Center for Scholars.

39. Han, *1990 Multi Party Democracy: General Elections.*

40. As discussed earlier, Aung San Suu Kyi's father was a major figure in the indepen-

dence movement and her mother was a minister and later ambassador during part of the 1948–62 civilian government. Many other early leaders of the NLD were also closely connected to important civilian or military figures.

41. South, A. 2008. *Ethnic Politics in Burma*, London: Routledge.

42. Zin, M. 2010. *Opposition Movements in Burma: The Question of Relevancy. Finding Dollars, Sense and Legitimacy in Burma.*

43. Ibid.

44. Han, *1990 Multi Party Democracy: General Elections*. As discussed earlier, one consequence of the 1942 violence had been to end the old patchwork of Rohingya and Rakhine communities and to produce a Muslim north and Buddhist south. As early as 1988, the Arakan League for Democracy was effectively calling for the displacement of the Rohingyas from the north of the province.

45. Arakan Rohingya National Organisation. 2013. 'Rakhine Extremist Gang ALD & RNDP Disguised and Merged as ANP' [Online]. Available: http://www. rohingya.org/portal/index.php/burma/63-news—article/1074-analysis-rakhine-extremist-gang-ald-a-rndp-disguised-and-merged-as-anp.html [Accessed 18 June 2015].

46. Interview with Rohingya politician, then sitting in parliament, 2015 (left anonymous for safety).

47. Interview with U Kyaw Min, Yangon, 30 June 2015.

48. Han, *1990 Multi Party Democracy: General Elections*.

49. Arakan Rohingya National Organisation. 2013. 'Rakhine Extremist Gang ALD & RNDP Disguised and Merged as ANP'.

50. Han, *1990 Multi Party Democracy: General Elections*.

51. Interview with U Kyaw Min, Yangon, 30 June 2015.

52. Interview with Rohingya politician, then sitting in parliament, 2015 (left anonymous for safety).

53. Karen News. 2013. 'Facts on Burma' [Online]. Available: http://karennews.org/facts-on-burma/ [Accessed 26 February 2014].

54. Smith, M. 2011b. 'Time for New Approach to Burma: War Crimes Mounting' [Online]. *The World Post*. Available: http://www.huffingtonpost.com/matthew-smith/burma-war-crimes_b_906660.html [Accessed 26 February 2014].

55. Stoisiek, J. 2012. 'The Killings of Ethnic Minorities in Myanmar (Burma): Change in Myanmar's Politics after Elections in April 2012'. *Genocide Prevention Now*, 12, 1215–20.

56. Human Rights Documentation Unit. 2007. 'Burma Human Rights Yearbook' [Online]. Available: http://www.burmalibrary.org/docs5/HRDU-archive/Burma%20Human%20Righ/maps.html [Accessed 7 March 2014].

57. Rangoon Suspense 2002. 'Report Card, Burma'.

58. Holmes, R. A. 1967. 'Burmese domestic policy: the politics of Burmanization'. *Asian Survey*, 7:3, 188–197.

59. Charney, M. W. 2009. *A History of Modern Burma.*

60. Talbot, I. & Singh, G. 2009. *The Partition of India*, Cambridge: Cambridge University Press.

61. Foley, M. 2010. *The Cold War and National Assertion in Southeast Asia: Britain, the United States and Burma, 1948–1962*, London: Routledge.

62. Ibid.

63. Ibid.

64. Abraham, I. 2008. 'From Bandung to NAM: Non-Alignment and Indian Foreign Policy, 1947–65'. *Commonwealth & Comparative Politics*, 46:2, 195–219.

65. Steinberg, D. I. 2010. 'The United States and Myanmar: a 'boutique issue'?' *International Affairs*, 86:1, 175–194.

66. Busczynski, L. 1986. *Soviet Foreign Policy and Southeast Asia*, London: Routledge.

67. International Crisis Group 2001. 'Myanmar: The Military Regime's View of the World'. Bangkok: International Crisis Group.

68. Goldston, J. 1990. 'Human Rights in Burma (Myanmar)', New York: Human Rights Watch; Images Asia 1997. 'No Childhood at all: A Report about Child Soldiers in Burma'. Geneva: UN Quaker Office; International Labour Organisation. 1998. 'Forced labour in Myanmar (Burma)'.

69. Lintner, B. 2013. 'Myanmar, North Korea stay brothers in arms' [Online]. *Asia Times*. Available: http://www.atimes.com/atimes/Southeast_Asia/SEA-01–050913.html [Accessed 27 June 2015].

70. Ibid.

71. Selth, A. 2004. 'Pariah Partners in Arms' [Online]. Rangoon: *The Irrawaddy*. Available: http://www2.irrawaddy.org/article.php?art_id=933 [Accessed 19 August 2015].

72. BBC. 2005. 'Rice names "outposts of tyranny"' [Online]. London: BBC. Available: http://news.bbc.co.uk/1/hi/world/americas/4186241.stm [Accessed 27 June 2015].

73. Lintner, B. 2013. 'Myanmar, North Korea stay brothers in arms'.

74. Mathieson, D. S. 2003. 'The March of Folly' [Online]. Rangoon: *The Irrawaddy*. Available: http://www2.irrawaddy.org/article.php?art_id=3050 [Accessed 27 June 2015].

75. Selth, A. 2004. 'Pariah Partners in Arms'.

76. Selth, A. 2008. 'Burma's continuing fear of invasion' [Online]. *The Interpreter*. Available: http://www.lowyinterpreter.org/post/2008/05/28/Burmas-continuing-fear-of-invasion.aspx [Accessed 27 June 2015].

77. Roughneen, S. 2010. 'China Backs Burma's Junta Leaders' [Online]. OilPrice. Available: http://oilprice.com/Geopolitics/Asia/China-Backs-Burmas-Junta-Leaders.html [Accessed 1 July 2015].

78. Lintner, B. 2013. 'Myanmar, North Korea stay brothers in arms'.

79. Selth, A. 2008. 'Burma's continuing fear of invasion'.

80. BBC. 2005. 'Rice names "outposts of tyranny"'.

81. Tucker, J. 2007. 'Enough! Electoral Fraud, Collective Action Problems, and Post-Communist Coloured Revolutions'. *Perspectives on Politics*, 5:3, 537–53.

82. Selth, A. 2008. 'Burma's continuing fear of invasion'.

83. International Crisis Group 2001. 'Myanmar: The Military Regime's View of the World'. Bangkok: International Crisis Group, p. 9; speech was by Senior General Saw Maung in 1989.

84. Boot, W. 2007. 'Step on the Gas' [Online]. Rangoon: *The Irrawaddy*. Available: http://www2.irrawaddy.org/article.php?art_id=7735 [Accessed 1 July 2015].

85. Roughneen, S. 2010. 'China Backs Burma's Junta Leaders'.

86. Irish Centre for Human Rights 2010. 'Crimes against Humanity in Western Burma: The Situation of the Rohingyas'. Galway: Irish Centre for Human Rights.

87. Quintana, T. O. 2014. 'Report of the Special Rapporteur on the situation of human rights in Myanmar'. Geneva: United Nations General Assembly.

88. Constituent Assembly 1947. 'The Constitution of the Union of Burma'. Rangoon: Foreign Office.

89. Article 19 1996. 'Burma: Beyond the Law'. London: Global Campaign for Free Expression.

90. Constituent Assembly 1947. 'The Constitution of the Union of Burma'. Rangoon: Foreign Office; FIDH 2000. 'Burma: repression, discrimination and ethnic cleansing in Arakan'. Paris: International Federation of Human Rights Leagues.

91. Lwin, N. S. 2012. 'Making Rohingya Stateless' [Online]. Rangoon: New Mandala. Available: http://asiapacific.anu.edu.au/newmandala/2012/10/29/making-rohingya-statelessness/ [Accessed 8 July 2015].

92. Shah, I. 2015. 'Rohingyas' demand Burmese Gov't: either historically disprove "the ethnical term Rohingya" or pay back their indigenous rights' [Online]. Rangoon: *Burma Times*. Available: http://burmatimes.net/rohingyas-demand-burmese-govt-either-historically-disprove-the-ethnical-term-rohingya-or-pay-back-their-indigenous-rights/ [Accessed 8 July 2015].

93. Baxter, J. 1941. *Report on Indian Immigration*. Rangoon: India Office.

94. Constituent Assembly 1947. 'The Constitution of the Union of Burma'. Rangoon: Foreign Office; FIDH 2000. 'Burma: repression, discrimination and ethnic cleansing in Arakan'.

95. Pugh, C. L. 2013. 'Is Citizenship the Answer? Constructions of belonging and exclusion for the stateless Rohingya of Burma'. Oxford: International Migration Institute.

96. Citizenship Election Officer 1948. 'Indigenous Race Recognition'.

97. Min, U. K. 2012. 'An Assessment of the Question of Rohingya's Nationality: Legal Nexus between Rohingya and the State'. Rangoon.

98. Tahay, A. 2014. *Challenges on Rohingya's Citizenship*. Japan.

99. Lwin, N. S. 2012. 'Making Rohingya Stateless'.

100. Min, U. K. 2012. 'An Assessment of the Question of Rohingya's Nationality: Legal Nexus between Rohingya and the State'.

101. Bank of Knowledge 1964. *Scripture of Myanmar Encyclopedia*, Rangoon, p. 89.

102. Pugh, C. L. 2013. 'Is Citizenship the Answer? Constructions of belonging and exclusion for the stateless Rohingya of Burma'.; and Venkateswaran, 'Burma: Beyond the Law'.

103. Government of the Union of Burma 1974. 'The Constitution of the Socialist Republic of the Union of Burma'. Rangoon.

104. Refworld. 1982. 'Burma Citizenship Law' [Online]. UNHCR. Available: http://www.refworld.org/docid/3ae6b4f71b.html [Accessed 2014 28 February].

105. This is in direct contravention of the Universal Declaration of Human Rights, art. 15(2) ('No one shall be arbitrarily deprived of his nationality'); International Convention on the Elimination of all Forms of Racial Discrimination, art. 5(d) (iii) (governments shall 'undertake … to guarantee the right of everyone, without distinction as to race, colour, or national or ethnic origin, to equality before the law, notably in … the right to nationality'); International Covenant on Civil and Political Rights, art. 26 ('The law shall … guarantee to all persons equal and effective protection against discrimination on any ground such as race').

106. Refworld. 1982. 'Burma Citizenship Law'.

107. Human Rights Watch. 2000. 'Malaysia/Burma: Living in Limbo' [Online]. Available: http://www.hrw.org/reports/2000/malaysia/maybr008–01.htm [Accessed 28 February 2014].

108. Pugh, C. L. 2013. 'Is Citizenship the Answer? Constructions of belonging and exclusion for the stateless Rohingya of Burma'.

109. Article 19 1996. 'Burma: Beyond the Law'. London: Global Campaign for Free Expression.

110. Interview with U Kyaw Min, Yangon, 30 June 2015.

111. Feeny, T. 2001. *Rohingya Refugee Children in Cox's Bazar, Bangladesh*. Oxford: Refugee Studies Centre; Kiragu, E., Rosi, A. L. & Morris, T. 2011. *States of Denial: A review of UNHCR's response to the protracted situation of stateless Rohingya refugees in Bangladesh*. UNHCR.

112. Amnesty International 2004. *Myanmar. The Rohingya Minority: Fundamental Rights Denied*, London: Amnesty International, p. 5.

113. Sharples, R. 2003. 'Repatriating the Rohingya'. *Burma Issues*, 13:3, 1–3.

114. Médecins Sans Frontières 2002. '10 Years for the Rohingya Refugees in Bangladesh: Past, Present and Future'. Médecins Sans Frontières, p. 10.

115. Ibid.

116. Interview with Rohingya politician, then sitting in parliament, 2015 (left anonymous for safety).

117. Interview with U Kyaw Min, Yangon, 30 June 2015.

118. International Labour Organisation. 1998. 'Forced labour in Myanmar (Burma)'

[Online]. Geneva: ILO. Available: http://www.ilo.org/public/english/standards/relm/gb/docs/gb273/myanmar3.htm [Accessed 1 March 2014], International Labour Organisation 2013a. 'Forced labour in Myanmar (Burma)'. Geneva: United Nations.

119. Medecins Sans Frontieres 2002. '10 Years for the Rohingyas Refugees in Bangladesh: Past, Present and Future', p. 11.

120. Irish Centre for Human Rights 2010. 'Crimes against Humanity in Western Burma: The Situation of the Rohingyas', Galway: Irish Centre for Human Rights.

121. Lewa, C. 2009. 'North Arakan: an open prison of the Rohingyas in Burma'. Forced Migration Review.

122. Lewa, C. 2003. 'We are like a soccer ball, kicked by Burma, kicked by Bangladesh!' Forum Asia.

123. FIDH 2000. 'Burma: repression, discrimination and ethnic cleansing in Arakan'. Paris: International Federation of Human Rights Leagues.

124. Ragland, T. K. 1994. 'Burma's Rohingyas in Crisis: Protection of "Humanitarian" Refugees under International Law'. *Boston College Third World Law Journal*, 14:2, 301–38.

125. Human Rights Watch. 2000. 'Malaysia/Burma: Living in Limbo'.

126. US Campaign For Burma. 2014. 'Top 4 Racist Laws against Rohingya Muslims in Burma' [Online]. Washington, D.C.: US Campaign For Burma. Available: https://uscampaignforburma.wordpress.com/2014/03/26/racism-in-burma-4-discriminatory-laws-against-rohingya-muslims/ [Accessed 20 February 2015].

127. Gutter, P. 2001. 'Law and Religion in Burma'. *Legal Issues of Burma Journal*, 8, 1–69.

128. Asian Human Rights Commission 2011. 'Diagnosing the un-rule of law in Burma: A submission to the UN Human Rights Council's Universal Periodic Review', Hong Kong: AHRC.

129. Ibid.

3. THE RETURN TO DEMOCRACY (2008–2015)

1. *The Economist*. 2007. 'How Myanmar's people rose up against its regime—and the regime rose up against its people' [Online]. London: *The Economist*. Available: http://www.economist.com/node/9868041 [Accessed 28 June 2015].

2. Walton, M. & Hayward, S. 2014. *Contesting Buddhist Narratives*.

3. Seekins, D. M. 2008. 'The Social, Political and Humanitarian Impact of Burma's Cyclone Nargis'. *Asia-Pacific Journal*.

4. Selth, A. 2008. 'Burma's continuing fear of invasion'.

5. In which case, under International Law, military intervention is acceptable, as the state is failing in its primary duty to protect its own population. See, for example: Alkire, S. 2003. *A Conceptual Framework for Human Security*. Oxford: Centre for Research on Inequality, Human Security and Ethnicity, CRISE; Doyle, M. W. &

Sambanis, N. 2006. *Making War and Building Peace*, Princeton, NJ: Princeton University Press; Kerr, P., Tow, W. T. & Hanson, M. 2003. 'The Utility of the Human Security Agenda for Policymakers'. *Asian Journal of Political Science*, 11:2, 89–114; Paris, R. 2001. 'Human Security: Paradigm Shift or Hot Air?' *International Security*, 26:2, 87–102.

6. Seekins, D. M. 2008. 'The Social, Political and Humanitarian Impact of Burma's Cyclone Nargis'.

7. Ibid., p. 4.

8. Linn, Z. 2015. 'Burma: Shattering of a democracy dream?' [Online]. The Stateless Rohingya. Available: http://www.thestateless.com/2015/08/burma-shattering-of-a-democracy-dream.html [Accessed 18 August 2015].

9. Myanmar 2008. 'Constitution of the Republic of the Union of Myanmar'.

10. Human Rights Watch. 1996. 'Burma: The Rohingyas Muslims: Ending a Cycle of Exodus?' [Online]. UNHCR. Available: http://www.refworld.org/cgi-bin/texis/vtx/rwmain?page=printdoc&docid=3ae6a84a2 [Accessed 28 February 2014].

11. The Rakhine Inquiry Commission, Final report, July 8, 2013, cited in Smith, M. 2014. 'Politics of Persecution'. Fortify Rights International, p. 22.

12. Zaw, A. & Yeni. 2010. 'The NLD Makes its Move' [Online]. Rangoon: *The Irrawaddy*. Available: http://www2.irrawaddy.org/article.php?art_id=18216 [Accessed 30 June 2015].

13. Zin, M. 2010. *Opposition Movements in Burma: The Question of Relevancy. Finding Dollars, Sense and Legitimacy in Burma*.

14. Humanitarian Information Unit 2012. *Burma 2010 Election Results: One small step for democracy?* Washington, D.C.: US Department of State, p. 1.

15. Kyaw, K. 2012. 'Analysis of Myanmar's NLD landslide'.

16. Hidalgo, F. D. & Nichter, S. 2015. 'Voter Buying: Shaping the Electorate through Clientelism'. *American Journal of Political Science*.

17. World Elections. 2012. 'Burma (Myanmar) by-elections 2012' [Online]. Available: http://welections.wordpress.com/2012/04/06/burma-by-elections-2012/ [Accessed 8 March 2014].

18. Kyaw, K. 2012. 'Analysis of Myanmar's NLD landslide'.

19. Heinemann, T. 2015. 'Misunderstanding Myanmar's Military'.

20. Ribeiro, E. H. 2013. 'Military can still be good state-builders in Myanmar'.

21. Ibid.

22. Heinemann, T. 2015. 'Misunderstanding Myanmar's Military'.

23. Zarni, M. 2012. 'Popular "Buddhist" racism and the generals' militarism' [Online]. Oslo: DVB. Available: https://www.dvb.no/analysis/popular-buddhist-racism-and-the-generals%E2%80%99-militarism/23595 [Accessed 21 February 2015].

24. Win, T. L. 2014a. 'Burmese journalist beseeches brethren: Stop with the Muslim hate speech'; Zin, M. 2014. 'Return of the Myanmar Military?'.

25. Macdonald, A. P. 2015. 'Time to engage Myanmar's military'.

26. Walton, M. & Hayward, S. 2014. *Contesting Buddhist Narratives*.

27. Zin, M. 2014. 'Return of the Myanmar Military?'.

28. Jagan, L. 2014. 'Suu Kyi shifts pre-election tack in Myanmar'.

29. Zin, M. 2014. 'Return of the Myanmar Military?'.

30. Ribeiro, E. H. 2013. 'Military can still be good state-builders in Myanmar'.

31. Jagan, L. 2014. 'Suu Kyi shifts pre-election tack in Myanmar'.

32. Lewis, S. & Doherty, B. 2015. 'Turmoil in Burma's military-backed ruling party as leaders are deposed' [Online]. London: *The Guardian*. Available: http://www.theguardian.com/world/2015/aug/13/burmese-forces-surround-ruling-party-headquarters-and-confine-mps-report [Accessed 13 August 2015].

33. Reuters. 2015b. 'Myanmar's ousted ruling party leader Shwe Mann meets Aung San Suu Kyi' [Online]. Available: http://www.rohingyablogger.com/2015/08/myanmars-ousted-ruling-party-leader.html [Accessed 18 August 2015].

34. Moe, W. 2015. 'Aung San Suu Kyi Calls Ex-Leader of Myanmar Governing Party an "Ally"' [Online]. Asia Pacific. Available: http://www.nytimes.com/2015/08/19/world/asia/myanmar-aung-san-suu-kyi-calls-shwe-mann-an-ally.html?_r=0 [Accessed 19 August 2015].

35. Linn, Z. 2015. 'Burma: Shattering of a democracy dream?'

36. Ibid.

37. Kyaw, K. 2012. 'Analysis of Myanmar's NLD landslide'.

38. Loyn, D. 2011. 'Suu Kyi's NLD democracy party to rejoin Burma politics' [Online]. London: BBC. Available: http://www.bbc.co.uk/news/world-asia-15787605 [Accessed 16 October 2015].

39. World Elections. 2012. 'Burma (Myanmar) by-elections 2012'.

40. Jagan, L. 2014. 'Suu Kyi shifts pre-election tack in Myanmar'.

41. Loyn, D. 2011. 'Suu Kyi's NLD democracy party to rejoin Burma politics'.

42. Chachavalpongpun, P. 2012. 'The Vexing Strategic Tug-of-War over Naypyidaw: ASEAN's View of the Sino-Burmese Ties'. *Journal of Current Southeast Asian Affairs*, 31:1, 97–114.

43. Zin, M. 2010. *Opposition Movements in Burma: The Question of Relevancy. Finding Dollars, Sense and Legitimacy in Burma*.

44. Moe, W. 2015. Aung San Suu Kyi Calls Ex-Leader of Myanmar Governing Party an "Ally"'.

45. Article 19. 2015. 'Myanmar: Government's handling of Par Gyi criticised at UN HRC' [Online]. London: Article 19. Available: https://www.article19.org/resources.php/resource/38106/en/myanmar:-government%E2%80%99s-handling-of-par-gyi-criticised-at-un-hrc [Accessed 19 September 2015].

46. Walton, M. & Hayward, S. 2014. *Contesting Buddhist Narratives*.

47. Ibid.

48. Marshall, A. R. C. 'Myanmar gives official blessing to anti-Muslim monks', Reuters,

27 June 2013, available online at http://uk.reuters.com/article/2013/06/27/us-myanmar-969-specialreport-idUSBRE95Q04720130627 (accessed 26 January 2016).

49. McGowan, W. 2012. 'Burma's Buddhist Chauvinism' [Online]. New York: *Wall Street Journal*. Available: http://www.wsj.com/articles/SB10000872396390443 84740457762887414752869 2 [Accessed 8 July 2015].

50. Zin, M. 2014. 'Return of the Myanmar Military?'.

51. Strathern, A. 2013. 'Why are Buddhist monks attacking Muslims?'.

52. Walton, M. 2013b. 'A Primer on the Roots of Buddhist/Muslim Conflict in Myanmar and a Way Forward'; Walton, M. & Hayward, S. 2014. *Contesting Buddhist Narratives*.

53. Bischoff, R. 1996. *Buddhism in Myanmar: A short history*.

54. Leider, J. P. 2008. 'Forging Buddhist Credentials as a Tool for Legitimacy and Ethnic Identity: A Study of Arakan's Subjection in Nineteenth Century Burma'. *Journal of the Economic and Social History of the Orient*, 51, 409–59.

55. Ruthven, M. 2002. *A Fury for God: The Islamist Attack on America*, London: Granta.

56. Ibrahim, A. 2014. *The Resurgence of Al-Qaeda in Syria and Iraq*. Washington, D.C.: SSI.

57. Walton, M. 2013a. 'Myanmar needs a new nationalism' [Online]. *Asia Times*. Available: http://www.atimes.com/atimes/Southeast_Asia/SEA-02-200513.html [Accessed 16 July 2015].

58. Galache, C. S. 2013. 'Who are the Monks behind Burma's "969" Campaign?' [Online]. Democratic Voice of Burma. Available: http://www.dvb.no/news/features-news/the-monks-behind-burmas-969-movement [Accessed 17 September 2015].

59. BBC. 2015a. 'Dalai Lama presses Aung San Suu Kyi over Rohingya migrants' [Online]. BBC: London. Available: http://www.bbc.co.uk/news/world-asia-3292 5805 [Accessed 15 June 2015].

60. Ibid.

61. Collins, G. 2015. 'Dalai Lama gets Mischievous' [Online]. New York: *New York Times*. Available: http://www.nytimes.com/2015/07/16/opinion/nicholas-kristof-dalai-lama-gets-mischievous.html?ref=opinion&_r=0 [Accessed 20 July 2015].

62. Sarkar, A. K. 1993. *The Mysteries of Vajrayana Buddhism: From Atisha to Dalai Lama*, Coburg, Au: South Asia Books.

63. Kyohan, B. 1995. *The Classification of Buddhism*, Wiesbaden: Harrassowitz Verlag.

64. Interview with local journalists from *Myanmar Times*, *Burma Times* and *The Guardian*.

65. Fuller, P. 31 August 2014. 'Ban Ki Moon Comments on Buddhist Extremism'. Available from: https://drpaulfuller.wordpress.com/category/burma/ [Accessed 28 June 2015].

66. Coclanis, P. A. 2013. 'Terror in Burma: Buddhists vs. Muslims' [Online]. Washington, D.C.: World Affairs. Available: http://www.worldaffairsjournal.org/article/terror-burma-buddhists-vs-muslims [Accessed 29 June 2015].

67. Preston, A. 2015. 'Saffron Terror: an audience with Burma's 'Buddhist Bin Laden' Ashin Wirathu' [Online]. London: *GQ*. Available: http://www.gq-magazine.co.uk/comment/articles/2015–02/12/ashin-wirathu-audience-with-the-buddhist-bin-laden-burma [Accessed 28 June 2015].

68. Ibid.

69. Justice Trust 2015. *Hidden Hands Behind Communal Violence in Myanmar: Case Study of the Mandalay Riots*. New York: Justice Trust; Keane, F. 2012. 'The Burmese monks who preach intolerance against Muslim Rohingyas' [Online]. London: BBC. Available: http://www.bbc.co.uk/news/world-asia-20427889 [Accessed 18 June 2015]; Tharor, I. 2015. 'Why does this Buddhist-majority nation hate these Muslims so much?' [Online]. Washington, D.C.: *The Washington Post*. Available: http://www.washingtonpost.com/blogs/worldviews/wp/2015/02/13/why-does-this-buddhist-majority-nation-hate-these-muslims-so-much/ [Accessed 18 February 2015].

70. Walton, M. & Hayward, S. 2014. *Contesting Buddhist Narratives*.

71. Preston, A. 2015. 'Saffron Terror: an audience with Burma's "Buddhist Bin Laden" Ashin Wirathu'.

72. Walton, M. & Hayward, S. 2014. *Contesting Buddhist Narratives*, p. 23.

73. Interview with U Kyaw Min, Yangon, 30 June 2015.

74. Walton, M. & Hayward, S. 2014. *Contesting Buddhist Narratives*.

75. Interview with U Kyaw Min, Yangon, 30 June 2015.

76. United Nations Human Rights. 2015. 'Myanmar: UN rights experts express alarm at adoption of first of four "protection of race and religion" bills' [Online]. New York: Office of the High Commissioner for Human Rights. Available: http://www.ohchr.org/EN/NewsEvents/Pages/DisplayNews.aspx?NewsID=16015&LangID=E [Accessed 28 June 2015].

77. Stratfor 2015. 'The Buddhist Core of Fractured Myanmar'. Washington, D.C.: Stratfor Global Intelligence.

78. Stout, D. 2015. 'Burma Jails New Zealander for 'Insulting Buddhism' in Facebook Post' [Online]. *Time Magazine*. Available: http://time.com/3747187/burma-buddhism-new-zealand-phil-blackwood/ [Accessed 28 June 2015].

79. Walton, M. 2014. 'What are Myanmar's Buddhist Sunday schools teaching?' [Online]. East Asia Forum. Available: http://www.eastasiaforum.org/2014/12/16/what-are-myanmars-buddhist-sunday-schools-teaching/ [Accessed 16 July 2015].

80. Walton, M. & Hayward, S. 2014. *Contesting Buddhist Narratives*.

81. Walton, M. 2014. 'What are Myanmar's Buddhist Sunday schools teaching?'.

82. Walton, M. 2013b. 'A Primer on the Roots of Buddhist/Muslim Conflict in Myanmar and a Way Forward'.

83. Win, S. 2015. 'Special Report—With official help, Myanmar's radical Buddhists target Muslim-owned businesses' [Online]. Rangoon: *Myanmar Now*. Available: http://www.myanmar-now.org/news/i/?id=9ba61afc-285d-49bd-8f73–8b9efaf941c0 [Accessed 21 September 2015].

84. Ibid.

85. Ibid.

86. Snaing, Y. 2014. 'Activists Face Violent Threats After Opposing Interfaith Marriage Bill' [Online]. Rangoon: *The Irrawaddy*. Available: http://www.irrawaddy.org/burma/activists-face-violent-threats-opposing-interfaith-marriage-bill.html [Accessed 16 July 2015].

87. Stratfor 2015. *The Buddhist Core of Fractured Myanmar*. Washington, D.C.: Stratfor Global Intelligence.

88. Win, T. L. 2014a. 'Burmese journalist beseeches brethren: Stop with the Muslim hate speech'.

89. Interview with U Kyaw Min, Yangon, 30 June 2015.

90. Stoakes, E. 2015. 'Monks, PowerPoint Presentations, and Ethnic Cleansing'.

91. Walton, M. 2013b. 'A Primer on the Roots of Buddhist/Muslim Conflict in Myanmar and a Way Forward'.

92. Win, T. L. 2014b. 'Myanmar activists launch anti-"hate speech" campaign'. Schissler, M. 2014. 'May Flowers' [Online]. New Mandala. Available: http://asiapacific.anu.edu.au/newmandala/2014/05/17/may-flowers/ [Accessed 16 July 2015].

93. Win, T. L. 2014b. 'Myanmar activists launch anti-"hate speech" campaign'.

94. Ibid.

95. Walton, M. & Hayward, S. 2014. *Contesting Buddhist Narratives*, p. 16.

96. Schissler, M. 2014. 'May Flowers'.

97. Michaels, S. 2014. 'Suu Kyi Meets Critics of "Protection of Race and Religion" Bills'.

98. Snaing, Y. 2014. 'Activists Face Violent Threats After Opposing Interfaith Marriage Bill'.

99. Win, T. L. 2014a. 'Burmese journalist beseeches brethren: Stop with the Muslim hate speech'.

100. Interview with local journalists from *Myanmar Times*, *Burma Times* and *The Guardian*.

101. Associated Press. 2013. 'Buddhist monks offer shelter to persecuted Burma Muslims' [Online]. Washington, D.C.: CBS News. Available: http://www.cbsnews.com/news/buddhist-monks-offer-shelter-to-persecuted-burma-muslims/ [Accessed 16 September 2015].

102. Ibid.

103. Interview with Steven Kiersons, Team Lead for Burma, Sentinel Project on Genocide Prevention, 24 October 2015.

104. Pitman, T. & Peck, G. 2013. 'Radical monks, prejudice fuel Myanmar violence' [Online]. Associated Press. Available: http://www.thejakartapost.com/news/2013/06/01/radical-monks-prejudice-fuel-myanmar-violence.html [Accessed 16 September 2015].

105. Walton, M. 2013a. 'Myanmar needs a new nationalism'.

106. Walton, M. & Hayward, S. 2014. *Contesting Buddhist Narratives*.

107. Walton, M. & Hayward, S. 2014. *Contesting Buddhist Narratives*, pp. 30–4.

108. Tun, A. H. 2014. 'Myanmar sees foreign investment topping $5 bln in 2014–15' [Online]. Reuters. Available: http://www.reuters.com/article/2014/09/16/myanmar-investment-idUSL3N0RH3EZ20140916 [Accessed 20 April 2015].

109. Triveldi, S. 2013. 'New role for India in Myanmar' [Online]. *Asia Times*. Available: http://www.atimes.com/atimes/Southeast_Asia/SEA-01–160913.html [Accessed 26 February 2014].

110. Ibid.

111. Egreteau, R. 2012. 'Burmese Tango: Indian and Chinese Games and Gains in Burma (Myanmar) since 1988'. *In:* Devare, S. T., Singh, S. & Marwah, R. (eds.) *Emerging China: Prospects of Partnership in Asia*. New Delhi: Routledge.

112. Li, Q. 2015. *North Myanmar Minority Issues and its Impact on China-Myanmar Relations. Burma/Myanmar in Transition: Connectivity, Changes and Challenges.* Chiang Mai University, Thailand.

113. Smith, M. 2015. 'How China Fuels Myanmar's Wars' [Online]. New York: *New York Times*. Available: http://www.nytimes.com/2015/03/05/opinion/how-china-fuels-myanmars-wars.html?_r=1 [Accessed 20 August 2015].

114. Quintana, T. O. 2014. 'Report of the Special Rapporteur on the situation of human rights in Myanmar'. Geneva: United Nations General Assembly.

115. Slim, W. J. 1956. *Defeat into Victory: Battling Japan in Burma and India 1942–1945*, New York: Cooper Square.

116. Preston, A. 2015. 'Saffron Terror: an audience with Burma's "Buddhist Bin Laden" Ashin Wirathu'.

117. Interview with Steven Kiersons, 24 October 2015.

118. Farrelly, N. 2015. 'On China, the Lady has no choice' [Online]. *Myanmar Times*. Available: http://asiapacific.anu.edu.au/newmandala/2015/07/08/on-china-the-lady-has-no-choice/ [Accessed 20 August 2015].

119. Ibid.

120. Preston, A. 2015. 'Saffron Terror: an audience with Burma's 'Buddhist Bin Laden' Ashin Wirathu'.

121. Alessi, C. & Xu, B. 2015. 'China in Africa' [Online]. Council for Foreign Relations. Available: http://www.cfr.org/china/china-africa/p9557 [Accessed 2 June 2015].

122. Selth, A. 2008. 'Burma's continuing fear of invasion'.

123. Macdonald, A. P. 2015. 'Time to engage Myanmar's military'.

124. *Pakistan Today*. 2011. 'Pakistan to facilitate Chinese investment in all sectors: PM' [Online]. Available: http://www.pakistantoday.com.pk/2011/06/pakistan-to-facilitate-chinese-investment-in-all-sectors-pm/ [Accessed 9 July 2011].

125. Dosch, J. & Sidhu, J. S. 2015. 'The European Union's Myanmar Policy: Focused or Directionless?' *Journal of Current Southeast Asian Affairs*, 34:2, 85–112.

126. Reuters. 2012. 'EU welcomes "measured" Myanmar response to rioting' [Online]. Brussels: Reuters. Available: http://uk.reuters.com/article/2012/06/11/us-myanmar-violence-idUSBRE85A01C20120611 [Accessed 18 June 2015].

127. EurActiv. 2013. 'EU lifts Myanmar sanctions, except arms embargo' [Online]. Brussels: EurActiv.com. Available: http://www.euractiv.com/global-europe/eu-lifts-myanmar-sanctions-arms-news-519303 [Accessed 15 January 2015].

128. Dosch, J. & Sidhu, J. S. 2015. 'The European Union's Myanmar Policy: Focused or Directionless?'

129. ASEAN Parliamentarians for Human Rights 2015. 'Disenfranchisement and Desperation in Myanmar's Rakhine State: Drivers of a Regional Crisis'. APHR; *Burma Times*. 2015. 'In Burma's historic elections, a Muslim minority is banned from voting but still the focus of the campaign' [Online]. Rangoon: *Burma Times*. Available: http://burmatimes.net/in-burmas-historic-elections-a-muslim-minority-is-banned-from-voting-but-still-the-focus-of-the-campaign/ [Accessed 19 October 2015]; Mepham, D. 2015. 'What Burma's Elections Mean for the Rohingyas' [Online]. Human Rights Watch. Available: https://www.hrw.org/news/2015/10/08/what-burmas-elections-mean-rohingya [Accessed 11 October 2015]; Wong, C. 2015. 'Burma: Activists Charged for Mocking Military Online' [Online]. Human Rights Watch. Available: https://www.hrw.org/news/2015/10/17/burma-activists-charged-mocking-military-online [Accessed 19 October 2015].

130. Selth, A. 2008. 'Burma's continuing fear of invasion'.

131. Interview conducted by the author with Rohingya politician, left anonymous for safety, in Yangon, June 2015.

132. Chachavalpongpun, P. 2012. 'The Vexing Strategic Tug-of-War over Naypyidaw: ASEAN's View of the Sino-Burmese Ties'. *Journal of Current Southeast Asian Affairs*, 31:1, 97–114.

133. Ibid.

134. Triveldi, S. 2013. 'New role for India in Myanmar' [Online]. *Asia Times*. Available: http://www.atimes.com/atimes/Southeast_Asia/SEA-01-160913.html [Accessed 26 February 2014].

135. Bünte, M. & Dosch, J. 2015. 'Myanmar: Political Reforms and the Recalibration of External Relations'. *Journal of Current Southeast Asian Affairs*, 34:2, 3–19.

136. Pugh, C. L. 2013. 'Is Citizenship the Answer? Constructions of belonging and exclusion for the stateless Rohingya of Burma'. Oxford: International Migration Institute.

137. Bünte, M. & Dosch, J. 2015. 'Myanmar: Political Reforms and the Recalibration of External Relations'.

138. Interview with Rohingya politician, then sitting in parliament, 2015 (left anonymous for safety).

139. Cockett, R. 2015. *Blood, Dreams and Gold: The Changing Face of Burma*, New Haven, CT: Yale University Press.

140. Interview with Rohingya politician, then sitting in parliament, 2015 (left anonymous for safety).

141. Ibid.

4. IMPLICATIONS FOR THE ROHINGYAS (2008–2015)

1. Han, K. K. 2003. '1990 Multi Party Democracy: General Elections'.

2. McLaughlin, T. 2015b. 'Rising Arakanese Party could further marginalize Rohingya' [Online]. Reuters. Available: http://www.thestateless.com/2015/10/03/rising-arakanese-party-could-further-marginalize-rohingya/ [Accessed 13 October 2015].

3. Mepham, D. 2015. 'What Burma's Elections Mean for the Rohingyas'.

4. Arakan Rohingya National Organisation. 2013. 'Rakhine Extremist Gang ALD & RNDP Disguised and Merged as ANP' [Online]. Available: http://www.rohingya.org/portal/index.php/burma/63-news—article/1074-analysis-rakhine-extremist-gang-ald-a-rndp-disguised-and-merged-as-anp.html [Accessed 18 June 2015].

5. And, as noted several times, to add to the confusion both names continue in use. Here, the contemporary name will be used except when citing other works.

6. Arakan Rohingya National Organisation. 2013. 'Rakhine Extremist Gang ALD & RNDP Disguised and Merged as ANP'.

7. Interview conducted by author with Rohingya activist (left anonymous for their safety), 2015.

8. Human Rights Watch 2013a. '"All You Can Do is Pray": Crimes Against Humanity and Ethnic Cleansing of Rohingya Muslims in Burma's Arakan State'. Washington, D.C.: Human Rights Watch, p. 10.

9. Interview with U Kyaw Min, Yangon, 30 June 2015.

10. US Commission on International Religious Freedom 2011. 'Countries of Particular Concern: Burma'. Washington, D.C.: US Commission on International Religious Freedom.

11. International Crisis Group 2013. 'The Dark Side of Transition: Violence Against Muslims in Myanmar'.

12. Human Rights Watch 2013a. '"All You Can Do is Pray": Crimes Against Humanity and Ethnic Cleansing of Rohingya Muslims in Burma's Arakan State'.

13. Ibid.

14. Ibid.

15. Human Rights Watch 2012. 'The Government should have stopped this'. New York: Human Rights Watch, pp. 20–29.

16. Ibid.
17. Human Rights Watch 2013a. '"All You Can Do is Pray": Crimes Against Humanity and Ethnic Cleansing of Rohingya Muslims in Burma's Arakan State', p. 15.
18. Ibid.
19. Reuters. 2012. 'EU welcomes "measured" Myanmar response to rioting'.
20. Human Rights Watch. 2014a. 'Burma: Communal Violence Undercuts Rights Gains'.
21. Human Rights Watch. 2013. '"All You Can Do is Pray": Crimes Against Humanity and Ethnic Cleansing of Rohingya Muslims in Burma's Arakan State' [Online]. Available: https://www.hrw.org/report/2013/04/22/all-you-can-do-pray/crimes-against-humanity-and-ethnic-cleansing-rohingya-muslims [Accessed 29 March 2016].
22. Smith, M. 2014. 'Politics of Persecution'. Fortify Rights International.
23. Human Rights Watch 2013a. '"All You Can Do is Pray": Crimes Against Humanity and Ethnic Cleansing of Rohingya Muslims in Burma's Arakan State'.
24. Smith, M. 2014. 'Politics of Persecution'.
25. Human Rights Watch 2012. 'The Government should have stopped this'.
26. Ibid.
27. Keane, F. 2012. 'The Burmese monks who preach intolerance against Muslim Rohingyas'.
28. Arakan Rohingya National Organisation. 2013. 'Rakhine Extremist Gang ALD & RNDP Disguised and Merged as ANP'.
29. Equal Rights Trust 2014. 'The Human Rights of the Stateless Rohingya in Thailand'. London: Equal Rights Trust.
30. Human Rights Council 2014. 'Hear our Screams'.
31. Human Rights Watch 2013a. '"All You Can Do is Pray": Crimes Against Humanity and Ethnic Cleansing of Rohingya Muslims in Burma's Arakan State'.
32. Smith, M. 2014. 'Politics of Persecution'.
33. Win, T. L. 2014a. 'Burmese journalist beseeches brethren: Stop with the Muslim hate speech'.
34. Allchin, J. 2012. 'The Rohingya, myths and misinformation' [Online]. DVB. Available: http://www.dvb.no/analysis/the-rohingya-myths-and-misinformation/22597 [Accessed 18 June 2015].
35. *The Economist*. 2012. 'War Among the Pagodas'.
36. Human Rights Council 2014. 'Hear our Screams'.
37. Human Rights Watch 2013a. '"All You Can Do is Pray": Crimes Against Humanity and Ethnic Cleansing of Rohingya Muslims in Burma's Arakan State'.
38. Ibid.
39. Ibid.
40. Refugees International 2013. 'Myanmar'.
41. Amnesty International 2014. 'Myanmar: The Rohingyas Minority: Fundamental

Rights Denied'. London: Amnesty International; Andrews, T. & Sullivan, D. 2014. 'Marching to Genocide in Burma'. Washington, D.C.: United to End Genocide; Human Rights Watch 2013a. '"All You Can Do is Pray": Crimes Against Humanity and Ethnic Cleansing of Rohingya Muslims in Burma's Arakan State'.

42. Ibid.
43. Ibid.
44. Ibid.
45. Human Rights Council 2014. 'Hear our Screams'.
46. United Nations 2013. 'Situation of human rights in Myanmar'. New York: UN.
47. Human Rights Watch 2013a. '"All You Can Do is Pray": Crimes Against Humanity and Ethnic Cleansing of Rohingya Muslims in Burma's Arakan State'.
48. Quintana, T. O. 2014. 'Report of the Special Rapporteur on the situation of human rights in Myanmar'.
49. Ibid.
50. McLaughlin, T. 2015a. 'Government failed to ensure justice after riots: UN chief' [Online]. Reuters. Available: http://www.thestateless.com/2015/10/03/govt-failed-to-ensure-justice-after-riots-un-chief/ [Accessed 13 October 2015].
51. Kiersons, S., Stein, S., Kalmats, D. & Mediratta, R. 2013. 'Burma Risk Assessment'. Toronto: Sentinel Project for Genocide Prevention.
52. Walton, M. & Hayward, S. 2014. *Contesting Buddhist Narratives*, p. 17.
53. Human Rights Watch. 2014a. 'Burma: Communal Violence Undercuts Rights Gains' [Online].
54. Human Rights Council 2014. 'Hear our Screams'.
55. Ibid.
56. Human Rights Watch. 2014a. 'Burma: Communal Violence Undercuts Rights Gains'.
57. A map showing these locations is provided below as it also shows the location of the current internal refugee camps.
58. Quintana, T. O. 2014. 'Report of the Special Rapporteur on the situation of human rights in Myanmar'.
59. Fortify Rights 2014. 'Policies of Persecution: Ending Abusive State Policies Against Rohingya Muslims in Myanmar'.
60. International Crisis Group 2013. 'The Dark Side of Transition: Violence Against Muslims in Myanmar'.
61. Justice Trust 2015. 'Hidden Hands Behind Communal Violence in Myanmar: Case Study of the Mandalay Riots'. New York: Justice Trust.
62. Fortify Rights 2014. 'Policies of Persecution: Ending Abusive State Policies Against Rohingya Muslims in Myanmar'.
63. Hodal, K. 2014. 'Burma tells Medécins Sans Frontières to leave state hit by sectarian violence' [Online]. London: *The Guardian*. Available: http://www.the-guardian.com/world/2014/feb/28/burma-medecins-sans-frontieres-rakhine-state [Accessed 1 March 2014].

64. Ibid.

65. Information from ASEAN Parliamentarians for Human Rights 2015. 'Disenfranchisement and Desperation in Myanmar's Rakhine State: Drivers of a Regional Crisis'. APHR., p. 3

66. Quintana, T. O. 2014. 'Report of the Special Rapporteur on the situation of human rights in Myanmar'.

67. Walton, M. 2013b. 'A Primer on the Roots of Buddhist/Muslim Conflict in Myanmar and a Way Forward'.

68. Interview with Rohingya politician, then sitting in parliament, 2015 (left anonymous for safety).

69. Win, T. L. 2014d. 'Will the Rohingya, driven from their homes, spend the rest of their lives segregated in ghettoes?' [Online]. Thomson Reuters. Available: http://www.trust.org/item/20140827082155-p627d/ [Accessed 20 July 2015].

70. Ibid.

71. Win, T. L. 2014c. 'Sexism, racism, poor education condemn Rohingya women in western Myanmar' [Online]. Thomson Reuters. Available: http://www.trust.org/item/20140709164452-re3s1/ [Accessed 20 July 2015].

72. Hodal, K. 2014. 'Burma tells Medécins Sans Frontières to leave state hit by sectarian violence '.

73. Interview with U Kyaw Min, Yangon, 30 June 2015.

74. Human Rights Watch. 2014b. 'Burma: Government Plan Would Segregate Rohingya'.

75. Ibid.

76. Interview with Steven Kiersons, 24 October 2015.

77. Thein, T. 2015a. 'Man assaulted by military refused treatment by hospitals' [Online]. Rangoon: *Burma Times*. Available: http://burmatimes.net/man-assaulted-by-military-refused-treatment-by-hospitals/?utm_medium=twitter&utm_source=twitterfeed [Accessed 1 July 2015].

78. Interview with Steven Kiersons, 24 October 2015.

79. Human Rights Watch. 2015. 'Southeast Asia: Accounts from Rohingya Boat People' [Online]. HRW. Available: http://www.hrw.org/news/2015/05/27/southeast-asia-accounts-rohingya-boat-people [Accessed 15 June 2015].

80. Ibid.

81. McElwee, J. J. 2015. 'Francis: Burmese treatment of Rohingya minority a form of 'war'' [Online]. Kansas City: National Catholic Reporter. Available: http://ncronline.org/news/vatican/francis-burmese-treatment-rohingya-minority-form-war [Accessed 18 August 2015].

82. Environmental Justice Foundation 2014. 'Slavery at Sea: The Continued Plight of Trafficked Migrants in Thailand's Fishing Industry'. London: Environmental Justice Foundation.

83. International Labour Organisation. 2013b. 'Trafficked into slavery on Thai trawl-

ers to catch food for prawns' [Online]. Geneva: ILO. Available: http://apflnet.
ilo.org/news/trafficked-into-slavery-on-thai-trawlers-to-catch-food-for-prawns
[Accessed 15 June 2015].

84. Ibid.

85. Bales, K. 2012. *Disposable People: New Slavery in the Global Economy*, Berkeley,
CA: University of California Press.

86. International Labour Organisation. 2013b. 'Trafficked into slavery on Thai trawlers to catch food for prawns'.

87. *Bangkok Post*. 2015. 'Crime Navy commander faces arrest over trafficking' [Online].
Bangkok. Available: http://www.bangkokpost.com/news/crime/699884/navy-
commander-faces-arrest-over-trafficking [Accessed 21 September 2015].

88. Hodal, K. & Kelly, C. 2014. 'Trafficked into slavery on Thai trawlers to catch food
for prawns'.

89. Stoakes, E., Kelly, A. & Kelly, C. 2015. 'Revealed: how the Thai fishing industry
traffics, imprisons and enslaves' [Online]. London: *The Guardian*. Available:
http://www.theguardian.com/global-development/2015/jul/20/thai-fishing-
industry-implicated-enslavement-deaths-rohingya [Accessed 20 July 2015].

90. US Department of State. 2014. 'Trafficking in Persons Report: 2014 Report'
[Online]. Washington, D.C.: US Department of State. Available: http://www.
state.gov/j/tip/rls/tiprpt/ [Accessed 15 June 2015].

91. Stoakes, E., Kelly, A. & Kelly, C. 2015. 'Revealed: how the Thai fishing industry
traffics, imprisons and enslaves'.

92. Hodal, K. & Kelly, C. 2014. 'Trafficked into slavery on Thai trawlers to catch food
for prawns'.

93. Rohingya National Organisation 2015. 'Press Release: Save Rohingyas from the
hands of the human traffickers and greedy exploiters'.

94. Stokes, E. & Kelly, C. 2015. 'Asian refugee crisis: trafficked migrants held off
Thailand in vast "camp boats"'.

95. Thein, T. 2015b. 'Refugee injured in construction site' [Online]. Rangoon: *Burma
Times*. Available: http://burmatimes.net/refugee-injured-in-construction-site/
[Accessed 1 July 2015].

96. Stoakes, E., Kelly, A. & Kelly, C. 2015. 'Revealed: how the Thai fishing industry
traffics, imprisons and enslaves'.

97. Buckley, C. & Barry, E. 2015. 'Rohingya women fleeing Burma sold into marriage'
[Online]. Dublin: *Irish Times*. Available: http://www.irishtimes.com/news/
world/asia-pacific/rohingya-women-fleeing-burma-sold-into-marriage-1.2319703
[Accessed 18 August 2015].

98. Stokes, E. & Kelly, C. 2015. 'Asian refugee crisis: trafficked migrants held off
Thailand in vast "camp boats"'.

99. Interview with Steven Kiersons, 24 October 2015.

100. Human Rights Watch. 2015. 'Southeast Asia: Accounts from Rohingya Boat People'.

101. BBC. 2015c. 'Why are so many Rohingya migrants stranded at sea?' [Online]. London: BBC. Available: http://www.bbc.co.uk/news/world-asia-32740637 [Accessed 15 June 2015].

102. Interview with Steven Kiersons, 24 October 2015.

103. Cochrane, J. 2015. 'In Reversal, Myanmar Agrees to Attend Meeting on Migrant Crisis' [Online]. New York: *New York Times*. Available: http://www.nytimes. com/2015/05/22/world/asia/myanmar-rohingya-migrant-crisis-malaysia-thai-land-indonesia.html?_r=0 [Accessed 15 June 2015].

104. Ibid.

105. Thein, T. 2015b. 'Refugee injured in construction site'.

106. Graham, D. 2015. 'Burma Doesn't Want the Rohingyas but Insists on Keeping Them' [Online]. *The Atlantic*. Available: http://www.theatlantic.com/interna-tional/archive/2015/06/burma-rohingya-migration-ban/395729/ [Accessed 15 June 2015].

107. Reuters. 2015a. 'Burma military chief claims refugees pretending to be Rohingya to get aid' [Online]. London: *The Guardian*. Available: http://www.theguard-ian.com/world/2015/may/22/burma-military-chief-claims-refugees-pretend-ing-to-be-rohingya-to-get-aid [Accessed 15 June 2015].

108. Graham-Harrison, E. 2015. 'Burma's boatpeople "faced choice of annihilation or risking their lives at sea"' [Online]. London: *The Observer*. Available: http://www.theguardian.com/world/2015/may/17/rohingya-burma-refugees-boat-migrants [Accessed 15 June 2015].

109. Interview with U Kyaw Min, Yangon, 30 June 2015.

110. Aung, N. L. 2015. 'First human trafficking case in Rakhine to head to court' [Online]. *Myanmar Times*. Available: http://www.mmtimes.com/index.php/national-news/15939-first-human-trafficking-case-in-rakhine-to-head-to-court. html [Accessed 19 August 2015].

111. US Department of State. 2015. 'Trafficking in Persons Report: 2015 Report', p. 104.

112. Ibid.

113. Lefevre, A. S. & Marshall, A. R. C. 2014. 'Special Report: Traffickers use abduc-tions, prison ships to feed Asian slave trade' [Online]. Reuters. Available: http://www.reuters.com/article/2014/10/22/us-thailand-trafficking-specialreport-id USKCN0IB0A320141022http://www.reuters.com/article/2014/10/22/us-thailand-trafficking-specialreport-idUSKCN0IB0A320141022 [Accessed 20 September 2015].

114. Associated Press. 2015. 'Myanmar ex-slave: Those with sympathy would not eat our fish' [Online]. Associated Press. Available: http://hosted.ap.org/dynamic/stories/A/AS_FACES_OF_SLAVERY_KYAW_ZAYAR?SITE=AP&SECTI

ON=HOME&TEMPLATE=DEFAULT&CTIME=2015–09–18–01–48–09 [Accessed 20 September 2015].

115. Slodkowski, A. 2015. 'Beaten and starving, some Rohingya flee boats, return to camps' [Online]. Reuters. Available: http://www.rohingyablogger.com/2015/05/beaten-and-starving-some-rohingya-flee.html [Accessed 18 August 2015].

116. Lin, K. M. Z. 2015. 'India and Myanmar monsoon rains leave dozens dead' [Online]. London: BBC. Available: http://www.bbc.co.uk/news/world-asia-33745840 [Accessed 18 August 2015].

117. Slodkowski, A. 2015. 'Beaten and starving, some Rohingya flee boats, return to camps'.

118. Aung, A. 2015. 'Rohingya in Komen Cyclone' [Online]. The Stateless Rohingya. Available: http://www.thestateless.com/2015/08/rohingya-in-komen-cyclone.html [Accessed 17 August 2015].

5. GENOCIDE AND INTERNATIONAL LAW

1. International Crisis Group 2013. 'The Dark Side of Transition: Violence Against Muslims in Myanmar'.

2. Winn, P. 2013. 'Suu Kyi spokesman: 'There is no Rohingya' [Online]. *Global Post*. Available: http://www.globalpost.com/dispatch/news/regions/asia-pacific/myanmar/130501/suu-kyi-no-rohingya [Accessed 26 February 2014].

3. Teff, M. & Gopallawa, S. 2013. 'Myanmar: Protecting Minority Rights is non-Negotiable'. Refugees International.

4. Interview with Steven Kiersons, 24 October 2015.

5. Kin, T. 2015. 'Risk of Mass Atrocities and Policies of Persecution in Burma' [Online]. Early Warning Project. Available: http://www.earlywarningproject.com/2015/07/16/policies-of-persecution-in-burma [Accessed 15 October 2015].

6. United Nations 1951. 'Convention on the Prevention and Punishment of the Crime of Genocide'. Geneva: United Nations.

7. Human Rights Watch. 2014b. 'Burma: Government Plan Would Segregate Rohingya'; Win, T. L. 2014d. 'Will the Rohingya, driven from their homes, spend the rest of their lives segregated in ghettoes?'

8. United Nations. 2002. 'Rome Statute of the International Criminal Court' [Online]. UN. Available: http://legal.un.org/icc/statute/romefra.htm [Accessed 23 February 2014].

9. Harff, B. 2005. 'Assessing Risks of Genocide and Politicide'. *In:* Marshall, M. G. & Gurr, T. R. (eds.) *Peace and Conflict*. College Park, MD: Center for International Development and Conflict Management.

10. Interview with Steven Kiersons, 24 October 2015.

11. Jones, A. 2008. 'Genocide and Mass Killing'. *In:* Williams, P. D. (ed.) *Security Studies: An Introduction*. London: Routledge; Tharoor, I. 2015. 'The risk of geno-

cide around the world' [Online]. Washington, D.C.: *Washington Post*. Available: https://www.washingtonpost.com/news/worldviews/wp/2015/09/21/map-the-risk-of-genocide-around-the-world/ [Accessed 22 September 2015], United Nations. 2015. 'Genocide in Rwanda' [Online]. Geneva: United Nations Human Rights Council. Available: http://www.unitedhumanrights.org/genocide/genocide_in_rwanda.htm [Accessed 22 February 2015].

12. Brass, P. R. 2003. *The Production of Hindu-Muslim Violence in Contemporary India*, Washington, D.C.: University of Washington Press; Varshney, A. 2002. *Ethnic Conflict, Civic Life*, New Haven, CT: Yale University Press.

13. Fearon, J. D. & Laitin, D. 1996. 'Explaining Interethnic Cooperation'. *The American Political Science Review*, 90:4, 715–735.

14. Varshney, A. 2002. *Ethnic Conflict, Civic Life*.

15. Fisk, R. 2001. *Pity the Nation: Lebanon at War*, 3rd, Oxford: Oxford University Press; Glenny, M. 1996. *The Fall of Yugoslavia*, London: Penguin; Simms, B. 2001. *Unfinest Hour: Britain and the Destruction of Bosnia*, London: Penguin.

16. Brass, P. R. 2003. *The Production of Hindu-Muslim Violence in Contemporary India*.

17. Fearon, J. D. & Laitin, D. D. '2000. Violence and the Social Construction of Ethnic Identity'. *International Organization*, 54:4, 845–77.

18. Ferroggiaro, W. 2001. 'The US and the Genocide in Rwanda 1994: Evidence of Inaction'. Washington, D.C.: National Security Archive; Pierson, P. 2004. *Politics in Time: History, Institutions, and Social Analysis*, Princeton, NJ: Princeton University Press.

19. Fisk, R. 2001. *Pity the Nation: Lebanon at War*.

20. United Nations 1951. 'Convention on the Prevention and Punishment of the Crime of Genocide'. Geneva: United Nations; United Nations 2002. 'Rome Statute of the International Criminal Court' [Online]. UN. Available: http://legal.un.org/icc/statute/romefra.htm [Accessed 23 February 2014].

21. Perry, D. M. 1983. *Stefan Stambolov and the Emergence of Modern Bulgaria, 1870–1895*, Durham, NC: Duke University Press.

22. Hill, R. C. 2000. *The Balkan Wars 1912–1913: Prelude to the First World War*, London: Routledge.

23. Ahmad, F. 2014. *The Young Turks and the Ottoman Nationalities: Armenians, Greeks, Albanians, Jews, and Arabs, 1908–1918*, Salt Lake City, UT: University of Utah Press.

24. Pohl, J. O. 1999. *Ethnic Cleansing in the USSR, 1937–1949*, Westport, CT: Greenwood Press.

25. LeDonne, J. P. 2004. *The Grand Strategy of the Russian Empire 1650–1831*, Oxford: Oxford University Press.

26. Aselius, G. 2012. 'The Ottoman Absence from the Battlefields of the Seven Years' War'. *In:* Danley, M. H. & Speelman, P. J. (eds.) *The Seven Years' War: Global Views*. Leiden: Brill.

27. United Nations. 2015. 'Genocide in Rwanda'.

28. Ibid.

29. Weikart, R. 1993. 'The Origins of Social Darwinism in Germany, 1859–1895'. *Journal of the History of Ideas*, 54:3, 469–88.

30. Fritz, S. G. 2011. *Ostkrieg: Hitler's War of Extermination in the East*, Lexington, KY: University of Kentucky Press.

31. United Nations. 2015. 'Genocide in Rwanda'.

32. Fritz, S. G. 2011. *Ostkrieg: Hitler's War of Extermination in the East*.

33. Bryce, J. & Toynbee, A. 2000. *The Treatment of Armenians in the Ottoman Empire 1915–1916*, Reading: Taderon Press.

34. Ferroggiaro, W. 2001. 'The US and the Genocide in Rwanda 1994: Evidence of Inaction'.

35. Andrews, T. & Sullivan, D. 2014. 'Marching to Genocide in Burma'. Washington, D.C.: United to End Genocide.

36. United Nations 1951. 'Convention on the Prevention and Punishment of the Crime of Genocide'.

37. International Court of Justice 2015. 'Case Concerning Application of the Convention on the Prevention and Punishment of the Crime of Genocide (Croatia v Serbia)'. The Hague: International Court of Justice.

38. Jones, A. 2008. 'Genocide and Mass Killing'. *In:* Williams, P. D. (ed.) *Security Studies: An Introduction*. London: Routledge.

39. Quintana, T. O. 2014. 'Report of the Special Rapporteur on the situation of human rights in Myanmar'. Geneva: United Nations General Assembly.

40. Ibid. pp. 13–14.

41. DNA India. 2015. 'United Nations rights envoy says meeting with Myanmar's Rohingya blocked' [Online]. DNA. Available: http://www.dnaindia.com/world/report-united-nations-rights-envoy-says-meeting-with-myanmar-s-rohingya-blocked-2112331 [Accessed 19 August 2015].

42. United Nations 2013. 'Situation of human rights in Myanmar'. New York: UN.

43. Interview with Shabnum Mayet, a human rights lawyer and activist, 17 May 2015.

44. Interview with Steven Kiersons, 24 October 2015.

6. CURRENT SITUATION

1. Khin, T. 2015. 'Risk of Mass Atrocities and Policies of Persecution in Burma'.

2. Harff, B. 2005. 'Assessing Risks of Genocide and Politicide'.

3. Andrews, T. & Sullivan, D. 2014. 'Marching to Genocide in Burma'.

4. Early Warning Project. 2015. 'Myanmar'.

5. Mathies, C. E. 2013. 'Managing Peace and Security in Southeast Asia: Does ASEAN have the Political Will?'

6. Yee, T. H. 2015. 'Expect further Rohingya exodus, report warns' [Online]. Singapore: *The Straits Times*. Available: http://www.straitstimes.com/asia/se-asia/expect-further-rohingya-exodus-report-warns [Accessed 19 October 2015].

7. *Sydney Morning Herald*. 2015. '"They are humans": Myanmar opposition says Rohingya people have rights' [Online]. Sydney: *Sydney Morning Herald*. Available: http://www.smh.com.au/world/they-are-humans-myanmar-opposition-says-rohingya-people-have-rights-20150519-gh4q8m.html [Accessed 23 September 2015].

8. Myintzu, S. Y., Ei, K. K., Thu, K. & Kyaw, N. R. 2015. 'Myanmar Election Body Rejects Muslim Parliamentary Candidates' [Online]. Radio Free Asia. Available: http://www.rfa.org/english/news/myanmar/election-body-rejects-muslim-parliamentary-candidates-09012015161036.html [Accessed 22 September 2015].

9. *Burma Times*. 2015. 'In Burma's historic elections, a Muslim minority is banned from voting but still the focus of the campaign' [Online]. *Rangoon: Burma Times*. Available: http://burmatimes.net/in-burmas-historic-elections-a-muslim-minority-is-banned-from-voting-but-still-the-focus-of-the-campaign/ [Accessed 19 October 2015]; Mepham, D. 2015. 'What Burma's Elections Mean for the Rohingyas'.

10. Philip Heijmans, *The Diplomat*, Sept 2014, 'Myanmar's Controversial Census', http://thediplomat.com/2014/09/myanmars-controversial-census/ [Accessed 20 November 2015]

11. Republic of the Union of Myanmar 2014. 'The Population and Housing Census of Myanmar 2014'. Yangon: Department of Population.

12. Ibid., p. 4

13. Human Rights Watch. 2014b. 'Burma: Government Plan Would Segregate Rohingya'.

14. UCANEWS. 2015. 'Refugee boats set sail as monsoon season ends' [Online]. UCANEWS. Available: http://www.ucanews.com/news/refugee-boats-set-sail-as-monsoon-season-ends/74455 [Accessed 21 October 2015].

15. ASEAN Parliamentarians for Human Rights 2015. 'Disenfranchisement and Desperation in Myanmar's Rakhine State: Drivers of a Regional Crisis'. APHR.

16. Heijmans, P. 2014. 'Myanmar's Controversial Census'[Online]. *The Diplomat*. Available: http://thediplomat.com/2014/09/myanmars-controversial-census/ [Accessed 20 February 2015].

17. Hindstrom, H. 2015. 'In Myanmar, Muslim minority is targeted for hate, not for votes' [Online]. Al Jazeera, America. Available: http://america.aljazeera.com/articles/2015/9/20/muslim-minority-cut-out-of-myanmar-vote.html [Accessed 22 September 2015].

18. Myintzu, S. Y., Ei, K. K., Thu, K. & Kyaw, N. R. 2015. 'Myanmar Election Body Rejects Muslim Parliamentary Candidates'.

19. Ibid.

20. Ibid.

21. Caralucci, T. 2015. 'Myanmar's Aung San Suu Kyi Dodging or Driving the Rohingyas Crisis?' [Online]. New Eastern Outlook. Available: http://journal-neo.org/2015/06/20/myanmar-s-aung-san-suu-kyi-dodging-or-driving-the-rohingya-crisis/ [Accessed 22 September 2015].

22. Human Rights Watch. 2014a. 'Burma: Communal Violence Undercuts Rights Gains'; Human Rights Watch. 2014b. 'Burma: Government Plan Would Segregate Rohingya'.

23. Sheridan, M. 2015. 'Myanmar 'effectively a state of apartheid' for Muslims' [Online]. *The Australian*. Available: http://www.theaustralian.com.au/news/world/myanmar-effectively-a-state-of-apartheid-for-muslims/story-fnb64oi6122 7537589783 [Accessed 22 September 2015].

24. Heijmans, P. 2014. 'Myanmar's Controversial Census'.

25. Interview with U Kyaw Min, Yangon, 30 June 2015.

26. Interview with Rohingya politician, then sitting in parliament, 2015 (left anonymous for safety).

27. Interview with Steven Kiersons, 24 October 2015.

28. Interview by author with Rohingya elders in Sittwe IDP camp, 26 October 2015.

29. Preston, A. 2015. 'Saffron Terror: an audience with Burma's "Buddhist Bin Laden" Ashin Wirathu'.

30. Kyi, A. S. S. 1991. *Freedom from Fear: And Other Writings*, London: Penguin Books, p. 27.

31. Interview with Steven Kiersons, 24 October 2015.

32. Shah, I. 2015. 'Rohingyas' demand Burmese Gov't: either historically disprove "the ethnical term Rohingya" or pay back their indigenous rights' [Online]. Rangoon: *Burma Times*. Available: http://burmatimes.net/rohingyas-demand-burmese-govt-either-historically-disprove-the-ethnical-term-rohingya-or-pay-back-their-indigenous-rights/ [Accessed 8 July 2015].

33. Michaels, S. 2014. 'Suu Kyi Meets Critics of 'Protection of Race and Religion' Bills' [Online]. Rangoon: *The Irrawaddy*. Available: http://www.irrawaddy.org/burma/suu-kyi-meets-critics-protection-race-religion-bills.html [Accessed 16 July 2015]; Snaing, Y. 2014. 'Activists Face Violent Threats After Opposing Interfaith Marriage Bill'; Win, T. L. 2014b. 'Myanmar activists launch anti-'hate speech' campaign' [Online]. Thomson Reuters. Available: http://www.trust.org/item/20140403131148–4mqvg/ [Accessed 20 July 2015].

34. UCANEWS. 2015. 'Refugee boats set sail as monsoon season ends'.

35. *Burma Times*. 2015. 'In Burma's historic elections, a Muslim minority is banned from voting but still the focus of the campaign'.

36. Simonson, T. 2015. 'The taming of the NLD... by the NLD' [Online]. New Mandala. Available: http://asiapacific.anu.edu.au/newmandala/2015/08/12/the-taming-of-the-nld-by-the-nld/ [Accessed 11 October 2015].

37. Ibid.

38. Sheridan, M. 2015. 'Myanmar 'effectively a state of apartheid' for Muslims'.

39. Moe, W. 2015. 'Aung San Suu Kyi Calls Ex-Leader of Myanmar Governing Party an 'Ally'; Reuters. 2015b. 'Myanmar's ousted ruling party leader Shwe Mann meets Aung San Suu Kyi'.

40. Myanmar 2008. 'Constitution of the Republic of the Union of Myanmar'.
41. Simonson, T. 2015. 'The taming of the NLD... by the NLD'.
42. Interview with Steven Kiersons, 24 October 2015.
43. Williams, D. C. 2014. 'What's so Bad about Burma's 2008 Constitution?' *In:* Crouch, M. & Lindsey, T. (eds.) *Law, Society and Transition In Myanmar.* Oxford: Hart Publishing.
44. Bünte, M. & Dosch, J. 2015. 'Myanmar: Political Reforms and the Recalibration of External Relations'. *Journal of Current Southeast Asian Affairs*, 34:2, 3–19.
45. Pedersen, M. B. 2014. 'Myanmar's Democratic Opening'. *In:* Cheesman, N., Farrelly, N. & Wilson, T. (eds.) *Debating Democratization in Myanmar.* Singapore: ISEAS Publishing.
46. Vrieze, P. 2015. 'Nikkei Asian Review: "Myanmar's coming elections spell r-i-s-k for investors"' [Online]. Yangon: Vriens and Partners. Available: http://www.vrienspartners.com/nikkei-asian-review-myanmars-coming-elections-spell-r-i-s-k-for-investors.html [Accessed 22 September 2015].
47. Win, T. L. 2014a. 'Burmese journalist beseeches brethren: Stop with the Muslim hate speech'.
48. Cockett, R. 2015. *Blood, Dreams and Gold: The Changing Face of Burma*, New Haven, CT: Yale University Press.
49. Pedersen, M. B. 2014. 'Myanmar's Democratic Opening'.
50. Arakan Rohingya National Organisation. 2013. 'Rakhine Extremist Gang ALD & RNDP Disguised and Merged as ANP'.
51. Thu, M. K. 2015. 'Rakhine National Party in "chaos"' [Online]. Rangoon: *Myanmar Times*. Available: http://www.mmtimes.com/index.php/national-news/15221-rakhine-national-party-in-chaos.html [Accessed 22 September 2015].
52. Fortify Rights 2014. 'Policies of Persecution: Ending Abusive State Policies Against Rohingya Muslims in Myanmar'.
53. Ibrahim, A. 2015. 'Who Is Instigating the Violence Against the Rohingyas in Myanmar?' [Online]. New York: *Huffington Post*. Available: http://www.huffingtonpost.com/azeem-ibrahim/who-is-instigating-the-vi_b_7810972.html [Accessed 17 July 2015].
54. Lee, P. 2012. 'Myanmar fixates on Rohingya calculation' [Online]. *Asia Times*. Available: http://www.atimes.com/atimes/Southeast_Asia/NK14Ae01.html [Accessed 22 September 2015].
55. McLaughlin, T. 2015b. 'Rising Arakanese Party could further marginalize Rohingya'.
56. ASEAN Parliamentarians for Human Rights 2015. 'Disenfranchisement and Desperation in Myanmar's Rakhine State: Drivers of a Regional Crisis'. APHR.
57. McLaughlin, T. 2015b. 'Rising Arakanese Party could further marginalize Rohingya'.

58. *Burma Times*. 2015. 'In Burma's historic elections, a Muslim minority is banned from voting but still the focus of the campaign'.

59. Thu, M. K. 2015. 'Rakhine National Party in "chaos"'.

60. Ibrahim, A. 2015. 'Who Is Instigating the Violence Against the Rohingyas in Myanmar?'.

61. Interview by author with Rohingya elders in Sittwe IDP camp, 26 October 2015.

62. McGowan, W. 2012. 'Burma's Buddhist Chauvinism' [Online]. New York: *Wall Street Journal*. Available: http://www.wsj.com/articles/SB10000872396390443 847404577628874147528692 [Accessed 8 July 2015].

63. ASEAN Parliamentarians for Human Rights 2015. 'Disenfranchisement and Desperation in Myanmar's Rakhine State: Drivers of a Regional Crisis'.

64. UCANEWS. 2015. 'Refugee boats set sail as monsoon season ends'.

65. Kin, T. 2015. 'Risk of Mass Atrocities and Policies of Persecution in Burma'.

66. UCANEWS. 2015. 'Refugee boats set sail as monsoon season ends'.

67. Mepham, D. 2015. 'What Burma's Elections Mean for the Rohingyas'.

68. ASEAN Parliamentarians for Human Rights 2015. 'Disenfranchisement and Desperation in Myanmar's Rakhine State: Drivers of a Regional Crisis'.

69. *Sydney Morning Herald*. 2015. '"They are humans": Myanmar opposition says Rohingya people have rights'.

70. Yee, T. H. 2015. 'Expect further Rohingya exodus, report warns' [Online]. Singapore: *The Straits Times*. Available: http://www.straitstimes.com/asia/se-asia/ expect-further-rohingya-exodus-report-warns [Accessed 19 October 2015].

71. ASEAN Parliamentarians for Human Rights 2015. 'Disenfranchisement and Desperation in Myanmar's Rakhine State: Drivers of a Regional Crisis', p. 8.

72. Topsfield, J. 2015. 'Australia criticised for inaction on Rohingya refugee crisis' [Online]. Sydney: *Sydney Morning Herald*. Available: http://www.smh.com.au/ world/fears-rohingya-death-toll-vastly-underestimated-20151021-gkeeee.html [Accessed 21 October 2015].

73. CNN. 2012. 'Arakan Rohingya National Organization Contacts with Al Qaeda' [Online]. CNN. Available: http://ireport.cnn.com/docs/DOC-803422 [Accessed 26 February 2014].

74. Walton, M. 2013b. 'A Primer on the Roots of Buddhist/Muslim Conflict in Myanmar and a Way Forward' [Online]. IslamiCommentary. Available: http:// islamicommentary.org/2013/10/matthew-walton-a-primer-on-the-roots-of-buddhistmuslim-conflict-in-myanmar-and-a-way-forward/ [Accessed 16 July 2015].

75. Wadhwaney, R. 2015. 'Fearing Radicalization Attempt, India ups Surveillance on Rohingya Refugees' [Online]. Benar News. Available: http://www.benarnews. org/english/news/bengali/rohingya-08172015155820.html [Accessed 18 August 2015].

76. Bhalla, N. 2015. 'Myanmar's Rohingya stuck in refugee limbo in India' [Online]. Reuters. Available: http://www.reuters.com/article/2014/09/15/us-foundation-

stateless-india-rohingya-idUSKBN0HA07F20140915 [Accessed 26 October 2015].

77. Wolf, S. O. 2015. 'The Rohingya: Humanitarian Crisis or Security Threat?'.

78. Dalby, S. 2008. 'Environmental Change'. *In:* Williams, P. D. (ed.) *Security Studies: An Introduction.* London: Routledge; Peterson, S. 2002. 'Epidemic Disease and National Security'. *Security Studies,* 12:2, 43–81.

79. Aung, A. 2015. 'Rohingya in Komen Cyclone' [Online]. The Stateless Rohingya. Available: http://www.thestateless.com/2015/08/rohingya-in-komen-cyclone.html [Accessed 17 August 2015].

7. WHAT CAN BE DONE?

1. ASEAN Parliamentarians for Human Rights 2015. 'Disenfranchisement and Desperation in Myanmar's Rakhine State: Drivers of a Regional Crisis'.

2. Ibid.

3. Interview by author with Rohingya elders in Sittwe IDP camp, 24 October 2015.

4. Interview with Steven Kiersons, 24 October 2015.

5. Andrews, T. & Sullivan, D. 2014. 'Marching to Genocide in Burma'. Washington, D.C.: United to End Genocide; Human Rights Council 2014. 'Hear our Screams'; McLaughlin, T. 2015b. 'Rising Arakanese Party could further marginalize Rohingya'.

6. Ibrahim, A. 2015. 'Who Is Instigating the Violence Against the Rohingyas in Myanmar?'; United Nations 2013. 'Situation of human rights in Myanmar'. New York: UN.

7. ASEAN Parliamentarians for Human Rights 2015. 'Disenfranchisement and Desperation in Myanmar's Rakhine State: Drivers of a Regional Crisis'; Interview with Steven Kiersons, 24 October 2015.

8. Hodal, K. 2013. 'Buddhist monk uses racism and rumours to spread hatred in Burma'; Keane, F. 2012. 'The Burmese monks who preach intolerance against Muslim Rohingyas'; Pitman, T. & Peck, G. 2013. 'Radical monks, prejudice fuel Myanmar violence' [Online]. Associated Press. Available: http://www.thejakartapost.com/news/2013/06/01/radical-monks-prejudice-fuel-myanmar-violence.html [Accessed 16 September 2015].

9. Interview with Jamila Hanan, 26 October 2015.

10. Human Rights Watch. 2014b. 'Burma: Government Plan Would Segregate Rohingya'; Khin, T. 2015. 'Risk of Mass Atrocities and Policies of Persecution in Burma'; Myintzu, S. Y., Ei, K. K., Thu, K. & Kyaw, N. R. 2015. 'Myanmar Election Body Rejects Muslim Parliamentary Candidates'; Sheridan, M. 2015. 'Myanmar "effectively a state of apartheid" for Muslims'.

11. Bünte, M. & Dosch, J. 2015. 'Myanmar: Political Reforms and the Recalibration of External Relations'. *Journal of Current Southeast Asian Affairs,* 34:2, 3–19; Chachavalpongpun, P. 2012. 'The Vexing Strategic Tug-of-War over Naypyidaw:

ASEAN's View of the Sino-Burmese Ties'. *Journal of Current Southeast Asian Affairs*, 31:1, 97–114.

12. Aung, N. L. 2015b. 'First human trafficking case in Rakhine to head to court' [Online]. *Myanmar Times*. Available: http://www.mmtimes.com/index.php/national-news/15939-first-human-trafficking-case-in-rakhine-to-head-to-court.html [Accessed 19 August 2015].

13. Yee, T. H. 2015. 'Expect further Rohingya exodus, report warns'.

14. Graham, D. 2015. 'Burma Doesn't Want the Rohingyas but Insists on Keeping Them'.

15. Interview with Jamila Hanan, 26 October 2015.

16. Interview with Rohingya politician, then sitting in parliament, 2015 (left anonymous for safety).

17. Organisation of Islamic Cooperation. 2015. 'OIC continues to Mobilize Efforts for Political and Humanitarian Assistance to Rohingya Refugees' [Online]. OIC. Available: http://www.oic-oci.org/oicv2/topic/?t_id=10123&ref=4006&lan=en&x_key=rohingya [Accessed 19 July 2015].

18. Interview with Rohingya politician, then sitting in parliament, 2015 (left anonymous for safety).

19. Fuller, P. 31 August 2014. 'Ban Ki Moon Comments on Buddhist Extremism'. Available from: https://drpaulfuller.wordpress.com/category/burma/ [Accessed 28 June 2015]; Quintana, T. O. 2014. 'Report of the Special Rapporteur on the situation of human rights in Myanmar'.

20. Al Jazeera. 2014b. 'UN calls for "full Rohingya citizenship"' [Online]. Al Jazeera. Available: http://www.aljazeera.com/news/americas/2014/12/un-calls-full-rohingya-citizenship-myanmar-monks-rakhin-2014123044246726211.html [Accessed 30 January 2015]; Article 19. 2015. 'Myanmar: Government's handling of Par Gyi criticised at UN HRC' [Online]. London: Article 19. Available: https://www.article19.org/resources.php/resource/38106/en/myanmar:-government%E2%80%99s-handling-of-par-gyi-criticised-at-un-hrc [Accessed 19 September 2015]; Weng, L. 2014. 'Burma Govt Rejects "Unacceptable" UN Statement on Rohingya Killings' [Online]. Rangoon: *The Irrawaddy*. Available: http://www.irrawaddy.org/burma/burma-govt-rejects-unacceptable-un-statement-rohingya-killings.html [Accessed 22 September 2015].

21. Human Rights Watch. 2014b. 'Burma: Government Plan Would Segregate Rohingya'.

22. Hodal, K. 2014. 'Burma tells Médecins Sans Frontières to leave state hit by sectarian violence'.

23. Weng, L. 2014. 'Burma Govt Rejects "Unacceptable" UN Statement on Rohingya Killings'.

24. Reuters. 2012. 'EU welcomes "measured" Myanmar response to rioting'.

25. Heinemann, T. 2015. 'Misunderstanding Myanmar's Military'; Macdonald,

A. P. 2015. 'Time to engage Myanmar's military'; Ribeiro, E. H. 2013. 'Military can still be good state-builders in Myanmar'.

26. BBC. 2005. 'Rice names "outposts of tyranny"'; US Commission on International Religious Freedom 2011. 'Countries of Particular Concern: Burma'.

27. Al Jazeera. 2014a. 'Obama casts doubt on Myanmar reforms' [Online]. Al Jazeera. Available: http://www.aljazeera.com/news/asia-pacific/2014/11/obama-casts-doubt-myanmar-reforms-2014111465258897877.html [Accessed 10 January 2015].

28. EurActiv. 2013. 'EU lifts Myanmar sanctions, except arms embargo' [Online]. Brussels: EurActiv.com. Available: http://www.euractiv.com/global-europe/eu-lifts-myanmar-sanctions-arms-news-519303 [Accessed 15 January 2015].

29. Smith, M. 2011a. 'Myanmar's Economy Needs Human Rights Reforms' [Online]. *The World Post*. Available: http://www.huffingtonpost.com/matthew-smith/myanmars-economy-needs-hu_b_4347843.html [Accessed 26 February 2014].

30. Roughneen, S. 2010. 'China Backs Burma's Junta Leaders'.

31. Smith, M. 2015. 'How China Fuels Myanmar's Wars' [Online]. New York: *New York Times*. Available: http://www.nytimes.com/2015/03/05/opinion/how-china-fuels-myanmars-wars.html?_r=1 [Accessed 2015 20 August].

32. Farrelly, N. 2015. 'On China, the Lady has no choice'.

33. McElwee, J. J. 2015. 'Francis: Burmese treatment of Rohingya minority a form of "war"' [Online]. Kansas City: *National Catholic Reporter*. Available: http://ncronline.org/news/vatican/francis-burmese-treatment-rohingya-minority-form-war [Accessed 18 August 2015].

34. BBC. 2015a. 'Dalai Lama presses Aung San Suu Kyi over Rohingya migrants' [Online]. BBC: London. Available: http://www.bbc.co.uk/news/world-asia-32925805 [Accessed 15 June 2015].

35. Fuller, P. 31 August 2014. 'Ban Ki Moon Comments on Buddhist Extremism'. Available from: https://drpaulfuller.wordpress.com/category/burma/ [Accessed 28 June 2015].

36. McGowan, W. 2012. 'Burma's Buddhist Chauvinism'.

37. Rakhine Investigation Committee 2013. 'Summary of Recommendations'.

38. Fortify Rights 2014. 'Policies of Persecution: Ending Abusive State Policies Against Rohingya Muslims in Myanmar'; Human Rights Council 2014. 'Hear our Screams'; International Crisis Group 2013. 'The Dark Side of Transition: Violence Against Muslims in Myanmar'; Smith, M. 2011b. 'Time for New Approach to Burma: War Crimes Mounting'.

39. Human Rights Watch. 2013b. 'International Criminal Court' [Online]. Human Rights Watch. Available: https://www.hrw.org/topic/international-justice/international-criminal-court [Accessed 24 February 2014]; United Nations. 2002. 'Rome Statute of the International Criminal Court'.

40. Human Rights Watch. 2013b. 'International Criminal Court'.

41. United Nations. 2002. 'Rome Statute of the International Criminal Court'.

42. Ibid.

43. Ibid.

44. Pedersen, M. B. 2014. 'Myanmar's Democratic Opening', in Cheesman, N., Farrelly, N. & Wilson, T. (eds.) *Debating Democratization in Myanmar*. Singapore: ISEAS Publishing; Schissler, M. 2014. 'May Flowers'.

45. Michaels, S. 2014. 'Suu Kyi Meets Critics of "Protection of Race and Religion" Bills'.

46. *Sydney Morning Herald*. 2015. '"They are humans": Myanmar opposition says Rohingya people have rights'.

47. Hindstrom, H. 2015. 'In Myanmar, Muslim minority is targeted for hate, not for votes' [Online]. Al Jazeera, America. Available: http://america.aljazeera.com/articles/2015/9/20/muslim-minority-cut-out-of-myanmar-vote.html [Accessed 22 September 2015]; Myintzu, S. Y., Ei, K. K., Thu, K. & Kyaw, N. R. 2015. 'Myanmar Election Body Rejects Muslim Parliamentary Candidates'.

CONCLUSION

1. Stoakes, E. 2015. 'Monks, PowerPoint Presentations, and Ethnic Cleansing'.

2. McLaughlin, T. 2015b. 'Rising Arakanese Party could further marginalize Rohingya'; Thu, M. K. 2015. 'Rakhine National Party in "chaos"'.

3. *Burma Times*. 2015. 'In Burma's historic elections, a Muslim minority is banned from voting but still the focus of the campaign'.

4. Hindstrom, H. 2015. 'In Myanmar, Muslim minority is targeted for hate, not for votes'.

5. Doyle, D. 2015. 'Burma elections: Aung San Suu Kyi steers clear of "stateless" minority the Rohingya'.

6. *Sydney Morning Herald*. 2015. '"They are humans": Myanmar opposition says Rohingya people have rights'.

APPENDIX 1: H. G. BELL ON THE ETHNIC GROUPS OF ARAKAN, 1852

1. Bell, H. G. 1852. *An Account of the Burman Empire, Compiled from the Works of Colonel Symes, Major Canning, Captain Cox, Dr. Leyden, Dr. Buchanan*, Calcutta: D'Rozario and Co.

APPENDIX 2: EXCERPT FROM PATON'S REPORT

1. Paton, C. 1826. *A Short Report on Arakan*. London: Colonial Office.

APPENDIX 3: STATEMENT OF CITIZENSHIP

1. Citizenship Election Officer 1948. 'Indigenous Race Recognition'.

APPENDIX 5: PRO-MILITARY SLOGAN

1. Ribeiro, E. H. 2013. 'Military can still be good state-builders in Myanmar' [Online]. Rangoon: New Mandala. Available: http://asiapacific.anu.edu.au/newman-dala/2013/10/15/military-can-still-be-good-state-builders-for-myanmar/ [Accessed 27 June 2015].

REFERENCES

Abraham, I. 2008. 'From Bandung to NAM: Non-Alignment and Indian Foreign Policy', 1947–65. *Commonwealth & Comparative Politics*, 46:2, 195–219.

Ahmad, F. 2014. *The Young Turks and the Ottoman Nationalities: Armenians, Greeks, Albanians, Jews, and Arabs, 1908–1918*, Salt Lake City, UT: University of Utah Press

Akins, H. 2013. 'No place for Islam? Buddhist nationalism in Myanmar' [Online]. Al Jazeera. Available: http://www.aljazeera.com/indepth/opinion/2013/10/no-place-islam-buddhist-nationalism-myanmar-2013101710411233906.html [Accessed 26 February 2014].

Alessi, C. & Xu, B. 2015. 'China in Africa' [Online]. Council for Foreign Relations. Available: http://www.cfr.org/china/china-africa/p9557 [Accessed 2 June 2015].

Al Jazeera. 2014a. 'Obama casts doubt on Myanmar reforms' [Online]. Al Jazeera. Available: http://www.aljazeera.com/news/asia-pacific/2014/11/obama-casts-doubt-myanmar-reforms-2014111465258897877.html [Accessed 10 January 2015].

Al Jazeera. 2014b. 'UN calls for "full Rohingya citizenship"' [Online]. Al Jazeera. Available: http://www.aljazeera.com/news/americas/2014/12/un-calls-full-rohingya-citizenship-myanmar-monks-rakhin-2014123044246726211.html [Accessed 30 January 2015].

Alkire, S. 2003. *A Conceptual Framework for Human Security*. Oxford: Centre for Research on Inequality, Human Security and Ethnicity, CRISE.

Allchin, J. 2012. 'The Rohingya, myths and misinformation' [Online]. DVB. Available: http://www.dvb.no/analysis/the-rohingya-myths-and-misinformation/22597 [Accessed 18 June 2015].

Amnesty International 2014. 'Myanmar: The Rohingyas Minority: Fundamental Rights Denied'. London: Amnesty International.

Andrews, T. & Sullivan, D. 2014. 'Marching to Genocide in Burma'. Washington, D.C.: United to End Genocide.

REFERENCES

Arakan Rohingya National Organisation. 2013. 'Rakhine Extremist Gang ALD & RNDP Disguised and Merged as ANP' [Online]. Available: http://www.rohingya. org/portal/index.php/burma/63-news—article/1074-analysis-rakhine-extremist-gang-ald-a-rndp-disguised-and-merged-as-anp.html [Accessed 18 June 2015].

Article 19 1996. Burma: Beyond the Law. London: Global Campaign for Free Expression.

Article 19. 2015. 'Myanmar: Government's handling of Par Gyi criticised at UN HRC' [Online]. London: Article 19. Available: https://www.article19.org/resources.php/resource/38106/en/myanmar:-government%E2%80%99s-handling-of-par-gyi-criticised-at-un-hrc [Accessed 19 September 2015].

ASEAN Parliamentarians for Human Rights 2015. 'Disenfranchisement and Desperation in Myanmar's Rakhine State: Drivers of a Regional Crisis'. APHR.

Aselius, G. 2012. 'The Ottoman Absence from the Battlefields of the Seven Years' War'. *In:* Danley, M. H. & Speelman, P. J. (eds.) *The Seven Years' War: Global Views.* Leiden: Brill.

Asian Human Rights Commission 2011. 'Diagnosing the un-rule of law in Burma: A submission to the UN Human Rights Council's Universal Periodic Review'. Hong Kong.

Associated Press. 2013. 'Buddhist monks offer shelter to persecuted Burma Muslims' [Online]. Washington, D.C.: CBS News. Available: http://www.cbsnews.com/news/buddhist-monks-offer-shelter-to-persecuted-burma-muslims/ [Accessed 16 September 2015].

Associated Press. 2015. 'Myanmar ex-slave: Those with sympathy would not eat our fish' [Online]. Associated Press. Available: http://hosted.ap.org/dynamic/stories/A/AS_FACES_OF_SLAVERY_KYAW_ZAYAR?SITE=AP&SECTION=HOME&TEMPLATE=DEFAULT&CTIME=2015–09–18–01–48–09 [Accessed 20 September 2015].

Aung, A. 2015. 'Rohingya in Komen Cyclone' [Online]. The Stateless Rohingya. Available: http://www.thestateless.com/2015/08/rohingya-in-komen-cyclone. html [Accessed 17 August 2015].

Aung, N. L. 2015. 'First human trafficking case in Rakhine to head to court' [Online]. *Myanmar Times.* Available: http://www.mmtimes.com/index.php/national-news/15939-first-human-trafficking-case-in-rakhine-to-head-to-court.html [Accessed 19 August 2015].

Aung, S. T. 1979. 'The Buddhist art of ancient Arakan: An eastern border state beyond ancient India, east of Vanga and Samatata', Rangoon: Daw Saw Saw.

Aung Thwin, M. 1985a. 'Burma Before Pagan: The Status of Archaeology Today', *Asian Perspectives,* 25:2, 1–22.

Aung Thwin, M. 1985b. *Pagan: the origins of modern Burma,* Honolulu, HI: University of Hawaii.

Bales, K. 2012. *Disposable People: New Slavery in the Global Economy,* Berkeley, CA: University of California Press.

REFERENCES

Bangkok Post. 2015. 'Crime Navy commander faces arrest over trafficking' [Online]. Bangkok. Available: http://www.bangkokpost.com/news/crime/699884/navy-commander-faces-arrest-over-trafficking [Accessed 21 September 2015].

Bank of Knowledge 1964. *Scripture of Myanmar Encyclopedia*, Rangoon.

Baxter, J. 1941. 'Report on Indian Immigration'. Rangoon: India Office.

BBC. 2005. 'Rice names "outposts of tyranny"' [Online]. London: BBC. Available: http://news.bbc.co.uk/1/hi/world/americas/4186241.stm [Accessed 27 June 2015].

—— 2007. 'Burma's 1988 protests' [Online]. London: BBC. Available: http://news.bbc.co.uk/1/hi/world/asia-pacific/7012158.stm [Accessed 28 June 2015].

—— 2012. 'Suu Kyi gives historic Parliament address' [Online]. London: BBC. Available: http://www.bbc.co.uk/news/uk-18543045 [Accessed 2 November 2014].

—— 2015a. 'Dalai Lama presses Aung San Suu Kyi over Rohingya migrants' [Online]. BBC: London. Available: http://www.bbc.co.uk/news/world-asia-3292 5805 [Accessed 15 June 2015].

—— 2015b. 'Why are so many Rohingya migrants stranded at sea?' [Online]. London: BBC. Available: http://www.bbc.co.uk/news/world-asia-32740637 [Accessed 15 June 2015].

Bell, H. G. 1852. *An Account of the Burmese Empire, Compiled from the Works of Colonel Symes, Major Canning, Captain Cox, Dr. Leyden, Dr. Buchanan*, Calcutta: D'Rozario and Co.

Bhalla, N. 2015. 'Myanmar's Rohingya stuck in refugee limbo in India' [Online]. Reuters. Available: http://www.reuters.com/article/2014/09/15/us-foundation-stateless-india-rohingya-idUSKBN0HA07F20140915 [Accessed 26 October 2015].

Bischoff, R. 1996. *Buddhism in Myanmar: A short history*, Kandy, Sri Lanka: Buddhist Publication Society.

Boot, W. 2007. 'Step on the Gas' [Online]. Rangoon: *The Irrawaddy*. Available: http://www2.irrawaddy.org/article.php?art_id=7735 [Accessed 1 July 2015].

Brass, P. R. 2003. *The Production of Hindu-Muslim Violence in Contemporary India*, Washington, D.C.: University of Washington Press.

Bryce, J. & Toynbee, A. 2000. *The Treatment of Armenians in the Ottoman Empire 1915–1916*, Reading: Taderon Press.

Buchanan, F. 1799. 'A Comparative Vocabularly of Some of the Languages spoken in the Burma Empire'. *Asiatic Researches*, 5, 219–240.

Buckley, C. & Barry, E. 2015. 'Rohingya women fleeing Burma sold into marriage' [Online]. Dublin: *Irish Times*. Available: http://www.irishtimes.com/news/world/asia-pacific/rohingya-women-fleeing-burma-sold-into-marriage-1.2319703 [Accessed 18 August 2015].

Bünte, M. & Dosch, J. 2015. 'Myanmar: Political Reforms and the Recalibration of External Relations'. *Journal of Current Southeast Asian Affairs*, 34:2, 3–19.

Burma Centrum Nederlands 2014. 'Ethnicity without Meaning, Data without Context: The 2014 Census, Identity and Citizenship in Burma/Myanma'. *Burma Policy Briefing*. Amsterdam: Burma Centrum Nederlands.

Burma Times. 2015. 'In Burma's historic elections, a Muslim minority is banned from voting but still the focus of the campaign' [Online]. Rangoon: *Burma Times*. Available: http://burmatimes.net/in-burmas-historic-elections-a-muslim-minority-is-banned-from-voting-but-still-the-focus-of-the-campaign/ [Accessed 19 October 2015].

Busczynski, L. 1986. *Soviet Foreign Policy and Southeast Asia*, London: Routledge.

Callahan, M. P. 2005. *Making Enemies: War and State Building in Burma*, Ithaca, NY: Cornell University Press.

Caralucci, T. 2015. 'Myanmar's Aung San Suu Kyi Dodging or Driving the Rohingyas Crisis?' [Online]. New Eastern Outlook. Available: http://journal-neo.org/2015/06/20/myanmar-s-aung-san-suu-kyi-dodging-or-driving-the-rohingya-crisis/ [Accessed 22 September 2015].

Case, W. 2002. *Politics in Southeast Asia: Democracy or Less*, Oxford: Routledge,

Chachavalpongpun, P. 2012. 'The Vexing Strategic Tug-of-War over Naypyidaw: ASEAN's View of the Sino-Burmese Ties'. *Journal of Current Southeast Asian Affairs*, 31:1, 97–114.

Chan, A. 2005. 'The Development of a Muslim Enclave in Arakan (Rakhine) State of Burma (Myanmar)'. *SOAS Bulletin of Burma Research*, 3:2, 396–420.

Charney, M. W. 2009. *A History of Modern Burma*, Cambridge: Cambridge University Press.

Citizenship Election Officer 1948. 'Indigenous Race Recognition'.

Classical Journal 1811. 'Numbers in 200 Tongues'. London, 535.

CNN. 2012. 'Arakan Rohingya National Organization Contacts with Al Qaeda' [Online]. CNN. Available: http://ireport.cnn.com/docs/DOC-803422 [Accessed 26 February 2014].

Cochrane, J. 2015. 'In Reversal, Myanmar Agrees to Attend Meeting on Migrant Crisis' [Online]. New York: *New York Times*. Available: http://www.nytimes.com/2015/05/22/world/asia/myanmar-rohingya-migrant-crisis-malaysia-thailand-indonesia.html?_r=0 [Accessed 15 June 2015].

Cockett, R. 2015. *Blood, Dreams and Gold: The Changing Face of Burma*, New Haven, CT: Yale University Press.

Coclanis, P. A. 2013. 'Terror in Burma: Buddhists vs. Muslims' [Online]. Washington, D.C.: World Affairs. Available: http://www.worldaffairsjournal.org/article/terror-burma-buddhists-vs-muslims [Accessed 29 June 2015].

Collins, G. 2015. 'Dalai Lama gets Mischievous' [Online]. New York: *New York Times*. Available:http://www.nytimes.com/2015/07/16/opinion/nicholas-kristof-dalai-lama-gets-mischievous.html?ref=opinion&_r=0 [Accessed 20 July 2015].

Collis, M. 1937. *Trials in Burma*, London: Faber and Faber.

REFERENCES

Colonial Office 1875. 'The Census of British Burma. Rangoon'.

────── 1911. 'Census of India: Burma'. Rangoon.

Constituent Assembly 1947. 'The Constitution of the Union of Burma'. Rangoon: Foreign Office.

CSIS. 2012. 'The Leaderboard: Aye Maung' [Online]. Center for Strategic and International Studies. Available: http://cogitasia.com/the-leaderboard-aye-maung/ [Accessed 22 September 2015].

Dalby, S. 2008. 'Environmental Change'. *In:* Williams, P. D. (ed.) *Security Studies: An Introduction.* London: Routledge.

DNA India. 2015. 'United Nations rights envoy says meeting with Myanmar's Rohingya blocked' [Online]. DNA. Available: http://www.dnaindia.com/world/report-united-nations-rights-envoy-says-meeting-with-myanmar-s-rohingya-blocked-2112331 [Accessed 19 August 2015].

Dosch, J. & Sidhu, J. S. 2015. 'The European Union's Myanmar Policy: Focused or Directionless?' *Journal of Current Southeast Asian Affairs,* 34:2, 85–112.

Doyle, D. 2015. 'Burma elections: Aung San Suu Kyi steers clear of "stateless" minority the Rohingyas' [Online]. London: *The Independent.* Available: http://www.independent.co.uk/news/world/asia/burma-elections-aung-san-suu-kyi-steers-clear-of-stateless-minority-the-rohingya-a6697341.html [Accessed 20 October 2015].

Doyle, M. W. & Sambanis, N. 2006. *Making War and Building Peace,* Princeton, NJ: Princeton University Press.

Drabble, J. H. 2000. *An economic history of Malaysia, c. 1800–1990: The transition to modern economic growth,* New York: St Martin's Press.

Early Warning Project. 2015. 'Myanmar' [Online]. Washington, D.C.: Early Warning Project. Available: http://www.earlywarningproject.com/countries/myanmar [Accessed 22 September 2015].

Egreteau, R. 2012. 'Burmese Tango: Indian and Chinese Games and Gains in Burma (Myanmar) since 1988'. *In:* Devare, S. T., Singh, S. & Marwah, R. (eds.) *Emerging China: Prospects of Partnership in Asia.* New Delhi: Routledge.

Environmental Justice Foundation 2014. 'Slavery at Sea: The Continued Plight of Trafficked Migrants in Thailand's Fishing Industry'. London: Environmental Justice Foundation.

Equal Rights Trust 2014. 'The Human Rights of the Stateless Rohingya in Thailand'. London: Equal Rights Trust.

EurActiv. 2013. 'EU lifts Myanmar sanctions, except arms embargo' [Online]. Brussels: EurActiv.com. Available: http://www.euractiv.com/global-europe/eu-lifts-myanmar-sanctions-arms-news-519303 [Accessed 15 January 2015].

Farrelly, N. 2015. 'On China, the Lady has no choice' [Online]. *Myanmar Times.* Available: http://asiapacific.anu.edu.au/newmandala/2015/07/08/on-china-the-lady-has-no-choice/ [Accessed 20 August 2015].

Fearon, J. D. & Laitin, D. 1996. 'Explaining Interethnic Cooperation.' *The American Political Science Review,* 90:4, 715–735.

—— 2000. 'Violence and the Social Construction of Ethnic Identity'. *International Organization*, 54:4, 845–877.

Feeny, T. 2001. 'Rohingya Refugee Children in Cox's Bazar, Bangladesh'. Oxford: Refugee Studies Centre.

Ferroggiaro, W. 2001. 'The US and the Genocide in Rwanda 1994: Evidence of Inaction'. Washington, D.C.: National Security Archive.

FIDH 2000. 'Burma: repression, discrimination and ethnic cleansing in Arakan'. Paris: International Federation of Human Rights Leagues.

Fisk, R. 2001. *Pity the Nation: Lebanon at War*, 3rd, Oxford: Oxford University Press.

Foley, M. 2010. *The Cold War and National Assertion in Southeast Asia: Britain, the United States and Burma, 1948–1962*, London: Routledge.

Fortify Rights 2014. 'Policies of Persecution: Ending Abusive State Policies Against Rohingya Muslims in Myanmar'. Fortify Rights.

Fritz, S. G. 2011. *Ostkrieg: Hitler's War of Extermination in the East*, Lexington, KY: University of Kentucky Press.

Fuller, P. 31 August 2014. 'Ban Ki Moon Comments on Buddhist Extremism'. Available from: https://drpaulfuller.wordpress.com/category/burma/ [Accessed 28 June 2015].

Galache, C. S. 2013. 'Who are the Monks behind Burma's "969" Campaign?' [Online]. Democratic Voice of Burma. Available: http://www.dvb.no/news/features-news/the-monks-behind-burmas-969-movement [Accessed 17 September 2015].

Galloway, C. K. 2007. *Burmese Buddhist Imagery of the Early Bagan Period (1044–1113)*. Australian National University.

Glenny, M. 1996. *The Fall of Yugoslavia*, London: Penguin.

Goldston, J. 1990. *Human Rights in Burma (Myanmar)*, New York: Human Rights Watch.

Government of the Union of Burma 1974. 'The Constitution of the Socialist Republic of the Union of Burma'. Rangoon.

Graham, D. 2015. 'Burma Doesn't Want the Rohingyas but Insists on Keeping Them' [Online]. The Atlantic. Available: http://www.theatlantic.com/international/archive/2015/06/burma-rohingya-migration-ban/395729/ [Accessed 15 June 2015].

Graham-Harrison, E. 2015. 'Burma's boatpeople "faced choice of annihilation or risking their lives at sea"' [Online]. London: *The Observer*. Available: http://www.theguardian.com/world/2015/may/17/rohingya-burma-refugees-boat-migrants [Accessed 15 June 2015].

Gutman, P. 2001. *Burma's Lost Kingdoms: Splendors Of Arakan*, Boulder, CO: Weatherhill.

Gutter, P. 2001. 'Law and Religion in Burma'. *Legal Issues of Burma Journal*, 8, 1–69.

Han, K. K. 2003. '1990 Multi Party Democracy: General Elections' [Online].

Rangoon: National League for Democracy. Available: http://www.ibiblio.org/obl/docs/1990_elections.htm [Accessed 2 July 2015].

Interview with Jamila Hanan, 26 October 2015.

Harff, B. 2005. 'Assessing Risks of Genocide and Politicide'. *In:* Marshall, M. G. & Gurr, T. R. (eds.) *Peace and Conflict*. College Park, MD: Center for International Development and Conflict Management.

Heijmans, P. 2014. 'Myanmar's Controversial Census' [Online]. *The Diplomat*. Available: http://thediplomat.com/2014/09/myanmars-controversial-census/ [Accessed 20 February 2015].

Heinemann, T. 2015. 'Misunderstanding Myanmar's Military' [Online]. *Asia Times*. Available: http://www.atimes.com/atimes/Southeast_Asia/SEA-01–110215.html [Accessed 27 June 2015].

Hidalgo, F. D. & Nichter, S. 2015. 'Voter Buying: Shaping the Electorate through Clientelism'. *American Journal of Political Science*, n/a-n/a.

Hill, R. C. 2000. *The Balkan Wars 1912–1913: Prelude to the First World War*, London: Routledge.

Hindstrom, H. 2015. 'In Myanmar, Muslim minority is targeted for hate, not for votes' [Online]. Al Jazeera, America. Available: http://america.aljazeera.com/articles/2015/9/20/muslim-minority-cut-out-of-myanmar-vote.html [Accessed 22 September 2015].

Hodal, K. 2013. 'Buddhist monk uses racism and rumours to spread hatred in Burma' [Online]. London: *The Guardian*. Available: http://www.theguardian.com/world/2013/apr/18/buddhist-monk-spreads-hatred-burma [Accessed 21 February 2015].

——— 2014. 'Burma tells Médecins Sans Frontières to leave state hit by sectarian violence' [Online]. London: *The Guardian*. Available: http://www.theguardian.com/world/2014/feb/28/burma-medecins-sans-frontieres-rakhine-state [Accessed 1 March 2014].

Hodal, K. & Kelly, C. 2014. 'Trafficked into slavery on Thai trawlers to catch food for prawns' [Online]. London: *The Guardian*. Available: http://www.theguardian.com/global-development/2014/jun/10/-sp-migrant-workers-new-life-enslaved-thai-fishing [Accessed 15 June 2015].

Holmes, R. A. 1967. 'Burmese domestic policy: the politics of Burmanization'. *Asian Survey*, 188–197.

Houtman, G. 1999. 'Remaking Myanmar and Human Origins'. *Anthropology Today*, 15:4, 13–19.

Htwe, R. 1990. 'Monthly Report: December'. Karen Refugee Council.

Human Rights Council 2014. 'Hear our Screams'.

Human Rights Documentation Unit. 2007. 'Burma Human Rights Yearbook' [Online]. Available: http://www.burmalibrary.org/docs5/HRDU-archive/Burma%20Human%20Righ/maps.html [Accessed 7 March 2014].

Human Rights Watch. 1996. 'Burma: The Rohingya Muslims: Ending a Cycle of

Exodus?' [Online]. UNHCR. Available: http://www.refworld.org/cgi-bin/texis/vtx/rwmain?page=printdoc&docid=3ae6a84a2 [Accessed 28 February 2014].

—— 2000. 'Malaysia/Burma: Living in Limbo' [Online]. Available: http://www.hrw.org/reports/2000/malaysia/maybr008–01.htm [Accessed 28 February 2014].

—— 2012. 'The Government should have stopped this'. New York: Human Rights Watch.

—— 2013a. '"All You Can Do is Pray": Crimes Against Humanity and Ethnic Cleansing of Rohingya Muslims in Burma's Arakan State'. Washington, D.C.: Human Rights Watch.

—— 2013b. 'International Criminal Court' [Online]. Human Rights Watch. Available: https://www.hrw.org/topic/international-justice/international-criminal-court [Accessed 24 February 2014].

—— 2014a. 'Burma: Communal Violence Undercuts Rights Gains' [Online]. Human Rights Watch. Available: http://www.hrw.org/news/2014/01/21/burma-communal-violence-undercuts-rights-gains [Accessed 8 March 2014].

—— 2014b. 'Burma: Government Plan Would Segregate Rohingya' [Online]. Human Rights Watch. Available: https://www.hrw.org/news/2014/10/03/burma-government-plan-would-segregate-rohingya [Accessed 20 September 2015].

—— 2015. 'Southeast Asia: Accounts from Rohingya Boat People' [Online]. HRW. Available: http://www.hrw.org/news/2015/05/27/southeast-asia-accounts-rohingya-boat-people [Accessed 15 June 2015].

Humanitarian Information Unit 2012. 'Burma 2010 Election Results: One small step for democracy?' Washington, D.C.: US Department of State.

Ibrahim, A. 2014. 'The Resurgence of Al-Qaeda in Syria and Iraq'. Washington, D.C.: SSI.

—— 2015. 'Who Is Instigating the Violence Against the Rohingyas in Myanmar?' [Online]. New York: *Huffington Post*. Available: http://www.huffingtonpost.com/azeem-ibrahim/who-is-instigating-the-vi_b_7810972.html [Accessed 17 July 2015].

Images Asia 1997. 'No Childhood at all: A Report about Child Soldiers in Burma.' Geneva: UN Quaker Office.

International Court of Justice 2015. 'Case Concerning Application of the Convention on the Prevention and Punishment of the Crime of Genocide (Croatia v Serbia)'. The Hague: International Court of Justice.

International Crisis Group 2001. 'Myanmar: The Military Regime's View of the World'. Bangkok: International Crisis Group.

—— 2013. 'The Dark Side of Transition: Violence Against Muslims in Myanmar'. Brussels.

International Labour Organisation. 1998. 'Forced labour in Myanmar (Burma)' [Online]. Geneva: ILO. Available: http://www.ilo.org/public/english/standards/relm/gb/docs/gb273/myanmar3.htm [Accessed 1 March 2014].

—— 2013a. 'Forced labour in Myanmar (Burma)'. Geneva: United Nations.

—— 2013b. 'Trafficked into slavery on Thai trawlers to catch food for prawns' [Online]. Geneva: ILO. Available: http://apflnet.ilo.org/news/trafficked-into-slavery-on-thai-trawlers-to-catch-food-for-prawns [Accessed 15 June 2015].

Irish Centre for Human Rights 2010. 'Crimes against Humanity in Western Burma: The Situation of the Rohingyas'. Galway: Irish Centre for Human Rights.

Jagan, L. 2014. 'Suu Kyi shifts pre-election tack in Myanmar' [Online]. *Asia Times*. Available: http://www.atimes.com/atimes/Southeast_Asia/SEA-01–120614.html [Accessed 30 June 2015].

James, H. 2000. 'The Fall of Ayutthaya: A Re-assessment'. *The Journal of Burma Studies*, 5, 75–108.

Jilani, A. 2006. 'The Muslim massacre of 1942' [Online]. Arakan Rohingya National Organisation (ARNO). Available: http://www.rohingya.org/portal/index.php/rohingya-library/26-rohingya-history/55-the-muslim-massacre-of-1942.html [Accessed 4 March 2014].

Jones, A. 2008. 'Genocide and Mass Killing'. *In:* Williams, P. D. (ed.) *Security Studies: An Introduction*. London: Routledge.

Justice Trust 2015. 'Hidden Hands Behind Communal Violence in Myanmar: Case Study of the Mandalay Riots'. New York: Justice Trust.

Karen News. 2013. 'Facts on Burma' [Online]. Available: http://karennews.org/facts-on-burma/ [Accessed 26 February 2014].

Keane, F. 2012. 'The Burmese monks who preach intolerance against Muslim Rohingyas' [Online]. London: BBC. Available: http://www.bbc.co.uk/news/world-asia-20427889 [Accessed 18 June 2015].

Kerr, P., Tow, W. T. & Hanson, M. 2003. 'The Utility of the Human Security Agenda for Policymakers'. *Asian Journal of Political Science*, 11:2, 89–114.

Khin, T. 2015. 'Risk of Mass Atrocities and Policies of Persecution in Burma' [Online]. Washington, D.C.: Early Warning Project. Available: http://www.early-warningproject.com/2015/07/16/policies-of-persecution-in-burma [Accessed 22 September 2015].

Kiersons, S., Stein, S., Kalmats, D. & Mediratta, R. 2013. 'Burma Risk Assessment'. Toronto: Sentinel Project for Genocide Prevention.

Kin, T. 2015. 'Risk of Mass Atrocities and Policies of Persecution in Burma' [Online]. Early Warning Project. Available: http://www.earlywarningproject.com/2015/07/16/policies-of-persecution-in-burma [Accessed 15 October 2015].

Kiragu, E., Rosi, A. L. & Morris, T. 2011. 'States of Denial: A review of UNHCR's response to the protracted situation of stateless Rohingya refugees in Bangladesh'. UNHCR.

Kyaw, K. 2012. 'Analysis of Myanmar's NLD landslide' [Online]. New Mandala. Available: http://asiapacific.anu.edu.au/newmandala/2012/05/01/analysis-of-myanmars-nld-landslide/ [Accessed 21 October 2015].

Kyi, A. S. S. 1991. *Freedom from Fear: And Other Writings*, London: Penguin Books.

REFERENCES

Kyohan, B. 1995. *The Classification of Buddhism*, Wiesbaden: Harrassowitz Verlag.

LeDonne, J. P. 2004. *The Grand Strategy of the Russian Empire 1650–1831*, Oxford: Oxford University Press.

Lee, J. 2013. 'A History of Broken Promises' [Online]. Alders Ledge. Available: http://aldersledge.blogspot.co.uk/2013/04/a-history-of-broken-promises.html [Accessed 4 March 2014].

Lee, P. 2012. 'Myanmar fixates on Rohingya calculation' [Online]. *Asia Times*. Available: http://www.atimes.com/atimes/Southeast_Asia/NK14Ae01.html [Accessed 22 September 2015].

Lefevre, A. S. & Marshall, A. R. C. 2014. 'Special Report: Traffickers use abductions, prison ships to feed Asian slave trade' [Online]. Reuters. Available: http://www.reuters.com/article/2014/10/22/us-thailand-trafficking-specialreport-idUSKC-N0IB0A320141022http://www.reuters.com/article/2014/10/22/us-thailand-trafficking-specialreport-idUSKCN0IB0A320141022 [Accessed 20 September 2015].

Leider, J. P. 2008. 'Forging Buddhist Credentials as a Tool for Legitimacy and Ethnic Identity: A Study of Arakan's Subjection in Nineteenth Century Burma'. *Journal of the Economic and Social History of the Orient*, 5:1,409–459.

—— 2012. '"Rohingya," Rakhaing and the Recent Outbreak of Violence—A Note' *Burma Studies*, 8–12.

—— 2014. 'Rohingya: The name, the movement, the quest for identity'. *Nation Building in Myanmar*. Yangon: Myanmar Egress & Myanmar Peace Center.

Lewa, C. 2003. 'We are like a soccer ball, kicked by Burma, kicked by Bangladesh!', Forum Asia.

Lewa, C. 2009. 'North Arakan: an open prison of the Rohingyas in Burma'. *Forced Migration Review*.

Lewis, S. & Doherty, B. 2015. 'Turmoil in Burma's military-backed ruling party as leaders are deposed' [Online]. London: *The Guardian*. Available: http://www.theguardian.com/world/2015/aug/13/burmese-forces-surround-ruling-party-headquarters-and-confine-mps-report [Accessed 13 August 2015].

Li, Q. 2015. 'North Myanmar Minority Issues and its Impact on China-Myanmar Relations'. *Burma/Myanmar in Transition: Connectivity, Changes and Challenges*. Chiang Mai University: Thailand.

Lin, K. M. Z. 2015. 'India and Myanmar monsoon rains leave dozens dead' [Online]. London: BBC. Available: http://www.bbc.co.uk/news/world-asia-33745840 [Accessed 18 August 2015].

Linn, Z. 2015. 'Burma: Shattering of a democracy dream?' [Online]. The Stateless Rohingya. Available: http://www.thestateless.com/2015/08/burma-shattering-of-a-democracy-dream.html [Accessed 18 August 2015].

Lintner, B. 1990. *The Rise and Fall of the Communist Party of Burma*, Ithaca, NY: Cornell University.

—— 2013. 'Myanmar, North Korea stay brothers in arms' [Online]. *Asia Times*. Available: http://www.atimes.com/atimes/Southeast_Asia/SEA-01–050913.html [Accessed 27 June 2015].

Loyn, D. 2011. 'Suu Kyi's NLD democracy party to rejoin Burma politics' [Online]. London: BBC. Available: http://www.bbc.co.uk/news/world-asia-15787605 [Accessed 16 October 2015].

Luce, G. H. 1986. *Phases of Pre-Pagan Burma*, Oxford: Oxford University Press.

Lwin, N. S. 2012. 'Making Rohingya Stateless' [Online]. Rangoon: New Mandala. Available: http://asiapacific.anu.edu.au/newmandala/2012/10/29/making-rohingya-statelessness/ [Accessed 8 July 2015].

Macdonald, A. P. 2015. 'Time to engage Myanmar's military' [Online]. *Asia Times*. Available: http://www.atimes.com/atimes/Southeast_Asia/SEA-01–040215.html [Accessed 27 June 2015].

Mathias, J. 2015. 'Foreign Influences on the Burmese Language'. *International Conference on Burma/Myanmar Studies: Burma/Myanmar in Transition: Connectivity, Changes and Challenges*. University Academic Service Centre (UNISERV), Chiang Mai University, Thailand, 24–26 July 2015.

Mathies, C. E. 2013. 'Managing Peace and Security in Southeast Asia: Does ASEAN have the Political Will?'

Mathieson, D. S. 2003. 'The March of Folly' [Online]. Rangoon: *The Irrawaddy*. Available: http://www2.irrawaddy.org/article.php?art_id=3050 [Accessed 27 June 2015].

—— 2004. 'The Enemy Within' [Online]. Rangoon: *The Irrawaddy*. Available: http://www2.irrawaddy.org/article.php?art_id=963 [Accessed 27 June 2015].

Maw, B. 1995. 'Research on Early Man in Myanmar'. *Myanmar Historical Research Journal*, 1, 1213–220.

McElwee, J. J. 2015. 'Francis: Burmese treatment of Rohingya minority a form of "war"' [Online]. Kansas City: *National Catholic Reporter*. Available: http://ncronline.org/news/vatican/francis-burmese-treatment-rohingya-minority-form-war [Accessed 18 August 2015].

McGowan, W. 2012. 'Burma's Buddhist Chauvinism' [Online]. New York: *Wall Street Journal*. Available: http://www.wsj.com/articles/SB10000872396390443847404577628874147528692 [Accessed 8 July 2015].

McLaughlin, T. 2015a. 'Government failed to ensure justice after riots: UN chief' [Online]. Reuters. Available: http://www.thestateless.com/2015/10/03/govt-failed-to-ensure-justice-after-riots-un-chief/ [Accessed 13 October 2015].

—— 2015b. 'Rising Arakanese Party could further marginalize Rohingya' [Online]. Reuters. Available: http://www.thestateless.com/2015/10/03/rising-arakanese-party-could-further-marginalize-rohingya/ [Accessed 13 October 2015].

Médecins Sans Frontières 2002. '10 Years for the Rohingyas Refugees in Bangladesh: Past, Present and Future'. Médecins Sans Frontières.

Mepham, D. 2015. 'What Burma's Elections Mean for the Rohingyas' [Online]. Human Rights Watch. Available: https://www.hrw.org/news/2015/10/08/what-burmas-elections-mean-rohingya [Accessed 11 October 2015].

Michaels, S. 2014. 'Suu Kyi Meets Critics of "Protection of Race and Religion" Bills '[Online]. Rangoon: *The Irrawaddy*. Available: http://www.irrawaddy.org/burma/suu-kyi-meets-critics-protection-race-religion-bills.html [Accessed 16 July 2015].

Min, U. K. 2012. 'An Assessment of the Question of Rohingya's Nationality: Legal Nexus between Rohingya and the State'. Rangoon.

Moe, W. 2015. 'Aung San Suu Kyi Calls Ex-Leader of Myanmar Governing Party an "Ally"' [Online]. Asia Pacific. Available: http://www.nytimes.com/2015/08/19/world/asia/myanmar-aung-san-suu-kyi-calls-shwe-mann-an-ally.html?_r=0 [Accessed 19 August 2015].

Moore, E. 2004. 'Interpreting Pyu material culture: Royal chronologies and finger-marked bricks'. *Myanmar Historical Research Journal*, 13:1, 1–57.

—— 2011. 'The Early Buddhist Archaeology of Myanmar: Tagaung, Thagara, and the Mon-Pyu Dichotomy', *In:* McCormick, P., Jenny, M. & Baker, C. (eds.) *The Mon over Two Millennia: Monuments, Manuscripts, Movements*. Bangkok: Institute of Asian Studies, Chulalongkorn University.

Myanmar 2008. 'Constitution of the Republic of the Union of Myanmar'.

Myintzu, S. Y., Ei, K. K., Thu, K. & Kyaw, N. R. 2015. 'Myanmar Election Body Rejects Muslim Parliamentary Candidates' [Online]. Radio Free Asia. Available: http://www.rfa.org/english/news/myanmar/election-body-rejects-muslim-parliamentary-candidates-09012015161036.html [Accessed 22 September 2015].

Organisation of Islamic Cooperation. 2015. 'OIC continues to Mobilize Efforts for Political and Humanitarian Assistance to Rohingya Refugees' [Online]. OIC. Available: http://www.oic-oci.org/oicv2/topic/?t_id=10123&ref=4006&lan=en&x_key=rohingya [Accessed 19 July 2015].

Pakistan Today. 2011. 'Pakistan to facilitate Chinese investment in all sectors: PM' [Online]. Available: http://www.pakistantoday.com.pk/2011/06/pakistan-to-facilitate-chinese-investment-in-all-sectors-pm/ [Accessed 9 July 2011].

Paris, R. 2001. 'Human Security: Paradigm Shift or Hot Air?' *International Security*, 26:2, 87–102.

Paton, C. 1826. 'A Short Report on Arakan'. London: Colonial Office.

Pearn, B. 1944. 'Arakan and the First Anglo-Burmese War, 1824–1825'. *The Far Eastern Quarterly*, 4:1, 27–40.

Pedersen, M. B. 2014. 'Myanmar's Democratic Opening'. *In:* Cheesman, N., Farrelly, N. & Wilson, T. (eds.) *Debating Democratization in Myanmar*. Singapore: ISEAS Publishing.

Perry, D. M. 1983. *Stefan Stambolov and the Emergence of Modern Bulgaria, 1870–1895*, Durham, NC: Duke University Press.

Peterson, S. 2002. 'Epidemic Disease and National Security'. *Security Studies*, 12:2, 43–81.

Pierson, P. 2004. *Politics in Time: History, Institutions, and Social Analysis*, Princeton, NJ: Princeton University Press.

Pitman, T. & Peck, G. 2013. 'Radical monks, prejudice fuel Myanmar violence' [Online]. Associated Press. Available: http://www.thejakartapost.com/news/2013/06/01/radical-monks-prejudice-fuel-myanmar-violence.html [Accessed 16 September 2015].

Pohl, J. O. 1999. *Ethnic Cleansing in the USSR, 1937–1949*, Westport, CT: Greenwood Press.

Preston, A. 2015. 'Saffron Terror: an audience with Burma's "Buddhist Bin Laden" Ashin Wirathu' [Online]. London: *GQ*. Available: http://www.gq-magazine.co.uk/comment/articles/2015–02/12/ashin-wirathu-audience-with-the-buddhist-bin-laden-burma [Accessed 28 June 2015].

Pugh, C. L. 2013. 'Is Citizenship the Answer? Constructions of belonging and exclusion for the stateless Rohingya of Burma'. Oxford: International Migration Institute.

Quintana, T. O. 2014. 'Report of the Special Rapporteur on the situation of human rights in Myanmar'. Geneva: United Nations General Assembly.

Ragland, T. K. 1994. 'Burma's Rohingyas in Crisis: Protection of "Humanitarian" Refugees under International Law'. *Boston College Third World Law Journal*, 14:2, 301–338.

Rakhine Investigation Committee 2013. 'Summary of Recommendations'. Government of Myanmar.

Rangoon Suspense 2002. 'Report Card, Burma'. Bangkok: Alternative ASEAN Network on Burma.

Refugees International. 2013. 'Myanmar' [Online]. Available: http://www.refugeesinternational.org/where-we-work/asia/myanmar [Accessed 26 February 2014].

refworld. 1982. 'Burma Citizenship Law' [Online]. UNHCR. Available: http://www.refworld.org/docid/3ae6b4f71b.html [Accessed 2014 28 February].

Republic of the Union of Myanmar 2014. 'The Population and Housing Census of Myanmar 2014'. Department of Population.

Reuters. 2012. 'EU welcomes "measured" Myanmar response to rioting' [Online]. Brussels: Reuters. Available: http://uk.reuters.com/article/2012/06/11/us-myanmar-violence-idUSBRE85A01C20120611 [Accessed 18 June 2015].

——— 2015a. 'Burma military chief claims refugees pretending to be Rohingya to get aid' [Online]. London: *The Guardian*. Available: http://www.theguardian.com/world/2015/may/22/burma-military-chief-claims-refugees-pretending-to-be-rohingya-to-get-aid [Accessed 15 June 2015].

——— 2015b. 'Myanmar's ousted ruling party leader Shwe Mann meets Aung San Suu Kyi' [Online]. Available: http://www.rohingyablogger.com/2015/08/myanmars-ousted-ruling-party-leader.html [Accessed 18 August 2015].

Ribeiro, E. H. 2013. 'Military can still be good state-builders in Myanmar' [Online]. Rangoon: New Mandala. Available: http://asiapacific.anu.edu.au/newmandala/2013/10/15/military-can-still-be-good-state-builders-for-myanmar/ [Accessed 27 June 2015].

Rohingya National Organisation 2015. 'Press Release: Save Rohingyas from the hands of the human traffickers and greedy exploiters'.

Roughneen, S. 2010. 'China Backs Burma's Junta Leaders' [Online]. OilPrice. Available: http://oilprice.com/Geopolitics/Asia/China-Backs-Burmas-Junta-Leaders.html [Accessed 1 July 2015].

Ruthven, M. 2002. *A Fury for God: The Islamist Attack on America*, London: Granta.

Sarkar, A. K. 1993. *The Mysteries of Vajrayana Buddhism: From Atisha to Dalai Lama*, Coburg: Au, South Asia Books.

Schissler, M. 2014. 'May Flowers' [Online]. New Mandala. Available: http://asiapacific.anu.edu.au/newmandala/2014/05/17/may-flowers/ [Accessed 16 July 2015].

Seekins, D. M. 2008. 'The Social, Political and Humanitarian Impact of Burma's Cyclone Nargis'. *The Asia-Pacific Journal*, 6:5.

Selth, A. 2004. 'Pariah Partners in Arms' [Online]. Rangoon: *The Irrawaddy*. Available: http://www2.irrawaddy.org/article.php?art_id=933 [Accessed 19 August 2015].

Selth, A. 2008. 'Burma's continuing fear of invasion' [Online]. The Interpreter. Available: http://www.lowyinterpreter.org/post/2008/05/28/Burmas-continuing-fear-of-invasion.aspx [Accessed 27 June 2015].

Shah, I. 2015. 'Rohingyas' demand Burmese Gov't: either historically disprove "the ethnical term Rohingya" or pay back their indigenous rights' [Online]. Rangoon: *Burma Times*. Available: http://burmatimes.net/rohingyas-demand-burmese-govt-either-historically-disprove-the-ethnical-term-rohingya-or-pay-back-their-indigenous-rights/ [Accessed 8 July 2015].

Sharples, R. 2003. 'Repatriating the Rohingya'. *Burma Issues*, 13:3, 1–3.

Sheridan, M. 2015. 'Myanmar "effectively a state of apartheid" for Muslims' [Online]. *The Australian*. Available: http://www.theaustralian.com.au/news/world/myanmar-effectively-a-state-of-apartheid-for-muslims/story-fnb64oi6–1227537589783 [Accessed 22 September 2015].

Shin, B. 1998. *From early Bama (Myanmar) up to the present Myanmar nation. Myanmar before Anawrahta*. Yangon: Innwa Publishing House.

SIL 2015. *Languages of Myanmar: An Ethnologue Country Report*, Dallas, TX: SIL.

Simms, B. 2001. *Unfinest Hour: Britain and the Destruction of Bosnia*, London: Penguin.

Simonson, T. 2015. 'The taming of the NLD... by the NLD' [Online]. New Mandala. Available: http://asiapacific.anu.edu.au/newmandala/2015/08/12/the-taming-of-the-nld-by-the-nld/ [Accessed 11 October 2015].

Slim, W. J. 1956. *Defeat into Victory: Battling Japan in Burma and India 1942–1945*, New York: Cooper Square.

Slodkowski, A. 2015. 'Beaten and starving, some Rohingya flee boats, return to camps'

REFERENCES

[Online]. Reuters. Available: http://www.rohingyablogger.com/2015/05/beaten-and-starving-some-rohingya-flee.html [Accessed 18 August 2015].

Smith, M. 2011a. 'Myanmar's Economy Needs Human Rights Reforms' [Online]. *The World Post*. Available: http://www.huffingtonpost.com/matthew-smith/myanmars-economy-needs-hu_b_4347843.html [Accessed 26 February 2014].

―――― 2011b. 'Time for New Approach to Burma: War Crimes Mounting' [Online]. *The World Post*. Available: http://www.huffingtonpost.com/matthew-smith/burma-war-crimes_b_906660.html [Accessed 26 February 2014].

―――― 2014. 'Politics of Persecution'. Fortify Rights International.

―――― 2015. 'How China Fuels Myanmar's Wars' [Online]. New York: *New York Times*. Available: http://www.nytimes.com/2015/03/05/opinion/how-china-fuels-myanmars-wars.html?_r=1 [Accessed 20 August 2015].

Smith, M. & Allsebrook, A. 1994. 'Ethnic Groups in Burma: Development, Democracy and Human Rights', London: Anti-Slavery International.

Snaing, Y. 2014. 'Activists Face Violent Threats After Opposing Interfaith Marriage Bill' [Online]. Rangoon: *The Irrawaddy*. Available: http://www.irrawaddy.org/burma/activists-face-violent-threats-opposing-interfaith-marriage-bill.html [Accessed 16 July 2015].

SOAS 2003. 'Burmese Buddhism in Colonial Burma'. *Bulletin of Burma Research*, 1:2, 42–47.

South, A. 2008. *Ethnic Politics in Burma*, London: Routledge.

Steinberg, D. I. 2001. *Burma: The State of Myanmar*, Washington, D.C.: Georgetown University Press.

Steinberg, D. I. 2010. 'The United States and Myanmar: a "boutique issue"?' *International Affairs*, 86:1, 175–194.

Stoakes, E. 2015. 'Monks, PowerPoint Presentations, and Ethnic Cleansing' [Online]. Washington, D.C.: Foreign Policy. Available: http://foreignpolicy.com/2015/10/26/evidence-links-myanmar-government-monks-ethnic-cleansing-rohingya/ [Accessed 28 October 2015].

Stoakes, E., Kelly, A. & Kelly, C. 2015. 'Revealed: how the Thai fishing industry traffics, imprisons and enslaves' [Online]. London: *The Guardian*. Available: http://www.theguardian.com/global-development/2015/jul/20/thai-fishing-industry-implicated-enslavement-deaths-rohingya [Accessed 20 July 2015].

Stoisiek, J. 2012. 'The Killings of Ethnic Minorities in Myanmar (Burma): Change in Myanmar's Politics after Elections in April 2012'. *Genocide Prevention Now*, 1215–20.

Stokes, E. & Kelly, C. 2015. 'Asian refugee crisis: trafficked migrants held off Thailand in vast "camp boats"' [Online]. London: *The Guardian*. Available: http://www.theguardian.com/global-development/2015/may/28/asian-refugee-crisis-trafficked-migrants-held-off-thailand-camp-boats [Accessed 15 June 2015].

Stout, D. 2015. 'Burma Jails New Zealander for "Insulting Buddhism" in Facebook

REFERENCES

Post' [Online]. *Time Magazine*. Available: http://time.com/3747187/burma-buddhism-new-zealand-phil-blackwood/ [Accessed 28 June 2015].

Stratfor 2015. 'The Buddhist Core of Fractured Myanmar'. Washington, D.C.: Stratfor Global Intelligence.

Strathern, A. 2013. 'Why are Buddhist monks attacking Muslims?' [Online]. London: BBC. Available: http://www.bbc.co.uk/news/magazine-22356306 [Accessed 28 June 2015].

Sydney Morning Herald. 2015. '"They are humans": Myanmar opposition says Rohingya people have rights' [Online]. Sydney: *Sydney Morning Herald*. Available: http://www.smh.com.au/world/they-are-humans-myanmar-opposition-says-rohingya-people-have-rights-20150519-gh4q8m.html [Accessed 23 September 2015].

Tahay, A. 2014. 'Challenges on Rohingya's Citizenship'. Japan.

Talbot, I. & Singh, G. 2009. *The Partition of India*, Cambridge: Cambridge University Press.

Teff, M. & Gopallawa, S. 2013. 'Myanmar: Protecting Minority Rights is non-Negotiable'. Refugees International.

Tha, B. 2013. 'Massacre of 1942' [Online]. Arakan Bumiputra. Available: http://www.arakanbumiputra.com/2013/04/massacre-of-1942-by-ba-tha-buthidaung.html [Accessed 4 March 2014].

Tharoor, I. 2015. 'The risk of genocide around the world' [Online]. Washington, D.C.: *Washington Post*. Available: https://www.washingtonpost.com/news/worldviews/wp/2015/09/21/map-the-risk-of-genocide-around-the-world/ [Accessed 22 September 2015].

―――― 2015. 'Why does this Buddhist-majority nation hate these Muslims so much?' [Online]. Washington, D.C.: *The Washington Post*. Available: http://www.washingtonpost.com/blogs/worldviews/wp/2015/02/13/why-does-this-buddhist-majority-nation-hate-these-muslims-so-much/ [Accessed 18 February 2015].

The Economist. 2007. 'How Myanmar's people rose up against its regime—and the regime rose up against its people' [Online]. London: *The Economist*. Available: http://www.economist.com/node/9868041 [Accessed 28 June 2015].

―――― 2012. 'War Among the Pagodas' [Online]. London: *The Economist*. Available: http://www.economist.com/blogs/banyan/2012/10/killings-myanmars-rakhine-state [Accessed 16 June 2015].

The Irrawaddy. 1997a. 'Slaughter of the Innocent Soldiers' [Online]. Rangoon: *The Irrawaddy*. Available: http://www2.irrawaddy.org/article.php?art_id=847 [Accessed 27 June 2015].

―――― 1997b. 'Who Killed Aung San?' [Online]. *The Irrawaddy*. Available: http://www2.irrawaddy.org/article.php?art_id=719 [Accessed 17 September 2015].

―――― 2007. 'Heroes and Villains' [Online]. Rangoon: *The Irrawaddy*. Available: http://www2.irrawaddy.org/article.php?art_id=6883 [Accessed 27 June 2015].

Thein, T. 2015a. 'Man assaulted by military refused treatment by hospitals' [Online]. Rangoon: *Burma Times*. Available: http://burmatimes.net/man-assaulted-by-

military-refused-treatment-by-hospitals/?utm_medium=twitter&utm_source=
twitterfeed [Accessed 1 July 2015].

—— 2015b. 'Refugee injured in construction site' [Online]. Rangoon: *Burma Times*. Available: http://burmatimes.net/refugee-injured-in-construction-site/ [Accessed 1 July 2015].

Thu, M. K. 2015. 'Rakhine National Party in "chaos"' [Online]. Rangoon: *Myanmar Times*. Available: http://www.mmtimes.com/index.php/national-news/15221-rakhine-national-party-in-chaos.html [Accessed 22 September 2015].

Tonkin, D. 2014a. 'Political Myths' [Online]. Network Myanmar. Available: http://www.networkmyanmar.org/index.php/political-myths [Accessed 28 February 2014].

—— 2014b. 'The "Rohingya" Identity: British experience in Arakan 1826–1948', Rangoon: Network Myanmar.

Topsfield, J. 2015. 'Australia criticised for inaction on Rohingya refugee crisis' [Online]. Sydney: *Sydney Morning Herald*. Available: http://www.smh.com.au/world/fears-rohingya-death-toll-vastly-underestimated-20151021-gkeeee.html [Accessed 21 October 2015].

Triveldi, S. 2013. 'New role for India in Myanmar' [Online]. *Asia Times*. Available: http://www.atimes.com/atimes/Southeast_Asia/SEA-01-160913.html [Accessed 26 February 2014].

Tucker, J. 2007. 'Enough! Electoral Fraud, Collective Action Problems, and Post-Communist Coloured Revolutions'. *Perspectives on Politics*, 5:3, 537–553.

Tun, A. H. 2014. 'Myanmar sees foreign investment topping $5 bln in 2014–15' [Online]. Reuters. Available: http://www.reuters.com/article/2014/09/16/myanmar-investment-idUSL3N0RH3EZ20140916 [Accessed 20 April 2015].

Tun, T. 1959. 'Religious Buildings of Burma AD 1000–1300'. *Journal of Burma Research Society*, 42:2, 71–81.

UCANEWS. 2015. 'Refugee boats set sail as monsoon season ends' [Online]. UCANEWS. Available: http://www.ucanews.com/news/refugee-boats-set-sail-as-monsoon-season-ends/74455 [Accessed 21 October 2015].

UNHCR. 2010. 'Burma Citizenship Law 1982' [Online]. UNHCR. Available: http://www.refworld.org/cgi-bin/texis/vtx/rwmain?page=printdoc&docid=3ae6b4f71b [Accessed 28 February 2014].

United Nations 1951. 'Convention on the Prevention and Punishment of the Crime of Genocide'. Geneva: United Nations.

—— 2002. 'Rome Statute of the International Criminal Court' [Online]. UN. Available: http://legal.un.org/icc/statute/romefra.htm [Accessed 23 February 2014].

—— 2013. 'Situation of human rights in Myanmar'. New York: UN.

—— 2015. 'Genocide in Rwanda' [Online]. Geneva: United Nations Human Rights Council. Available: http://www.unitedhumanrights.org/genocide/genocide_in_rwanda.htm [Accessed 22 February 2015].

REFERENCES

United Nations Human Rights. 2015. 'Myanmar: UN rights experts express alarm at adoption of first of four "protection of race and religion" bills' [Online]. New York: Office of the High Commissioner for Human Rights. Available: http://www.ohchr. org/EN/NewsEvents/Pages/DisplayNews.aspx?NewsID=16015&LangID=E [Accessed 28 June 2015].

US Campaign For Burma. 2014. 'Top 4 Racist Laws against Rohingya Muslims in Burma' [Online]. Washington, D.C.: US Campaign For Burma. Available: https:// uscampaignforburma.wordpress.com/2014/03/26/racism-in-burma-4-discrimina-tory-laws-against-rohingya-muslims/ [Accessed 20 February 2015].

US Commission on International Religious Freedom 2011. 'Countries of Particular Concern: Burma'. Washington, D.C.: US Commission on International Religious Freedom.

US Department of State. 2014. 'Trafficking in Persons Report: 2014 Report' [Online]. Washington, D.C.: US Department of State. Available: http://www.state.gov/j/ tip/rls/tiprpt/ [Accessed 15 June 2015].

——— 2015. 'Trafficking in Persons Report: 2015 Report' [Online]. Washington, D.C.: US Department of State. Available: http://www.state.gov/j/tip/rls/ tiprpt/2015/index.htm [Accessed 19 August 2015].

Varshney, A. 2002. *Ethnic Conflict, Civic Life*, New Haven, CT: Yale University Press.

Vateri, J. S. 1815. *Linguarum totius orbis Index*, Berlin.

Venkateswaran, K. S. 1996. 'Burma: Beyond the Law'. Article 19. Available: https:// www.article19.org/data/files/pdfs/publications/burma-beyond-law.pdf [Accessed 23 November 2015].

Vrieze, P. 2015. 'Nikkei Asian Review: "Myanmar's coming elections spell r-i-s-k for investors"' [Online]. Yangon: Vriens and Partners. Available: http://www. vrienspartners.com/nikkei-asian-review-myanmars-coming-elections-spell-r-i-s-k-for-investors.html [Accessed 22 September 2015].

Wadhwaney, R. 2015. 'Fearing Radicalization Attempt, India ups Surveillance on Rohingya Refugees' [Online]. Benar News. Available: http://www.benarnews.org/ english/news/bengali/rohingya-08172015155820.html [Accessed 18 August 2015].

Walton, M. 2013a. 'Myanmar needs a new nationalism' [Online]. *Asia Times*. Available: http://www.atimes.com/atimes/Southeast_Asia/SEA-02–200513.html [Accessed 16 July 2015].

——— 2013b. 'A Primer on the Roots of Buddhist/Muslim Conflict in Myanmar and a Way Forward' [Online]. IslamiCommentary. Available: http://islamicommentary. org/2013/10/matthew-walton-a-primer-on-the-roots-of-buddhistmuslim-conflict-in-myanmar-and-a-way-forward/ [Accessed 16 July 2015].

——— 2014. 'What are Myanmar's Buddhist Sunday schools teaching?' [Online]. East Asia Forum. Available: http://www.eastasiaforum.org/2014/12/16/what-are-myanmars-buddhist-sunday-schools-teaching/ [Accessed 16 July 2015].

Walton, M. & Hayward, S. 2014. *Contesting Buddhist Narratives: Democratization, Nationalism, and Communal Violence in Myanmar*. Honolulu, HI: East-West Centre.

Weikart, R. 1993. 'The Origins of Social Darwinism in Germany, 1859–1895'. *Journal of the History of Ideas*, 54:3, 469–488.

Weng, L. 2014. 'Burma Govt Rejects "Unacceptable" UN Statement on Rohingya Killings' [Online]. Rangoon: *The Irrawaddy*. Available: http://www.irrawaddy.org/burma/burma-govt-rejects-unacceptable-un-statement-rohingya-killings.html [Accessed 22 September 2015].

WikiCommons. 2012. 'Map of Burma' [Online]. Available: https://en.wikipedia.org/wiki/Myanmar [Accessed 13 September 2015].

Williams, D. C. 2014. 'What's so Bad about Burma's 2008 Constitution?' *In:* Crouch, M. & Lindsey, T. (eds.) *Law Society and Transition In Myanmar*. Oxford: Hart Publishing.

Wilson, H. H. 1817. *The History of British India*, London: Baldwin, Cradock and Joy.

Win, S. 2015. 'Special Report—With official help, Myanmar's radical Buddhists target Muslim-owned businesses' [Online]. Rangoon: Myanmar Now. Available: http://www.myanmar-now.org/news/i/?id=9ba61afc-285d-49bd-8f73–8b9efaf941c0 [Accessed 21 September 2015].

Win, T. L. 2014a. 'Burmese journalist beseeches brethren: Stop with the Muslim hate speech' [Online]. Thomson Reuters. Available: http://www.trust.org/item/201 40313074529–3vfw4/ [Accessed 20 July 2015].

—— 2014b. 'Myanmar activists launch anti-"hate speech" campaign' [Online]. Thomson Reuters. Available: http://www.trust.org/item/20140403131148–4mqvg/ [Accessed 20 July 2015].

—— 2014c. 'Sexism, racism, poor education condemn Rohingya women in western Myanmar' [Online]. Thomson Reuters. Available: http://www.trust.org/item/20140709164452-re3s1/ [Accessed 20 July 2015].

—— 2014d. 'Will the Rohingya, driven from their homes, spend the rest of their lives segregated in ghettoes?' [Online]. Thomson Reuters. Available: http://www.trust.org/item/20140827082155-p627d/ [Accessed 20 July 2015].

Winn, P. 2013. 'Suu Kyi spokesman: "There is no Rohingya"' [Online]. *Global Post*. Available: http://www.globalpost.com/dispatch/news/regions/asia-pacific/myanmar/130501/suu-kyi-no-rohingya [Accessed 26 February 2014].

Wolf, S. O. 2015. 'The Rohingya: Humanitarian Crisis or Security Threat?' [Online]. *The Diplomat*. Available: http://thediplomat.com/2015/10/the-rohingya-humanitarian-crisis-or-security-threat/ [Accessed 12 October 2015].

Wong, C. 2015. 'Burma: Activists Charged for Mocking Military Online' [Online]. Human Rights Watch. Available: https://www.hrw.org/news/2015/10/17/burma-activists-charged-mocking-military-online [Accessed 19 October 2015].

Woolacott, M. 2015. 'Why Burma still needs Aung San Suu Kyi' [Online]. London:

REFERENCES

The Guardian. Available: http://www.theguardian.com/commentisfree/2015/apr/06/burma-aung-san-suu-kyi-democracy-election [Accessed 1 July 2015].

World Elections. 2012. 'Burma (Myanmar) by-elections 2012' [Online]. Available: http://welections.wordpress.com/2012/04/06/burma-by-elections-2012/ [Accessed 8 March 2014].

Yee, T. H. 2015. 'Expect further Rohingya exodus, report warns' [Online]. Singapore: *The Straits Times.* Available: http://www.straitstimes.com/asia/se-asia/expect-further-rohingya-exodus-report-warns [Accessed 19 October 2015].

Yegar, M. 1972. *The Muslims of Burma: A Study of a Minority Group*, Wiesbaden: Otto Harrassowitz.

Yeni. 2005. 'An Enduring Legacy Written in Blood' [Online]. Rangoon: *The Irrawaddy.* Available: http://www2.irrawaddy.org/article.php?art_id=4498&page=2 [Accessed 27 June 2015].

Zan, U. S. & Chan, A. 2005. *Influx Viruses: The Illegal Muslims in Arakan*, New York: Arakanese in United States.

Zarni, M. 2012. 'Popular "Buddhist" racism and the generals' militarism' [Online]. Oslo: DVB. Available: https://www.dvb.no/analysis/popular-buddhist-racism-and-the-generals%E2%80%99-militarism/23595 [Accessed 21 February 2015].

Zaw, A. & Yeni. 2010. 'The NLD Makes its Move' [Online]. Rangoon: *The Irrawaddy.* Available: http://www2.irrawaddy.org/article.php?art_id=18216 [Accessed 30 June 2015].

Zin, M. 2010. *Opposition Movements in Burma: The Question of Relevancy. Finding Dollars, Sense and Legitimacy in Burma.* Washington, D.C.: Woodrow Wilson International Center for Scholars.

——— 2014. 'Return of the Myanmar Military?' [Online]. New York: *New York Times.* Available: http://www.nytimes.com/2014/11/18/opinion/return-of-the-myanmar-military.html?partner=rss&emc=rss&_r=1 [Accessed 27 June 2015].

INDEX

Abbott, Anthony 'Tony', 91, 97
aboriginal cultures, 20
Afghanistan, 6, 24, 66
agriculture, 7, 9, 18, 35, 49, 52, 56, 95
aid agencies, 38, 87
Akyab District, Arakan, 30
Ananda Chandra Inscriptions, Shitethaung Temple, 21
Anawrahta, Emperor of Pagan, 21
Andaman Sea, 74, 93, 96, 97, 129
Anglo-Burmese Wars
    First (1824–6), 3, 5–6, 18, 25–6, 28, 35, 50–1, 65, 79
    Second (1852–3), 26
    Third (1885–6), 26
animism, 18, 19, 22
anti-colonial riots (1938), 27
anti-extremism, 11, 14, 70–2, 135–6
anti-Semitism, 106–7
Arabic, 21
Arakan, 4–8, 18, 20–1, 23–33, 35, 41, 47, 48, 51, 56, 79, 141
Arakan League for Democracy (ALD), 13, 41, 42, 79, 121–3
Arakan National Party (ANP), 79, 80, 121–3, 130, 140
Armed Forces Day, 28

Armenian Genocide (1915–16), 104, 107, 109
arms trade, 2, 16, 44, 45, 47, 74, 75, 108, 131, 134
arson, 71, 81, 83, 84, 86
Ashton, Catherine, 81
Association of Southeast Asian Nations (ASEAN), 15, 45, 56, 62, 74–5, 94, 117, 124–5, 129, 131, 132, 133, 134, 136
Aung Gyi, 40
Aung Mingalar, Sittwe, 89
Aung San, 2, 11, 28, 36, 40, 130, 139
Aung San Suu Kyi, 1, 2, 10, 12, 13, 40, 43, 46, 60, 61, 66, 69, 71, 99, 118–21, 122, 133, 135, 139
    election boycott (2010), 13, 61
    presidential bar, 60, 120–1
    Rohingya persecution, silence on, 2, 66, 99, 118–21, 122
    Thein Sein, relations with, 60
Australia, 20, 43, 47, 91, 97, 125
Austro-Hungarian Empire (1867–1918), 108
authoritarianism, 2, 3, 15, 73, 76, 100, 134
Ava Kingdom (1287–1752), 22

Aye Maung, 82, 122

Balkans, 104
Ban Ki-moon, 66, 75, 85, 134
Bangladesh, xiii, 4, 8, 9, 18, 24, 27, 44, 52, 55, 56, 66, 82, 87, 91, 93, 94, 100, 126, 133
Barroso, José Manuel, 74
Baxter, James, 29–30, 49
Bay of Bengal, 6, 18, 20, 55, 73
begging, 95
Belarus, 46
Belgium, 105, 108
Bell, Henry G., 143
Bengal, 3, 4, 6, 10, 18, 20, 21, 24, 25, 29, 31, 32, 55, 73, 90, 94, 99, 115, 116, 117, 119
birth control, 53, 68, 80, 90, 100, 109
Blair, Anthony 'Tony', 74
boycotts
   of businesses, 14, 67, 69, 82
   of elections, 13, 58, 61
Britain, 2, 4, 5–7, 18, 22–3, 24, 25–32, 35, 40, 43–4, 46, 48, 49, 50, 65, 76, 79, 105, 108
   1824 First Anglo-Burmese War begins, 3, 5–6, 8, 25, 26, 28, 35
   1825 Charles Paton begins survey of Arakan, 6, 29, 145
   1826 annexation of Arakan, 5–6, 18, 22–3, 26, 28, 31, 65, 79; census of Arakan completed, 6, 29, 31, 145
   1852 Second Anglo-Burmese War begins, 26
   1871 census in Arakan, 29, 32
   1885 Third Anglo-Burmese War begins, 26
   1886 annexation of Burma to British India, 5, 18, 22–3, 26
   1911 Burmese census, 6
   1930 Saya San Uprising, 27

1937 Burma made separate colony, 5, 26, 29, 35
1938 anti-colonial riots in Burma, 27
1941 James Baxter publishes report on Burma, 29–30, 49
1946 BIA insurgency in Burma, 28
1948 Burma gains Independence, 2, 5, 7, 8, 18, 27, 28, 30, 35, 43–4
2008 warships sent to Myanmar to aid after Cyclone Nargis, 46, 56
2012 Tony Blair visits Myanmar, 74; David Cameron visits Myanmar, 74
British Broadcasting Corporation (BBC), 82
Buchanan, Francis, 24, 25
Buddhism, 2–16, 18–30, 32–3, 35–43, 46–7, 48, 53, 55, 57, 59, 63–72, 80–90, 91, 96, 97, 99, 101, 102, 105, 117, 118–19, 120, 122–3, 124, 130, 135–6, 140–1
   anti-extremism, 11, 14, 70–2, 135–6
   citizenship, 3, 4, 8, 10, 11, 28, 35–6, 37, 41, 47, 53, 59, 63, 71, 80, 87, 103, 117, 120
   dehumanisation, 3, 65, 68
   education, 14, 55, 68–9, 99, 140
   extremism, 3–4, 5, 6, 9, 11, 13, 14–15, 16, 29, 32, 33, 59, 63–72, 80–90, 91, 96, 97, 99, 101, 102, 105, 117, 118–19, 120, 122–3, 124, 130, 135–6
   hate speech, 11, 68, 70
   inter-communal violence, 2, 64–5, 67, 69, 141
   Mahayana, 66, 141
   monasteries, 22–3, 36, 37, 39, 66, 71, 80, 140
   nationalism, 5, 9, 23, 26, 46, 64, 65, 69, 87, 89

pagodas, 80
peaceful religion, perception as, 2, 140
reincarnation, 70
sangha, 11, 12, 13, 23, 37, 39, 40, 43, 55, 57, 63–72, 80, 82, 85, 101, 139, 140
sasana (teaching), 64–5
state, just rule, 3, 21–3, 35–6, 37–9, 46, 64–5, 87, 141
Theravada, 2, 19, 21, 23, 36, 38, 64–5, 141
Vajrayana tradition, 66
Burma Campaign UK, 118–19
Burma Road, 73
Burmese Communist Party, 7, 11, 28, 36, 47
Burmese Independence Army (BIA), 28
Burmese Road to Socialism, 9, 11, 37, 39, 42, 50, 53, 63
Burmese Socialist Programme Party, 8, 11, 38, 42, 49
Bush, George Walker, 46
Buthidaung, Rakhine State, 27, 80
Buy Buddhist campaigns, 69

Cambodia, 19, 44, 101
Cameron, David, 74
Caspian Sea, 105
Caucasus, 105
censuses, 6, 8, 10, 29–32, 49, 90, 115–17, 133
Central Intelligence Agency (CIA), 37
Chan, Aye, 32
children
    family planning, 53, 68, 80, 90, 100, 109
    infant mortality, 90
    murder of, 84, 87
    sexual exploitation, 93, 95

soldiers, 38
Chin people, 20, 24, 35, 51, 53
China, 16, 17, 20, 28, 36–7, 43, 44, 45–6, 47, 72–5, 131, 133, 134, 141
    1927–50 Civil War, 37
    1950 CIA begins funding exiled Kuomintang in Burma, 37, 43
    1960–89 Sino–Soviet split, 44
    2009 funding of pipeline from Kunming to Sittwe begins, 47
    2015 Aung San Suu Kyi visits Beijing, 73
Chinese Civil War (1927–50), 37
Christianity, 2, 7, 18, 23, 27, 53, 63, 104
citizenship, xiii, 3–10, 17, 32–3, 36, 41, 47–53, 57, 63, 75, 79, 80–1, 99, 103, 115–24, 129, 131–2, 136, 139, 141, 147
    and Buddhism, 3, 4, 8, 10, 11, 28, 35–6, 37, 41, 47, 53, 59, 63, 71, 80, 87, 103, 117, 120
civil service, 49, 58
civil society, 11, 15, 16, 70–2, 105, 107, 119, 135–6
Classical Journal, 24, 25
Clinton, Hillary, 74
colour revolutions, 46, 135
Committee Representing the People's Parliament (CRPP), 42
Commonwealth, 2, 43
Communism, 7, 11, 28, 36, 40, 43, 44, 47
Congo, Democratic Republic of the, 114
corruption, 61, 73, 92
Crimea, 105
crimes against humanity, 135
Croatia, 109
Cyclone Komen (2015), 97, 126
Cyclone Nargis (2008), 9, 46, 126

Dai Nat people, 50
Dalai Lama (Tenzin Gyatso), 66, 134, 140–1
dehumanisation, 3, 65, 68
democracy, xiii–xiv, 1–2, 3, 9–10, 12–15, 38–42, 48–50, 52–3, 56–63, 71–6, 80, 99, 100, 114–23, 124, 126, 131, 134, 139
Democracy and Human Rights Party, 120
Democratic Republic of the Congo, 114
demographics, 28–32, 109
Dragon King campaign (1977), 52
drug trade, 38
Duchiradan, Maungdaw, 86

Early Warning Project, 113
East Pakistan (1955–71), 7, 27, 44, 49
economic problems, 9, 22, 39, 43, 53, 55, 63, 114, 133
education, 14, 51, 55, 68–9, 80, 99, 140
Ei Ei Lwin, 92
8888 Uprising (1988), 9, 12, 14, 38, 39, 46, 52, 55, 67, 72, 120, 139, 140
elections
    1990 general election, 9, 12, 40, 41, 42, 46, 51, 52, 63, 114–15, 120, 122
    2010 general election, 10, 11, 13, 47, 56–8, 61, 72, 115
    2012 by-elections, 13, 58, 75, 120
    2015 general election, 1, 2, 10, 13–15, 59, 60–2, 90, 108, 114–23, 129, 132, 134, 136, 140
Electoral Commission, 10, 117
Emergency Immigration Act (1974), 50, 57
ethnic cleansing, xiii, 1, 9, 13, 33, 42, 52, 79, 81–97, 100, 117, 118, 122, 133

European Union (EU), 46, 71, 72, 74, 81, 134
eviction campaigns, *see* ethnic cleansing
extremism, 3–4, 5, 6, 9, 11, 13, 14–15, 16, 29, 32, 33, 59, 63–72, 80–90, 91, 96, 97, 99, 101, 102, 105, 117, 118–19, 120, 122–3, 124, 130, 135–6

Facebook, 83, 86
family planning, 53, 68, 80, 90, 100, 109
Farai-di movement, 31
Farmaner, Mark, 118–19
federalism, 44, 59, 130
fishing, 7, 9, 18, 49, 91–4, 96
forced labour, xiii, 39, 52, 80, 95
foreign investment, 38, 58, 59, 72, 73, 75, 76, 132
Foreign Policy, 75
Foreign Registration Cards, 50
France, 46, 108
Francis, Pope, 91, 134
freedom of movement, xiii, 51, 53, 80, 110, 129

Ganges Valley, 20
gas, 47, 72
genocide, 1, 3, 16, 48, 70, 76, 91, 96, 100–11, 113–27, 129–30, 132, 135, 136, 139, 141
    and international community, 99–100, 103, 108–9, 110–11, 129, 132, 136–7
    international law, 100–1, 103, 109–10, 135
    trigger events, 103, 107–8, 110, 114–27
Germany, 104, 105, 106–9, 132
GlobalPost, 99
Gutman, Pamela, 20

Habyarimana, Juvénal, 106, 107
Hagel, Chuck, 46
Harff, Barbara, 113
Harkat-ul-Jihad al-Islami (HuJI), 126
hate speech, 11, 68, 70
healthcare, 16, 89, 90, 91, 110, 124
heroin, 38
hill tribes, 38, 42
Hinduism, 2, 6, 19, 21, 24, 29
Hitler, Adolf, 107
Holocaust (1941–5), 104, 106–9, 132
Hong Kong, 4
Horthy, Miklós, 107
human rights, xiv, 9, 16, 38, 39, 44, 45,
    52, 62, 73–4, 75, 83, 85, 87, 89, 100,
    101, 109–10, 113, 131, 134, 136
Human Rights Watch, 115, 124
human trafficking, 89, 91–7, 124, 125,
    131–2
Hungary, 107
Hutus, 105–6, 107, 108–9

identity cards, 8, 9, 10, 41, 42, 49, 50,
    115, 116, 117, 119, 129
India, 5, 6, 7, 17, 18, 19, 20, 21, 22, 24,
    25, 26, 29, 30, 35, 43, 44, 45, 47,
    49, 50, 72–3, 74, 75, 102, 126, 131,
    139, 141
Indian Congress Party, 27
Indo–Aryan peoples, languages, 6, 20,
    21, 24
Indonesia, 18, 20, 66, 91, 92, 93, 94,
    95, 96, 125
infant mortality, 90
Influx Viruses (Zan and Chan), 32
inter-communal violence, 1, 2–3, 7, 10,
    11, 13, 14, 27, 38, 41, 70–2, 74, 79,
    81–90, 99, 102, 104, 107, 120, 121,
    122, 126, 131, 134, 135, 141
internal refugee camps, 1, 13, 16, 38,
    42, 81, 84, 86, *88*, 89–90, 100, 102,

110, 115, 116, 117, 118, 120, 124,
    126, 127, 135
international community, 1, 2, 5, 12,
    16, 32, 33, 38, 43–7, 72–7, 82, 85,
    86, 90, 91, 95–7, 99–100, 103,
    108–9, 110–1, 120, 125, 129–35,
    136–7, 141
International Court of Justice (ICJ),
    109
International Criminal Court (ICC),
    109–10, 129, 131, 135
international law, 2, 5, 33, 100–1, 103,
    109–10, 124, 129, 135
Internet, 83, 86
Iran, 46, 103
Iraq, 66
Irrawaddy region, 5, 7, 17, 18, 20, 21,
    22, 26, 35, 56
Islam, 30, 65, 69, 82, 86, 89, 103, 125;
    see also Muslims
    jihadism, 30, 65, 86, 89, 125
    Koran, 125
    mosques, 80, 83, 86, 125
    Ramadan, 86
    Sunni vs Shi'a, 103
    Wahhabism, 31
Islamic State of Iraq and al-Sham
    (ISIS), 125
Islamism, 30, 82, 125–6
isolationism, 16, 43, 46, 131
Israel, 45
Italy, 107

jade, 95
Jama'atul Mujahideen Bangladesh
    (JMB), 126
Japan, 2, 7, 27, 28, 40
Jewish people, 104, 106–9
jihadism, 30, 65, 86, 89, 125

Kachin people, 8, 35, 48, 51, 63, 73,
    95, 116

Kaman people, 6, 24, 30, 83–4
Karachi, Pakistan, 74
Karen people, 7, 8, 9, 11, 27, 35, 36–7, 38, 44, 47, 48, 50, 51, 56, 59
Karen State, 35
Kayah people, 8, 48, 51
Kayin State, 116
Khin Kyi, 2, 36
KhMee people, 50
Khmers, 19
Khmer Rouge, 101
Kiersons, Steven, 91
Kila Dong, Maungdaw, 86
Kolkata, West Bengal, 102
Konbaung Dynasty (1752–1885), 22, 25
Koran, 125
Kumi people, 20, 22
Kunming, Yunnan, 47
Kuomintang, 37, 43
Kyauk Pyu, District, Rakhine State, 83–4
Kyaukse, Mandalay Region, 22
Kyaw Min, 120
Kyaw Zay, 36

labour substitution, 7, 49–50
Labutta, Rakhine State, 69
land rights, xiii, 4, 51, 52, 63, 73
languages, 4, 6, 8, 19, 20, 21, 24–5, 29, 31, 48, 53
Laos, 17
Lashio, Shan State, 71–2
Lashkar-e-Taiba (LeT), 126
Leider, Jacques, 29, 31, 32
liberalism, 3, 15, 75
logging, 44

MaBaTha, 11, 12, 14, 15, 68–72, 118, 120, 123, 136, 140
Mahayana Buddhism, 66, 141

Malaysia, 9, 18, 44, 52, 75, 86, 91, 92, 93, 94, 95, 96, 124, 125, 133
Mandalay, Mandalay Region, 19, 22, 72, 86
marriage rights, 11, 15, 53, 67, 71, 100, 109, 110, 117, 118, 119, 122, 135
mass movements, 40, 57, 63, 139
Mathieson, David, 115
Maung Maung Ohn, 123
Maungdaw, Rakhine State, 27, 80, 86
Mayu Region, 30, 49, 50
Medécins Sans Frontières (MSF), 87, 90, 133
Mediterranean, 93
Meiktila, Mandalay Region, 70, 86
migration, 5–7, 16, 26, 29, 32, 48, 49, 50, 75, 76, 86, 90–7, 114, 124–5, 132, 136
military, 2, 3, 4, 8, 9, 10, 11–12, 14–15, 21, 36–40, 42–7, 50–3, 55–61, 62, 72–7, 80, 81, 86, 91, 99, 108, 120–1, 124, 131–4, 139, 141, 151
    arms trade, 2, 16, 44, 45, 47, 74, 75, 108, 131, 134
    Buddhism, 3, 12, 14–15, 38, 39, 46, 53, 59, 70, 117, 140
    child soldiers, 38
    drug trade, 38
    economic interests, 10, 12, 38–9, 47, 59, 62, 72, 76–7, 108, 140
    extremism, support for, 3, 12, 14–15, 59, 64, 81, 83–5, 113, 117, 136
    factionalism, 12, 38, 40, 60, 61
    international relations, 2, 12, 16, 44–7, 59, 72–7, 85, 94, 95, 108, 121, 125, 131–4
    scapegoating of Rohingyas, 3, 4, 8, 114
    security of state, 11, 36, 46–7, 59, 61, 121

Union Solidarity and Development Party (USDP), 3, 10–14, 58, 59–63, 67, 69, 76, 80, 115, 117–18, 120–1, 130, 136, 139–40, 141
Min Aung Hlaing, 95
Minbya, District, Rakhine State, 83
minerals, mining, 4, 9, 44, 47, 59, 75, 95
Ministry of Home Affairs, 49
Mon Mon Myat, 71
Mon people, 8, 19, 20, 21, 22, 48, 51
Mon State, 18, 19
monasteries, 22–3, 36, 37, 39, 66, 71, 80, 140
Mongol Empire (1206–1368), 5, 22, 105
monks, *see under* sangha
mosques, 80, 83, 86, 125
Moulmein, Mon State, 6, 30
Mrauk-U District, Rakhine State, 83
Mrauk-U Kingdom (1429–1785), 24
Mru people, 20, 24
Mughals, 21
Mumbai, Maharashtra, 102
Muslim Free Areas, 80
Muslim Free Hospital, Rangoon, 89
Muslims, Islam, 2–4, 6–10, 13, 14, 17, 18, 21, 24–5, 27, 29, 31–2, 48, 53, 65–7, 69–72, 82–97, 104–5, 117, 118–27, 130
birth control, 53, 68, 80, 90, 100, 109
boycotts of businesses, 14, 67, 69, 82
elections, exclusion from, 9, 13, 41–2, 79, 114–23, 124, 140
Islamism, 30, 82, 125–6
jihadism, 30, 65, 86, 89, 125
Koran, 125
marriage rights, 11, 15, 53, 67, 71, 100, 117, 118, 119, 122, 135
mosques, 80, 83, 86, 125

Ramadan, 86
slaughterhouses, campaign against, 69
Sunni vs Shi'a, 103
Wahhabism, 31
Mussolini, Benito, 107
Myanmar/Burma
1286 Mongol invasion of Pagan, 5, 22
1784 conquest of Arakan, 5, 6, 18, 22, 25, 26, 65, 141
1824 First Anglo-Burmese War begins, 3, 5–6, 8, 25, 26, 28, 35, 50
1825 Charles Paton begins survey of Arakan, 6, 29, 145
1826 Britain annexes Arakan, 5–6, 18, 22–3, 26, 28, 31, 51, 65, 79; census of Arakan completed, 6, 29, 31, 145
1852 Second Anglo-Burmese War begins, 26
1857 foundation of Mandalay, 22
1871 census in Arakan, 29, 32
1885 Third Anglo-Burmese War begins, 26
1886 annexation to British India, 5, 18, 22–3, 26
1911 census, 6
1930 Saya San Uprising, 27
1937 becomes separate British colony, 5, 26, 29, 35
1938 anti-colonial riots, 27
1941 Aung San visits Japan, 28; James Baxter publishes report, 29–30, 49
1942 Japanese invasion, 7, 27, 28; formation of BIA, 28; inter-communal violence in Arakan, 7, 27, 79–80
1945 BNA uprising against Japanese, 28

1946 BIA begins insurgency against British, 28

1947 assassination of Aung San, 11, 36; drafting of Constitution, 1, 47, 49, 50, 118; Rohingya revolt, 7, 9, 27, 30, 47, 49, 50

1948 Independence, 2, 5, 7, 8, 18, 27, 28, 30, 35, 43–4; Arakan renamed Rakhine, 18, 35; Muslims petition for integration of Maungdaw and Buthidaung into East Pakistan, 7, 27–8, 49; Communist Party begins insurgency, 28, 36, 47

1949 Karen conflict begins, 36, 47, 49

1950 CIA begins funding exiled Chinese Kuomintang units, 37, 43

1958 establishment of Ne Win caretaker government, 37

1959 Rohingya student association at Rangoon University approved, 49, 149

1961 census, 8; creation of Mayu Frontier District, 30, 49; U Thant elected UN Secretary General, 44

1962 coup d'état; Ne Win comes to power, 2, 4, 8, 11, 30, 36, 37, 44, 50

1964 Mayu Frontier District reincorporated into Rakhine, 30, 49

1974 Constitution; establishment of one-party state, 8, 9, 11, 38, 42, 50, 57; Emergency Immigration Act, 8, 9, 42, 50, 57

1976 failed coup d'état; resignation of Tin Oo, 2, 40, 139

1977 Nagamin campaign, 52

1978 partial return of Rohingya refugees, 133

1982 Burmese Citizenship Law, xiv, 8, 41, 50, 79

1983 North Korea bombs South Korean delegation in Rangoon, 45

1987 Ne Win cancels 'unlucky' banknotes, 39

1988 8888 uprising, 9, 12, 13, 14, 38, 39, 40, 46, 52, 55, 63, 67, 72, 120, 139, 140; Ne Win removed from power, 38; establishment of NLD, 12, 40

1989 establishment of SLORC, 1, 9, 39–40; name changed to Myanmar, 1, 39–40

1990 general election, 9, 12, 40, 41, 42, 46, 51, 52, 63, 114–15, 120, 122; EU and US begin imposing sanctions, 46, 74

1991 military campaign against Rohingyas begins, 9, 52

1994 partial return of Rohingya refugees, 133

1998 NLD forms CRPP, 42

2001 failed internal military coup, 43

2007 discovery of offshore oil and gas supplies, 47; Saffron Revolution, 9, 43, 46, 55, 56, 63, 70, 140

2008 Cyclone Nargis, 9, 46, 55–6, 126; Constitution, 9, 42, 56–7, 60, 79, 120, 121

2009 China begins funding pipeline from Sittwe to Kunming, 47

2010 foundation of MaBaTha, 14, 70; general election, 10, 11, 13, 47, 56–8, 61, 72, 115

2011 Than Shwe steps down; dissolution of SPDC, 3, 38, 58; Hillary Clinton makes visit, 74

2012 Tony Blair makes visit, 74; by-elections, 13, 58, 75, 120; David

Cameron makes visit, 74; first wave of Rakhine State violence, 10, 13, 14, 41, 74, 79, 81–2, 87, 93, 99, 122, 126, 129, 130, 134; Thein Sein suggests Rakhine responsibility for violence, 82; second wave of Rakhine State violence, 10, 13, 14, 41, 74, 79, 82, 87, 93, 99, 122, 126, 129, 130, 134; José Manuel Barroso makes visit, 74; Thein Sein writes to Ban Ki-moon acknowledging communal violence, 85; Barack Obama makes visit, 74, 85, 131; *Foreign Policy* names Thein Sein 'Thinker of the Year', 75

2013 Meiktila anti-Muslim riots, 70, 86; EU lifts sanctions, 74; Lashio anti-Muslim riots, 71–2; formation of ANP, 79; government commission blames Rohingyas for 2012 violence, 82; Rakhine State violence, 10, 13, 14, 71, 87, 99, 122, 129; USDP indicates support for repeal of Aung San Suu Kyi's ban from presidency, 60; USDP supports votes for White Card holders, 117

2014 ASEAN chairmanship begins, 62, 75; massacres in Maungdaw, 86, 87; MSF banned from country, 87, 133; USDP withdraws support for repeal of Aung San Suu Kyi's ban from presidency, 60; census, 10, 90, 115–17, 133; Par Gyi shot in police custody, 62; Hin Lin Oo arrested for criticising 969 Movement, 68

2015 advertisers arrested for depiction of Buddha wearing headphones, 68; expiration of White Cards, 10, 117, 119; refugee crisis, 16, 75, 76, 86, 90–7, 114, 124–5, 132, 136; Population Control Health Care Bill passed, 68; ASEAN summit on refugee crisis, 94, 132; Shwe Mann arrested; removed from post, 60, 62; Cyclone Komen, 97, 126; Interfaith Marriage Law passed, 11, 15, 53, 67, 70–1, 117, 118, 119, 122, 135; Aung San Suu Kyi visits Beijing, 73; general election, 1, 2, 10, 13–15, 59, 60–2, 90, 108, 114–23, 129, 132, 134, 136, 140

Myanmar Oil and Gas Enterprise (MOGE), 47

Myo people, 50

Nagamin campaign (1977), 52

Nat River, 42

National League for Democracy (NLD), 1–3, 9–15, 40–2, 55, 57–64, 67, 71, 73, 79, 99, 114–15, 117–23, 124, 130, 134, 135–6, 139–40, 141
  Buddhism, 3, 11, 12–13, 14, 40, 55, 57, 63, 71, 117, 120, 136
  Committee Representing the People's Parliament (CRPP), 42
  election boycott (2010), 13, 58, 61
  establishment of, 12, 40
  ethnic minorities, relations with, 2, 9, 11, 13, 40–1, 63, 79, 114–15, 117–18, 140
  military links, 2, 40, 139
  Muslims, relations with, 9, 13, 14, 71, 80, 114–15, 117–23, 124, 135
  USDP, relations with, 62

National Registration Certificates, 49, 50

National Unity Party (NUP), 9, 12, 41

nationalism, 5, 9, 23, 26, 27, 28, 46, 64, 65, 69, 87, 89, 104
natural disasters, 9, 46, 97, 126–7
naturalisation, 51
Nazi Germany (1933–45), 104, 106–9, 132
Ne Win, 11–12, 36
Nepal, 66
New Zealand, 43, 68
Nigeria, 114
969 Movement, 9, 11, 14, 15, 32, 65, 67–8, 70–2, 117, 119, 136
Nobel Peace Prize, 2, 10, 99
Non-Aligned Movement, 44, 131
non-governmental organisations (NGOs), 86, 87
non-violent resistance, 40
North Korea, 45–6, 74, 75, 92, 131
Nu, 8, 44, 48
nuclear weapons, 45
Nyam Min, 136
Nyan Win, 99, 117

Obama, Barack, 61, 74, 85, 131
oil, 47, 72
Olympic Games, 106
Organisation for the Protection of Race and Religion, 68
Organisation of Islamic Cooperation (OIC), 133
othering, 102–3
Ottoman Empire (1299–1922), 104, 107, 108, 109, 132

Pagan Kingdom (849–1297), 5, 19, 21–2, 23–4, 64
pagodas, 80
Pakistan, 7, 27, 43, 44, 45, 49, 74
palm oil, 95
Pan Zagar, 11, 15, 70
Par Gyi, 61

partition, 130
Paton, Charles, 6, 29, 145
Patriotic Association of Myanmar, *see* MaBaTha
Pauktaw District, Rakhine State, 83
Persian language, 21
pluralism, 22
Poland, 106, 107
police, 81, 84–5, 86, 91
Pope Francis, 91, 134
Population Control Health Care Bill (2015), 53, 68
prawn fishing, 91–6
precious stones, 95
Prussia (1525–1947), 105
Pyu people, 19–20, 21

al-Qaeda, 30, 82, 125

racism, 3, 4, 11, 17, 53, 70, 101, 105, 113, 114
Rakhine National Party (RNP), 121
Rakhine Nationalities Development Party (RNDP), 13, 14, 15, 41, 79, 80, 82, 83, 121–3, 140
Rakhine people, 6–9, 11, 13, 16, 18, 21, 23, 27, 29, 32, 33, 41–2, 48, 50–2, 79, 80, 82–4, 87, 89, 91, 96, 100, 115, 121–3, 124, 130–1, 135, 136, 140
Rakhine State, xiii, 1, 4, 9, 10, 17, 27, 31, 35, 41, 52, 53, 59, 61, 69, 71, 73, 79–97, 100–1, 115–16, 118, 120, 121–3, 124, 125, 130–1, 133, 140
Ramadan, 86
Rangoon, 26, 37, 45, 56, 89, 122, 149
Rangoon University, 49, 149
rape, 52, 81, 86, 110
Rathedaung, Rakhine State, 80
real estate, 72
refugees, xiv, 1, 8–10, 13, 15, 16, 38,

42, 52, 72–3, 75, 76, 81, 84, 86, *88*,
     89–97, 99–100, 102, 110, 115, 116,
     121, 123–7, 131–2, 133
  camps, 1, 10, 13, 15, 16, 38, 42, 81,
     84, 86, *88*, 89–90, 94, 100, 102,
     110, 115, 116, 117, 118, 120, 124,
     126, 127, 129, 135
  crisis (2015), 16, 75, 76, 86, 90–1,
     94, 114, 124–5, 132, 136
regional political parties, 11, 13
reincarnation, 70
Resistance Day, 28
Reuters, 96
rice, 7, 35, 49, 56
Rohingyas
  arson of property, 71, 81, 83, 84, 86
  birth control, 53, 68, 80, 90, 100,
     109
  boycott of businesses, 14, 67, 69, 82
  citizenship rights, xiii, 3–10, 17,
     32–3, 41, 48–53, 57, 75, 79,
     80–1, 99, 103, 115–24, 129,
     131–2, 136, 139, 141, 147
  education, denial of, 51, 80
  elections, exclusion from, 9, 13,
     41–2, 79, 114–23, 124, 129, 140
  ethnic cleansing of, xiii, 1, 9, 13, 33,
     42, 52, 79, 81–97, 100, 117, 118,
     122, 133
  forced labour, xiii, 52, 80, 95
  healthcare, denial of, 16, 89, 90, 91,
     110, 124
  identity cards, 8, 9, 10, 41, 42, 49,
     50, 115, 116, 117, 119, 129
  infant mortality, 90
  land rights, xiii, 51, 52
  language, 4, 6, 8, 20, 24–5, 29, 31,
     48, 53
  marriage rights, 11, 15, 53, 67, 71,
     100, 109, 110, 117, 118, 119, 122,
     135

mosques, destruction of, 80, 83
movement, restriction of, xiii, 51, 53,
     80, 110, 129
racism against, 4, 11, 17, 53, 70, 101,
     105, 113, 114
rape, 52, 86, 110
refugees, xiv, 1, 8, 9, 10, 13, 15, 16,
     52, 72, 76, 81, 84, 86, *88*, 89–97,
     99–100, 102, 110, 115, 116, 121,
     123–5, 126, 127, 129, 131–2, 133
segregation of, 1, 13, 16, 38, 42, 81,
     84, 86, *88*, 89–90, 100, 102, 110,
     115, 116, 117, 118, 120, 122, 124,
     126, 127, 130, 135
sexual exploitation, 93, 95
torture of, xiii, 110
trafficking, slavery, 89, 91–7, 124,
     125, 131–2
violence against, xiii, 1, 3, 8, 10, 11,
     13–16, 38, 48, 51–3, 70–2, 74,
     79, 81–90, 93, 99, 122, 126, 129,
     130, 134, 135
Rohingya Solidarity Organization, 83
Rohingya Student Association, Ran-
     goon University, 49, 149
Rome Statute (2002), 109–10, 135
rubber, 7, 49, 50, 95
Russian Empire (1721–1917), 104,
     105
Russian Federation, 133
Rwanda, 3, 76, 104, 105–6, 107,
     108–9, 129, 132, 133, 136–7
Rwandan Patriotic Front, 105

Saffron Revolution (2007), 9, 43, 46,
     55, 56, 70, 140
Sagaing people, 35
Sak people, 20, 22
sanctions, 46, 71, 72, 74, 76, 133
sangha, 11, 12, 13, 23, 37, 39, 40, 43,
     55, 57, 63–72, 80, 82, 85, 101, 139,
     140

sasana, 64–5

Saudi Arabia, 31, 105, 125, 126, 130

Saw Maung, 39

Saya San Uprising (1930), 27

secularism, 23, 26, 36, 40

segregation, 1, 13, 16, 38, 42, 81, 84, 86, *88*, 89–90, 100, 102, 110, 115, 116, 117, 118, 120, 122, 124, 126, 127, 130, 135

Sentinel Project for Genocide Prevention, 91

sexual exploitation, 93, 95–6

Shan Nationalities League for Democracy (SNLD), 41

Shan people, 8, 9, 11, 22, 35, 36–7, 47, 48, 50, 51, 59, 73, 95

Shi'a Islam, 103

Shwe Mann, 60–2, 121

Shwe Maung, 115, 117

Siam, 5, 18, 22, 25

Sino–Soviet split (1960–89), 44

Sitagu Sayadaw, 72

Sittwe, Rakhine State, 9, 47, 80, 84, 89, 110

slaughterhouses, 69

slavery, 91–7, 125

Smith, Martin, 5

social media, 83, 86

socialism, 8, 9, 11, 37–8, 39, 42, 44, 49, 50, 53, 63, 131

Songkhla, Thailand, 92

South Korea, 45, 47

Soviet Union (1922–91), 2, 44, 45, 46, 104–5, 106, 107, 108, 131, 132

Sri Lanka, 2, 18, 19, 64, 67, 69, 141

State Department, US, 92, 95, 96, 131

State Electoral Commission, 10, 117

state employees, 58, 61

students, 12, 39, 40, 63, 149

Sudan, 114

Sunni Islam, 103

Tanintharyi Region, 18

Tatmadaw, 36, 151; *see also* military

telecommunications, 72

terrorism, 30, 83, 123, 125–6

Thailand, 2, 5, 17, 18, 19, 22, 25, 38, 42, 44, 64, 69, 86, 91–6, 100, 141

Than Shwe, 38, 61

Thant, 44

Thaton, Mon State, 19

Thein Sein, 60–1, 68, 75, 81, 83, 85, 117, 120, 121

Theravada Buddhism, 2, 19, 21, 23, 36, 38, 64–5, 141

Tibet, 5, 18, 19, 20, 66, 141

Tin Maung Swe, 97

Tin Moe Wei, 40

Tin Oo, 2, 12, 40, 139

Tonkin, Derek, 29, 30, 31, 32

torture, xiii, 110

tourism, 72

Trafficking in Persons Report, 95

trigger events, 103, 107–8, 110, 114–27

Tun Khin, 113

Tun Min Soe, 117

Turkey, 66, 104, 107, 108, 109, 132

Turkic peoples, 105, 108

Tutsis, 105–6, 107, 108–9

Ukraine, 104

Union Solidarity and Development Party (USDP), 3, 10–14, 58, 59–63, 67, 69, 76, 80, 115, 117–18, 120–1, 130, 136, 139–40, 141

United Nations (UN), xiv, 5, 6, 33, 42, 44, 48, 50, 52, 56, 66, 71, 75, 76, 85–6, 87, 93, 95, 100–1, 103, 108, 109, 115, 124, 125, 129, 133, 135

Charter, 5, 33, 50, 93, 129, 135

Convention on the Prevention and Punishment of the Crime of Genocide, 100

Convention on the Reduction of Statelessness, 57

High Commissioner for Refugees (UNHCR), 42, 86, 95

Secretary General, 44, 66, 75, 85, 134

Security Council, 46, 85, 108, 109, 133

Special Rapporteur on Myanmar, 85, 89, 109

United States (US), 28, 37, 43, 44, 45–6, 59, 61, 73–5, 80, 81, 95, 96, 106, 107, 108, 109, 131, 132, 133, 134, 135

1950 CIA begins funding Kuomintang units in Burma, 37, 43

2008 warships sent to Myanmar to aid after Cyclone Nargis, 46, 56

2011 Hillary Clinton visits Myanmar, 74

2012 Barack Obama visits Myanmar, 74, 85

2015 publication of *Trafficking in Persons Report*, 95

United to End Genocide, 113

Unity for Peace Network, 125

Vajrayana tradition, 66

Varshney, Ashutosh, 102

Vateri, J.S., 25

Vietnam, 22, 44

violence

against children, 84, 87

inter-communal, xiii, 1, 2–3, 7, 10, 11, 13, 27, 70–2, 74, 79, 81–90, 99, 102, 104, 107, 120, 121, 122, 126, 131, 134, 135, 141

against women, xiii, 52, 71, 81, 86

Wahhabism, 31

Walton, Matthew, 65, 68

White Cards, 10, 117, 119

Wilson, Horace Hayman, 20

Wirathu, 67, 85, 119

women

birth control, 53, 68, 80, 90, 100, 109

and marriage laws, 15, 70–1, 119, 123, 135

rape of, 52, 81, 86, 110

sexual exploitation of, 93, 95–6

violence against, xiii, 52, 71, 81, 86

World War I (1914–18), 104, 105

World War II (1939–45), 2, 7, 8, 27, 28, 73, 103, 105, 106–7

Yan Thei, Rakhine State, 84

Yangon, Yangon Region, 26, 37, 45, 56, 89, 122, 149

Ye Myint Aung, 4

Young Turk Revolution (1908), 104

YouTube, 67

Yugoslavia, SFR (1945–1992), 2

Yunnan, China, 47, 73

Zan, Shw, 32

Zaw Htay, 94

Zimbabwe, 46